CW01465960

PRAISE FOR *DIAGNOSIS HUMAN*

"*Diagnosis Human* is a critical book for our time. While we, as doctors, have been focusing on the individuals' mental health we have forgotten that individuals exist in relationships with family and friends and that oftentimes, the problems that individuals' face can be addressed by bringing the family together with experts in family therapy. The stories in this book are truly fascinating, and once you start to read them, you will quickly see the important role that highly skilled family therapists can play in improving the life of a family and every individual within it. Begel and Keith take us inside their offices and show us that what we see as an individual's 'symptoms' is actually the result of subtle family dynamics. As a family physician with many years of experience. I am grateful that we have this precious chance to gain important insight's from these authors' experiences. Every family will see themselves somewhere in these stories as the authors bring peace and healing where there was turmoil and dysfunction. As a family physician for over 40 years, I highly recommend this book to professionals and struggling families alike."

—**Neil Calman**, MD, FAAFP, president and CEO of the Institute for Family Health, professor and chair of Family Medicine and Community Health at Mount Sinai Hospital

"As a marriage and family therapist for over thirty years, and a parent for over forty years, I applaud the authors for finally saying what so many systemic therapists know . . . that problems are relational. This book is a breath of fresh air, providing those who read it with new ways of envisioning problems, by healing relationships, which then heal behaviors. Parents who read this book will be reassured that things are not hopeless, when diagnoses are given out too freely to their children. That hope may result in better interactions at home, as hope emerges and worry decreases. Children will benefit when their parents focus on the family's relationships and watch those they love restore peace at home. This book offers a glance at what magic can occur when we look beyond a person's issue, into the interactions of the family system for solutions."

—**Linda Metcalf**, PhD, author of *Parenting Toward Solutions*

"*Diagnosis Human* by Amy Begel and David Keith offers an intelligent window into the workings of psychotherapy. Understanding the mechanisms that empower psychotherapy enables consumers to more easily benefit from treatment. *Diagnosis Human* presents reparative relationships as a refreshing alternative to a medical model. Symptoms are multifaceted and can be the result of underlying ruptures in family relationships. Symptoms are not merely biochemical abnormalities requiring medication."

—**Jeffrey K. Zeig**, PhD, director of The
Milton H. Erickson Foundation

"This book is healing! With vivid storytelling, this book is an illuminating dive into family therapy and can help us all unlearn the rigid patterns that prevent us from connecting with our partners and families."

—**Katie O'Grady**, MD, family medicine physician

Diagnosis Human

Diagnosis Human

How Unlocking Hidden
Relationship Patterns
Can Transform and
Heal Our Children, Our
Partners, Ourselves

Amy Begel and David V. Keith

ROWMAN & LITTLEFIELD
Lanham • Boulder • New York • London

Published by Rowman & Littlefield
An imprint of The Rowman & Littlefield Publishing Group, Inc.
4501 Forbes Boulevard, Suite 200, Lanham, Maryland 20706
www.rowman.com

86-90 Paul Street, London EC2A 4NE

British Library Cataloguing in Publication Information Available

Library of Congress Cataloging-in-Publication Data

Names: Begel, Amy, author. | Keith, David V., author. Title: Diagnosis human :
  how unlocking hidden relationship patterns can
  transform and heal our children, our partners, ourselves / Amy Begel and
  David V. Keith.
Description: Lanham : Rowman & Littlefield, [2023] | Includes
  bibliographical references and index.
Identifiers: LCCN 2023014635 (print) | LCCN 2023014636 (ebook) | ISBN
  9781538182727 (cloth) | ISBN 9781538182734 (ebook)
Subjects: LCSH: Families--Mental health--Popular works. | Family
  psychotherapy--Popular works. | Couples therapy--Popular works. |
  Depressed persons--Family relationships--Popular works. | Children of
  depressed persons--Mental health--Popular works.
Classification: LCC RC455.4.F3 B44 2023 (print) | LCC RC455.4.F3 (ebook)
  | DDC 616.89/156--dc23/eng/20230623
LC record available at https://lccn.loc.gov/2023014635
LC ebook record available at https://lccn.loc.gov/2023014636

Contents

Introduction: You're Not Sick   1

Couples

Chapter 1: Never Waste a Good Depression   7

Chapter 2: The Predivorce Couple   27

Chapter 3: Affair Repair   51

Chapter 4: The Couples Where Sex Went to Die   69

Families

Chapter 5: Little Kids Behaving Badly   89

Chapter 6: It's a Tough Job Raising Parents   113

Chapter 7: ADHD: Replacing Medications with Family Members   133

Chapter 8: Teens Who Hurt Themselves: Beneath the Mask of Family Unity   151

Chapter 9: Control Freak: Transmission of Intergenerational Trauma   173

Conclusion

Chapter 10: Looking for What's Right   197

Notes   211

Bibliography   213

Index   215

About the Authors   219

Introduction

You're Not Sick

When Meg walked into my office for her first therapy appointment, I was struck by the rather hollowed out appearance of this naturally beautiful woman, with her abundant dark curly hair. Settling herself on the couch, she began describing her "uncontrollable crying" and feelings of "hopelessness." She said, almost apologetically, "I used to be happy." Meg wondered if her mood was due to a chemical imbalance, in part because her brother suffered from periods of depression. She thought she might be genetically predisposed to depression, which she thought of as a disease. It soon became clear, however, that her marriage of four years was in trouble. In a near whisper as she said, "My husband and I barely talk anymore. He's always busy. I feel like he's avoiding me." Since I think of "mood" as an interpersonal experience, I suspected her depression was related to the dismal state of her marriage. I invited her husband to join for the next session.

Meg's husband, Brian, worked as a writer for a well-known progressive think tank. He wore his political passions on his sleeve. Handsome, with tousled red hair, Brian projected a kind of tight energy, like a coiled spring. His work commitments occupied a large share of his time and energy, which he recounted with great passion.

The couple had a three-year-old toddler, Adam. Meg and Brian described their relationship prior to Adam's arrival as having a free-wheeling quality, where they enjoyed a high degree of individual freedom. The transition from couple to family put new demands on them. They used to be two free spirits who bumped into each other when

1

they felt like it. That no longer worked. It looked to me like Meg and Brian had managed to avoid addressing some areas of conflict while they were childless. But the complexities of becoming a three-person family made these unresolved issues more pressing. At the end of this first visit I commented, "It looks to me like Meg's depression is more of a duet, not a solo." They didn't disagree.

At the second meeting Meg opened up about her depression. She clearly felt that her husband's strict adherence to his political principles didn't allow enough room for her voice, or her perspective. "It feels like there is no room for me, for what I want," she said. Meg talked about the time she looked forward to preparing a lovely omelet for their son, but Brian opposed it, based on his own strict vegan diet. Meg tried to reassure him it was okay, painting a picture of happy cage-free chickens eating organic feed, but Brian was adamant in his opposition. For Meg, Brian's passions felt exclusive rather than inclusive.

Meg was especially animated as she described preparing a meal: "Food, and feeding people is how I show love." She added, smiling, "I learned that from my mom." She understood and respected her husband's beliefs, but she didn't share them to the same degree. She wanted decision-making flexibility with their son, who was now caught in the confusion between the couple. I said, "I think your son will be happy to see that his dad loves his mom more than he loves chickens." Meg paused. "I don't know if he loves me more than he loves chickens." Brian's ears got red. I think he recognized the truth of what she said.

We met for eight sessions, some of them tumultuous. Brian opened up about his worry that he couldn't make Meg happy, and he was destined to be a failure as a husband. He said, almost under his breath, "I guess, in the back of my mind, I've been worried about losing her. I'm realizing now that when I'm anxious I run away." He added, "And I know I can be a bit of a bastard about the food thing." Meg was looking at her husband like she was just seeing this guy for the first time. I'm pretty sure she had no idea Brian was scared she would leave him.

As we began exploring and challenging some of the subtle patterns in their relationship, these two people began to be more honest with each other—in a good way. This was the first time either of them had taken the time to look at their way of operating as a couple.

There was a fundamental goodwill between Meg and Brian which helped them open up to each other. Their relationship had trust at its core. Our eighth and last meeting showed that Meg and Brian made the most of our sessions. Meg's depression had lifted. She said, "For the first time in a long time I feel that Brian is listening to me." She looked at him and smiled. "Actually, more important, I feel that he is finally hearing me." The wall had come down. The session ended, and we agreed they'd call as needed.

This small snapshot gives a glimpse into how depression can be relieved through therapy when treated not as a disease of the brain but as a reflection of a troubled relationship. Meg initially believed she had a chemical imbalance. She thought her ongoing depression was perhaps because she was not taking antidepressants and wondered if she should start medication. The phrase "chemical imbalance" has been so woven into our culture that Meg, like many of us, barely stop to question it. Even though we don't know exactly what it means, we accept that it is a real thing. But is it?

As family therapists, we would like to offer you a different narrative about emotional suffering. We want to tell you about the pain behind the pain. The stories we share, cases from our office, come from our many years of treating distressed adults and children in a family therapy setting. Some of these case illustrations, with their quick resolution, may seem as fantastic as a fairy tale. But our stories are true. They show how symptoms of depression, anxiety, or behavior problems in children are most often a response to a troubling relationship dynamic hidden from view. We view *symptom*s of mental distress, including behavioral problems in children, depression in adults, and various kinds of psychosomatic illness, as related to subtle and powerful dynamic patterns in families and relationships. Treating the symptom is like taking pain relievers for a fever—it may temporarily treat the symptom, but it doesn't cure the cold.

Many people who come to us for help have been treated individually by other therapists. They are often considered, or consider themselves, sick. These folks can usually tell us what is wrong with them but don't have much experience with what is right with them. When we include the couple or family in what was previously an individual therapy, we begin to uncover the distress buried in intimate patterns of relationship. We don't only look for what's wrong, however: we also pay attention to health, to areas of competence and caring. We assume that most people are doing the best they can and are trying to make things work. All of us, however, carry rigidities and wounds from our upbringing into the creation of our own families. Many of these patterns are outside of our awareness but may show up in the form of marital distress or behavior problems in kids.

Our therapeutic approach stems from many years of training and practice, working with whole families to try to understand the nature of their relationship operating system, and how to relieve suffering. Almost everyone comes to us experiencing some kind of painful impasse: ongoing family tensions, mood or behavior problems in themselves or someone in their family, maybe a child, that they haven't been able to fix despite the best of intentions. People often feel that they have "tried everything," but in fact they have tried mostly one thing, over and over. This "stuck" quality, where family members unknowingly repeat the same troubling interactions, without resolution, is the very definition of suffering. The dynamic approach of family therapy disrupts these repetitive patterns, helping families move beyond their painful stalemate into a more satisfying, life-giving experience with each other. Once the family becomes the "patient," individual symptoms typically recede.

Our perspective comes from the world of family therapy, or "family systems theory." This interpersonal, relationship-oriented approach is a powerful therapeutic model with a rich history that has never been discredited or proven wrong. This way of working is rarely practiced today in the larger psychiatric/psychotherapy community, however, due to the dominance of the brain chemistry focus in mental health, which is supported by powerful economic and political forces.

As we present these dynamic patterns of the couples and families who come to us for therapy, we are aware that we are speaking a language that has become unfamiliar in mainstream culture. We believe that our alternative perspective, where individual distress is understood and often healed in the context of a relationship, offers a fresh, empowering tool to address one's suffering.

We invite you into our office to take part in our family therapy sessions, where you can experience first-hand what these intimate relationship patterns look and feel like. As part of each therapy session, we include our therapeutic reflections, inviting you to sit beside us as we discuss the case, how we made various therapeutic choices, share our observations, and reveal our confusion, anxiety, or joy when the case goes well. Therapists are real, flawed people too; it is our hope to humanize the therapeutic process as we share our reactions and decision-making. We show how every patient needs to be considered in their own context, and we want to empower you to recognize yours. Of course, the identifying data of our patients is disguised in order to protect their privacy.

As you recognize yourself in our stories, you may begin to think about yourself and your relationships in a new way. We encourage you to sit with these narratives; the patterns may unravel and reveal insights into your own situation over time. We hope our stories of struggling couples, adults suffering from depression, or therapy sessions with distressed kids and their families, can help open new paths for you to understand and address whatever problems you, like all of us, wrestle with. That does not mean we are sick. Just deeply human.

Chapter 1

Never Waste a Good Depression

THE PROBLEM OF THE NICE BOYFRIEND

When Julie showed up for her first therapy appointment, she seemed like an old woman trapped in a young woman's body. She was thirty-two and talked about being incredibly depressed for the past couple of years. While she managed to function well enough at her job as an environmental researcher, she described how she spent her weekends: sleeping a lot, not eating much, and crying "at the drop of a hat." She was referred to me by her family physician, who had started her on antidepressants, which she had taken regularly, without much change, for about three years. Julie thought individual therapy might help her with what she called her "depression and mood disorder."

During the first few sessions I tried to get beneath Julie's emotional surface. I learned that she had been thinking a lot about her ex-boyfriend, whom she described, with a hint of longing, as "bipolar." It sounded like she missed the intense highs and lows that were the hallmark of their relationship. She added, "But I was exhausted by all the emotional drama by the time we broke up." It seemed to me that, despite the upheaval, this relationship made her feel alive. Julie described the "relief" she felt when she met David, her live-in boyfriend for the last six years. I asked her to invite David to come in with her.

He showed up with Julie for the next session. I was struck by the almost corpse-like quality of this couple. They sat nearly motionless.

7

This was one of the quietest couples I had ever seen. David, a slim young man with an impish grin and an intense gaze, had moved to the East Coast from Southern California. The impression he left me with was that he was a kind, gentle guy who tried to maintain peace at all costs.

"Boy, you guys are really going at it," I said, which probably sounded bizarre since they were sitting quietly on my pink couch. My take on the couple was that they were fighting like cats and dogs, only really politely.

Most striking was David's exaggerated calm. For some strange reason he thought he could convince me (and Julie) that he "didn't mind" that she regularly spurned his sexual moves, which she deemed were "half-hearted," or that he could give up his previous identity as a party animal for a life of Netflix and couch. They were like two old people. Two grouchy old people.

I began to challenge David's politeness with Julie, letting him know I wasn't fooled by his pretense at not caring. To me, David seemed depressed. When I suggested this, he didn't disagree.

"The problem is, you're a pretender," I said. "You pretend you don't want anything from Julie. You don't make any requests; you have no demands. In fact, you don't seem to expect or want anything from Julie, one way or another. That's a recipe for depression."

Julie nodded.

I looked at David. "I'm not talking about her depression. I'm talking about yours."

Julie, with quiet fury in her voice, said, "I have absolutely no idea if he cares about me one way or another. He falls asleep in front of the TV every night. He goes along with what I want to do, but I have no idea what HE wants. I'm not sure why we're in this relationship." She added, "This wasn't the guy I fell in love with." THAT guy, according to Julie, was a sweet, fun party guy.

I said, "It sounded like maybe you needed to tame him a bit, but this much?"

Could she untame him now? Slowly, David began talking about his acquired caution with his girlfriend. "I worry about Julie's mental health. She's been depressed, so I try to stay out of the way, not add any more weight to what she's already dealing with. She had a panic attack a couple of years ago, and that really scared me. I'm not sure she can take much stress."

I wanted to get to know David, to get a better sense of where his tendency toward emotional caution came from. He described his own mother as boisterous and opinionated. He said, "I could never win an argument with her."

David's parents divorced when he was a teenager, and it sounded to me like David reacted to this seismic event by burying his feelings, especially his anger. He talked about how he hated fighting, especially because of what he witnessed with his parents. He described his dad as emotionally unpredictable.

"My old man would fly off the handle for no reason," he said.

These memories were raw for David, and he clearly went out of his way to avoid being anything like his dad. But his aversion to fighting and his strenuous politeness with Julie ended up creating another, different kind of problem. He now had a very depressed girlfriend on his hands. David needed to learn that his emotional caution, though perhaps well intentioned, was experienced as uncaring indifference by his partner.

David's carefulness felt extremely painful to Julie. Every lively relationship requires some element of risk-taking, of exposure of vulnerability. Otherwise, couples can end up feeling like strangers to each other. This was the relationship in which Julie's soul was drying up.

She looked at David. "You make me feel like I'm not attractive to you. I feel so awful about myself, like I'm not even worth caring about. You don't even want to have sex with me anymore. Why are we together?"

Just so we don't put all the blame on David, remember that all intimate relationships are a duet. Julie, too, helped shape their hands-off relationship dance, though she didn't know it. This was vividly captured by an incident that took place a few months into therapy.

David opened a session saying, "We almost had a fight this past week."

I joked, "Oh, no, how *terrible!*"

They realized by now that I was rooting for them to have a good old-fashioned heated argument. David told me how they were in the kitchen preparing sauce for a spaghetti dinner, and he tried to show Julie a new way to chop onions.

"I'm a good cook, it's something I love to do, and she acted like I mugged her! So I backed off," he said.

Julie remembered it slightly differently. She recalled, "I was busy chopping the onions and David just inserted himself into what I was doing. It annoyed me and I told him that!"

David's interpretation: She won't let me teach her anything. Better stay in my lane. As we talked, they recognized this as was an all-too familiar pattern: Julie raising her hackles, David retreating. He was scared to stand up for himself, which, of course, made Julie (inwardly, unconsciously) furious. She didn't get mad, though. She just got depressed. This couple desperately needed to learn to fight.

Over the course of the next few months, using the "Onion Flareup" as a touchstone, David helped Julie to understand her power over him. She held some strong beliefs about "how things should be," and David sensed that she didn't want to be challenged. Beneath Julie's apparent vulnerability lay a very strong woman with strong ideas. She was actually quite powerful despite her apparent fragility. Since Julie didn't see herself as having any impact in the relationship, she was shocked to learn that David had grown afraid of her. He wanted to avoid upsetting her at all costs.

David began responding to what he was learning in our therapy sessions by beginning to take a few risks with his girlfriend—both in session and out. He coaxed her out of her comfort zone socially, got her to go with him to some of his favorite clubs, where they danced and partied like when they had first met. At first, Julie responded to his new level of connection warily, but then began to clearly enjoy her "new" boyfriend. And they started fighting more, which showed up in therapy sessions. A few times in the office, when tensions arose, the fur would fly. But no harm done. Their relationship had come alive.

About six months after I first met them, Julie mentioned in passing that she had stopped taking her antidepressants. She was feeling much better.

When Julie first came to the office, she seemed so stuck, convinced that her depression was biochemical, and not really in touch with what her mood, or her life, was about. When David came in, I saw the stuck-ness belonged to the relationship, not just Julie. I had the idea, as I usually do, that if the relationship feels alive, that translates to a person's individual experience. The mood of a relationship is infectious.

In the therapy, I knew I had to challenge David's hands-off, pseudo polite, no-demands posture with Julie. Being with a guy who seems to have no needs can be incredibly painful and confusing. It creates a profound disconnect, one which burrows its way into the relationship and can stay there, creating depression in one or both partners. David seemed to welcome the chance to take a look at himself, both as a boyfriend and in terms of his own background. If he had been less curious or engaged in the therapy, the outcome probably would have been different.

Bringing David into therapy with Julie, and reframing her depression as dynamic, relational, and within their capacity to change, had a healing impact on this couple. Julie and David's story shows one of the ways symptoms like depression live in the world of our intimate relationships.

David's conflict-avoidance left Julie feeling abandoned and angry, though she wasn't much in touch with her anger. She longed for connection, and David's carefulness in the relationship left her feeling isolated and alone. Through the course of therapy Julie, too, learned about herself and how her own rigid behavior helped to create a seemingly emotionally distant boyfriend. Her (unconscious) resistance to being changed by David disabled him and left him feeling impotent. He withdrew.

Through their therapy sessions, Julie's realization that her boyfriend was terrified of upsetting her began to open up possibilities for change. She was tuned in to her own feelings and the ways in which David let her down, but she had no clue how she affected him. She found out that her boyfriend muted his own desires so as not to provoke or destabilize her. And Julie didn't imagine that David was depressed. She didn't know he had any feelings at all, one way or another. On David's part, he discovered that Julie wouldn't collapse if he made emotional demands or argued with her; that, in fact, a good, occasional fight would do them good. He woke up.

Most of us are like Julie and David: we don't know how to see the subtle but profound dynamics in our relationships. These folks functioned well in society, had jobs, lived apparently normal lives, but their rhythmic undercurrents as a couple were pulling the relationship tensions underground, where they festered. Though Julie's depression was her ticket of admission for therapy, once her boyfriend joined the sessions, she, and they, had a chance to learn about the pain hidden in their relationship. This paved the way for Julie's recovery from what she thought of as an individual problem of mood.

THE WOMAN WHO MISPLACED HER VOICE

Jake, a surgeon in his mid-fifties, called to make an appointment for a consultation. He wanted to bring his family in. His oldest son was away at college and couldn't join us for the session. Jake said, "He's a star in every way, a great kid. And he never gives me a hard time. We understand each other." His primary concern revolved around his stormy relationship with his twenty-six-year-old daughter Sally. He said, "We need help. My daughter is having real psychological problems."

Jake was clearly the powerhouse of the family. His wife, Paula, characterized him as "the kind of guy who knows right from wrong." He prided himself on maintaining order and decorum, though in a rather subtle and sophisticated way.

His daughter's recent decision to apply to divinity school drove him mad. "This is a good example of her impulsive streak," he sneered. Though Jake clearly cared about his daughter, he specialized in demeaning Sally's way of operating in the world.

Sally, a bright, thoughtful, intuitive young woman, didn't back away from battles with her father. She had backbone. Her decision to attend divinity school seemed like a perfect fit for this humanistic, spiritual young woman. Sally both wanted her dad's approval and had launched a one-woman crusade to free her father from his destructive rigidities. During one therapy session she told her father, "You think you have all the answers. Maybe if you stop and listen to some other ideas, everyone would be better off!"

Jake's wife, Paula came across as unbearably cautious, speaking like she was stepping between land mines, afraid to set one off. Her timidity was troubling, since I suspected her point of view would be helpful for everyone. When she guardedly offered her impression of the family dynamic, I encouraged her: "Paula, I'm not sure why you're so careful since it looks like you're a great observer of your family. I'm impressed by your perceptive comments," I said.

I imagine Paula got the idea that I thought she was, perhaps, the smartest one in the room. I also suspected that Sally was worried about her mother's emotional withdrawal and was perhaps taking on the work that Paula should have been doing. Perhaps Sally was trying to show her mom how to fight? I guessed that Paula had given up trying to penetrate her husband's powerful rigidities, and Sally stepped in to save the day. I have seen a variation in these dynamics many times in my office. After a couple of rather turbulent sessions where Sally and her father went at it, Paula suggested a meeting for just herself and Jake. I wasn't sure what prompted her request, but it seemed like a good idea.

The session with Paula and Jake initially felt stilted. They clearly were not used to talking about their own intimate patterns and were more comfortable talking about Sally.

I noticed how Paula seemed empowered by our previous sessions. She looked different, slightly younger, and more alive than when I had first met her.

Jake initially expressed skepticism about my way of working, particularly since I didn't honor his script. For the first few sessions he seemed like he hated me. For instance, at the end of our first session, I asked the family not to speak about the meeting for twenty-four hours, something I often do. Jake, almost literally looking down his nose at me, scoffed, "That's absurd!" I told him, "It's better for you." With a slight smile, I added, "You'll thank me later."

Of course, it's never fun to be hated, even momentarily, as a therapist. But I'm used to it, as are most experienced therapists. I knew that Jake didn't really hate me. He was mad that I was the one in charge, that I was there to help, which meant that I would see things differently than him. As a surgeon, Jake was used to being in charge, and I think he was furious that I didn't dance to his tune. I knew if I did, however, it was game over and I would end up duplicating the unhealthy dynamic of the family, where everyone kowtowed to him, except the "troublesome" daughter.

In our first few meetings I respectfully indicated that I thought Jake was full of hot air, and that his bravado could use some major tweaking. At this session, however, his skepticism gave way to what felt like a new kind of engagement—a slight softening. Jake might have felt some grudging respect for me. I was clearly not a pushover.

Now, to his credit, Jake appeared almost eager to talk about his way of operating. He said with a slight smile on his lips, "Paula and I have been talking about my tunnel vision."

I looked puzzled.

He reminded me, saying, "A few meetings ago you said I was trapped by tunnel vision." Jake had taken up my challenge.

"And you're keeping your family in the tunnel with you. I think your daughter's trying to help you get out," I said.

As we talked, I wondered openly about Paula's reluctance to express herself. I figured it had something to do with the dynamics I'd observed between her and her husband. Paula looked like she was afraid to cross or contradict Jake.

"When did you lose your voice?" I asked her.

After pausing a moment, she said, "I know exactly when. It happened over eight years ago."

Jake raised his eyebrows with surprise.

Paula told me about a typical, though more heated, conflict over some little thing Sally had done that offended Jake's sense of order. "Jake went way over the top with Sally. He was insanely angry. I tried to stop him. He shut me down. Hard. I realized then that I couldn't change him," she said. "That's when my depression really hit me."

Paula had been on antidepressants for the past fifteen years. When I asked her what her depression was about, she asked, "What do you mean?"

She paused. "I've never thought about that."

This was the first time Paula considered that her depression was a mood with meaning. As we explored her family background, Paula painted a picture of her parents' turbulent marriage, which was marked by huge battles, mostly waged by Paula's tempestuous, grandiose father. They separated when Paula was a teenager.

"It was all traumatic, both my parents' marriage and what happened after," she said. Her mother sank into a depression after the separation, which took many years to recover from. This prolonged instability made a huge imprint on Paula. I think she (unconsciously) decided she wanted a peaceful home, no matter what.

At this session, Jake seemed taken aback when Paula recounted her version of being shut down. He said, "I don't even remember that day. Why didn't you say something?"

"You wouldn't have believed me. You were too angry," she said. I was heartened that Paula and Jake appeared to enjoy—if that's the right word—our conversation about Paula's loss of voice. I noted that Paula seemed to be taking a bit more risks with her husband, not tiptoeing around him as much. Her voice became bolder. Their relationship looked like it had a strong foundation; they seemed ready, almost eager, to open up some closed channels. Paula seemed to be letting go of an invisible blockage, and Jake didn't back away. Some of the long-held patterns began to give way.

At our next session, Sally and her mom came in by themselves because Jake had to attend a last-minute work meeting. Shortly after it began Paula began to talk about her depression. She said she had been thinking about trying to wean herself off her antidepressant medication.

"I'm feeling much better, and I'd like to see if I can do without it," she said.

Sally began talking about her own history of depression. "I've always thought of depression as a spiritual problem," she said, and I nodded.

"I like that," I said. I added, "Our intimate relationships are powerful mood-regulators."

Paula smiled as she said, "You know, before we came to see you, I was feeling very depressed. I thought I needed some other medication, and I called my psychiatrist to see if he could prescribe something else for me. He had a waiting list and couldn't see me for a month. And now look what's happened!"

Sally laughed. "Sometimes waiting lists are a good thing!"

Paula began to think of her problems as dynamic—a mood state that has context and meaning, that can change. I was struck that she had never had these conversations with a professional before. The only way Paula knew how to think about depression is that it's something you have, a checklist of symptoms, not a mood that is part of a larger, relational picture. Paula lacked ownership when it came to how she felt. Depression was something like weather—we don't have any responsibility for it, we just have to find a way to deal with it.

I saw Paula's depression as a reflection of her experience of disempowerment. She was self-aware enough to realize that her rather chaotic upbringing made her husband's assertive conduct attractive. She wanted relief from instability, not anticipating the downside to her husband's ultraconfidence in his positions. An amateur when it came to conflict,

Paula, a dedicated peace-seeker, took the escape route when it came to conflict. But, of course, in the long run, escape never really works.

When they first came to therapy, this family saw themselves as discreet individuals, with individual problems. They had names for their individual problems which, until now, had individual solutions. However, this framework didn't do much for them in terms of pain relief. Only when they began to connect their personal distress to their relationships with each other did the family patterns begin to transform. This acted as an antidepressant for the whole family. And the initial side effects were good.

Much of the fighting died down between Sally and her father, and both Sally and her mother seemed less depressed. Jake became slightly more self-reflective, though he still didn't seem to understand his daughter in any meaningful way. Sally prepared to move to Boston to begin divinity school and our therapy came to an end, after about eight sessions. But family patterns had begun to shift.

My rather relentless yet caring challenging of Jake, undoubtedly contributed to the loosening of this family's stuck dynamics. I knew as I was doing it that I was breaking an invisible family rule—don't mess with the King. I knew that for many years Sally had been fighting to get her father to be more flexible, more open, and it was hurting her. But I also knew that she had been trying to do this for many years, and it was hurting her. I believed that Sally's failed attempts to rebalance her family's power dynamic contributed to her emotional pain, to her depression. She had become the family scapegoat.

I wanted to relieve Sally of her thankless mission to demote her father. As I "fought" with him, I hoped to show Paula that it was okay, necessary, to fight with Jake. He needed to get off his high horse. If I was going to tiptoe around Jake, I wouldn't be interrupting these prob-lematic patterns; I would be reinforcing them.

As we said goodbye at our last session, I felt rather warm and fuzzy toward this family. I knew our sessions had been intense for them and they each emerged from this experience looking like life would be bet-ter. I was impressed by how they embraced the therapy. Unfortunately, as the family dynamics initially began to shift, apparently nothing sub-stantial changed, at least in the long run. I got a call from Jake nearly five years later, saying his daughter was coming home from divinity school and he would like to set up a meeting. He said, "We're still not getting along."

Indeed, when I saw them again, Jake and Paula had reverted to form. The picture was not pretty. Jake's superiority was on full unattractive display, with Paula sitting mostly silently by his side, appearing to agree with whatever he said. Ouch.

I naturally asked myself, What happened? What could I have done during our first meetings to help nail down some of the early progress they had made? Were the changes that I had observed in the family superficial, insubstantial? As I thought about it, I realized that we had only completed Phase I of the therapy. Phase II included addressing some of the underlying patterns the couple had created that contributed to so much depression in Paula and kept Jake in his role as Dr. Know-it-All.

I'm not sure what would have happened if I had encouraged Paula and Jake to continue with therapy in order to address some of the issues we'd uncovered. I don't know if they would have taken me up on it. The conflict between Paula and Jake had been concealed for many years, and, while they began to open up some of the old wounds, especially Paula's, they weren't used to thinking of themselves as a couple with "problems." They thought the problem was with their daughter. She was used as a sacrificial lamb so the parents could maintain their self-image as a close-knit, happy couple. In retrospect, I wish I had invited them to continue with therapy instead of assuming we were done once Sally moved away.

I met with Sally and her parents for two sessions before she returned to Boston. I tried to encourage this family by reminding them of the good work they had done five years earlier. At one point in our session Jake became tearful when talking about his relationship with his daughter. I took this as a good sign, that perhaps there was a crack in the armor of this man who seemed so self-satisfied. But after Sally returned to school, Jake and Paula declined to continue therapy. I hadn't been successful in getting Jake to be curious enough about himself and his contribution to the family distress. He seems to want to keep his daughter as the only patient in the family.

Sally, now a young, independent woman, and I have developed a therapeutic relationship. We meet occasionally by phone. I continue to be impressed by her thoughtful ability to look both at herself and her family. She appears to find our meetings helpful and is open to learning. I'm not yet sure about her parents.

No matter what happens, therapy provides endless opportunities to learn, to grow, to deepen our understanding of ourselves. As therapists, we all have our own strengths and limitations as a result of our upbringing and from life circumstances; we're neither saints nor perfectly crafted human beings. What this case illustrates is that even if the full family dynamic doesn't shift, confronting the patterns can still help individuals to heal. In this case, Sally felt affirmed in her experience as the family scapegoat, and that affirmation of her reality empowered her to begin to see herself and her life in a new way.

THE MAN WITH THE STONE-FACED MASK

In this next case the presenting problem isn't depression, but a relationship gone awry. Depression emerges from the shadows through the looking glass of the relationship.

When Francis called me, he didn't beat around the bush, "My relationship is in terrible shape. It may be too late." He agreed to bring in his partner, though he said, "He may not want to come."

When Francis and Oba showed up for their first appointment, I don't think I had ever seen a more disconnected couple. Francis, a rather stocky, handsome man in his early forties had an open, buoyant demeanor; he looked almost cheerful, despite his dire prediction of relationship doom. Oba, on the other hand, appeared nearly comatose. Tall and elegantly slim, he wore a nearly expressionless mask, though I suspected a simmering anger lying beneath. Francis eagerly declared himself a "veteran of therapy." He said, nodding at Oba, "He didn't want to come, but I insisted."

Oba looked like he'd rather be anywhere else but sitting in a therapist's office. He said simply, "I am here," as if that ended the discussion.

My standard question, "How can I help?" was met with silence.

Then Francis began to open up. According to him, Oba had fallen for another guy, Rafael, and was thinking about moving out. Strangely, Francis denied being jealous. I got the feeling early on that Francis didn't want to admit to any "negative" emotions. My initial impression was that he was committed to presenting an upbeat version of himself.

He talked about Rafael in an almost factual way, as if Oba's new relationship was a mere annoyance, an interference, nothing more. Oba, for his part, said, "This isn't about Rafael. We've been having problems for many years. I can't continue like this." I subsequently learned that Oba had been suffering from a deep, though unspoken, depression. Several months before they came to see me, he had attempted suicide by swallowing aspirin, which only made him sick. I found out later that Francis and Oba never talked about this incident.

Francis and Oba had been living together as a couple for the past twenty years. Francis was the only son of a well-to-do family in California. His mother had passed away several years earlier, and he had a distant, semiformal relationship with his only sister. Francis remained close to his elderly father, whom Francis spoke of fondly. Francis described a complicated relationship with his mother.

"I'm pretty sure she didn't love me unconditionally," he said. He never felt she really approved of him, though his biggest wound occurred after he came out as gay. He said, "She threw me out of the house and didn't speak to me for two years." They eventually reconnected, though, in the style of his family, never spoke about it.

Francis's father, who went along with the mother's banishment of their only son, later told him, "That was the biggest regret of my life."

Oba, the second oldest in a large and loving family, was born in Nigeria. Many of his siblings were in the United States, enjoying successful careers as lawyers and accountants. Oba, a physician, had gone to medical school in Nigeria and came to the United States for his residency. After a few sessions, he began to open up about the pain of his beloved mother's death a few years before. Oba's siblings formed a large and important source of support and strength for him.

"We talk about everything," he said. Oba was lucky to have the kind of family that he did. Despite homosexuality being taboo in much of Africa, Oba said, "My family almost shrugged it off. No one had an issue with it." Even when he used to put on his sisters' makeup and dance around the house, his parents reacted with benign acceptance. During the course of their long relationship, Francis had of course met Oba's family. He nodded in agreement to Oba's description of his familial bonds.

Francis and Oba were parents to two boys, fifteen and twelve years old, whom they had adopted nine years earlier. As I got to know the couple, it became obvious that their lives as parents created a huge strain in their relationship, magnifying their differences and building emotional walls between them.

Francis, whose job as a professional recruiter allowed him to work from home, was the "mother hen," watching over his brood, shepherding them to activities, ever alert to protecting them from danger, especially of the emotional kind. The problem was that Oba had become identified as a source of that danger. Over the course of several months of meeting, it became clear that Oba held the unofficial label as the family "bad guy." Francis and the kids both viewed him as the stern, angry parent whose job it was to stand in the way of all fun. It became obvious to me that Oba had been marginalized, and I suspected this isolation helped to create his despair, which led to his suicide attempt.

Oba, by his own admission, had certain ideas about what children needed. Accountability and respect ranked high on his roster of what parents should expect from their kids. Raised in a poor country, Oba and his siblings developed a powerful work ethic that they hoped would lift them from poverty. They knew no one would hand them anything. As a young man, Oba worked hard, both at home and at school, and he expected his kids to do the same. He was also a bit of a self-declared neat freak and a hoarder, both of which were his way of (unconsciously) warding off potential disaster. These tendencies drove Francis up the wall, and I surmised by the couple's comments that their kids picked up on Francis's irritation.

Oba's stern style of parenting stood in contrast to the more freewheeling approach of Francis. His well-off upbringing, with a successful father who guaranteed that they would want for nothing, gave Francis a freedom that allowed him to take chances, knowing that a financial safety net would catch him if he fell. By contrast, Oba was always on edge, guarding against whatever adversity might strike, and his anxiety grew as their kids got older. At times, he was nearly frantic at the thought of his sons, young Black men, becoming potential victims of racism or police brutality. This race consciousness was something Oba developed since leaving Africa. In Nigeria, he didn't think of himself as Black. He only learned what that meant when he came to the United States.

The therapy, though intense, lasted a fairly short time—only a few months. From our initial visit it appeared the couple was on their way to separation, with Oba making plans to move in with Rafael. It didn't sound to me like Oba was in any way in love with this new guy; he framed it more that Rafael needed him, and he was answering the call. And there was no sign that Francis was especially hurt or angry about this betrayal; he cast it mostly in terms of his dislike for Rafael, and that he was angry at Oba for his bad taste. I was clearly sitting with two men not much good at getting in touch with their feelings.

During this time, I asked them to bring their children in, which they did. These two young men showed that, as usual, kids know what's going on with their folks. I admit that, before I met them, I was worried about these children. The boys, biological brothers, had been adopted at a fairly late age, six and three years old, and I was afraid that their parents' separation was going to be a painful, unconscious reabandonment trauma for them. The boys, Anton and Michael, talked about their folks with a lot of concern. They said, "Daddy Oba seems depressed," and "Papa Francis will be fine, but we think he worries about us too much." They were quite cautious and reserved in our sessions; it looked to me like they tried to stay out of the way as their parents engaged in their (mostly silent) emotional battles.

One session stands out for me as symbolic of how this couple became so emotionally crippled. Oba had gotten the hang of this therapy thing; he started to bring more of himself to our meetings, giving me a chance to see what was behind the early, stone-faced mask. He revealed some of what his pain was made of, mostly with Francis, but also with his children.

"I always felt wrong, like I was making everyone's life worse. Whatever I did, Francis would make a face, or let me know that I was getting in the way of the family flow. I felt like a real burden." Though he didn't say so, and at that moment I didn't ask, I assumed this was the kind of hurt and anger that gave rise to his suicidal attempt.

The atmosphere in the room was still, and I was absorbing Oba's painful narrative, when Francis jumped in with something completely out of left field.

"All's well that ends well," he chirped happily.

I almost felt dizzy. I said, "I'm having an out-of-body experience," only sort of joking. It felt so strange, in the midst of such a meaningful, poignant outpouring of emotion from Oba, to hear Francis's chipper reaction. It told me a lot about this couple.

They both looked at me quizzically.

"What was that?" I asked Francis. He looked surprised. He had no idea that he had just imposed a breezy alternate reality on top of his partner's moving account of vulnerability. It's what mixing Metallica with Mozart must sound like. Of course, Francis meant no deliberate harm. But for him, expression of feelings, especially the painful kind, felt dangerous.

Francis had been raised in a family where his parents measured the quality of their life by how much "fun" they had and how many trips they took. Meaningful, serious connection was considered a downer. Things had to be kept moving, all the time: escape and avoidance were the name of the game. In this atmosphere Francis learned to fear emotional exposure of all kinds, his own and that of his partner. He acted like the tension in the room was as invisible as the air. But here it was in living color, Francis trying to cast a rosy glow on his long-time partner's honest expression of distress. And typical of this couple, when Francis struck a la-dee-dah tone, Oba withdrew. This dance undoubtedly repeated itself hundreds, thousands, of times during their twenty years together. Each partner ended up alone, invisibly nursing their hurt.

As the time drew close for Oba to move out, I think I may have been more upset at their separation than they were. I had hoped I could have helped them to create a new relationship, one that offered more of a life-giving spirit to their dance as a couple. As it turned out, however, shortly after Oba left, Francis decided to move to France with their sons. He had a friend who lived in the outskirts of Paris who offered to show them around, and both Francis and Oba thought this would be a good opportunity for their children to develop a real-world, international cultural education.

I continued to meet with them until Francis and the boys moved. The kids were excited about their new adventure and looked forward to learning a new language and checking out the French girls.

I have had only sporadic contact with Francis since the move, but our conversations are honest, and I try to offer help in whatever way I can. Occasionally, he contacts me when he is upset with one of his sons or is stuck in terms of his social life and wants to talk something through. Sometimes we discuss his relationship with Oba. Francis and

I have spoken a good deal about his fear of conflict, and how hard it is for Francis to openly express his needs and wants. We talk about his self-esteem issues, which are slowly getting better, and about how his need to put on a happy face interferes with his being able to establish a truly intimate, romantic connection. Francis is an intelligent, caring man, and I hope that he will, in time, take a few more risks in the relationship department.

Oba's life turned out to be a remarkable story. He and Rafael parted ways not too long after they moved in together, clearing the way for Oba to live on his own for the first time in many years. This man, the stone-faced physician whom I first met, this therapy-hater, had now blossomed into a funny, warm, outwardly caring, expressive individual with a full life. As I've told him more than once, "You're showing how not to waste a good depression."

Oba periodically continues therapy with me to this day. He has also shared his story with his extended family, many of whom I've now met in the office, including his sisters and beloved nieces and nephews. Oba often functions as an informal therapist for them.

As part of his self-care, Oba has become a devotee of mindfulness meditation and discontinued his antidepressants, which he began taking shortly after his suicide attempt.

"I don't need it now. I feel like I have more of a handle on how to deal with my stress, and how to handle it when I'm upset. Breathe in and breathe out," he said with a smile.

Oba not only learned how to take care of himself, but he's also learning how to let himself be taken care of. Where previously he was racked with worry over whatever drama his siblings were going through, feeling like he had to fix it, now he allows himself to be there for them in a different way, as a support, as needed. Shockingly, he also has learned to let his siblings take care of him, at least a little bit. If he is upset, they know it, calling to inquire and to offer care. At one session Oba proudly announced that his brother had surprised him by sending him a TV as a birthday gift. What made Oba so proud was that he was able to accept the gift, unabashedly, without feeling like he needed to reciprocate.

Oba's depression and suicide attempt scared him, something we talked about after he and Francis broke up. While he said, "I don't think I really wanted to die, I felt so desperate I didn't know what to do." In our post-Francis therapy sessions, I saw how Oba used this difficult period in his life to look deeply at himself, and his relationships. He showed great courage in looking honestly at his shortcomings and the ways in which he contributed to the distress in his relationship to Francis. In looking at his partnership with Francis, Oba knows too well that he became avoidant, that he didn't pursue important conversations, that he allowed his need for connection to go unmet, and unaddressed. When he talked about his siblings, he said almost proudly, "We argue about everything." Oba smiled, knowing that this "arguing" is part of their intimacy. He regrets backing away from arguing with Francis, appearing to accommodate instead of talking about how he really felt. He vows that in his next relationship, "I won't be afraid to argue."

But perhaps the biggest change of all is with his children. Though the boys moved to Paris with Francis, they came back relatively often, for holidays or family visits. Oba, therapy-maven that he has become, often insisted the kids come and see me for a visit, both on their own and with him. One meeting with Oba and his kids stands out. At this session, these young men were weighing in on their family, their parents, and, in particular, Oba. Suddenly, the oldest son, Anton, then seventeen, a highly sensitive, bright young man, quietly nodded toward his father sitting before him.

"I've been afraid of him for a long time," he said. A hush fell over the office. Oba didn't move, but you could tell he felt this like a blow. Oba didn't say anything while I praised this young man for taking a risk by opening up this painful issue.

I was not surprised that his sons feared him. Francis had alluded to this in our joint sessions, but I didn't expect Anton to address it so directly. You could tell that Oba's heart broke at that moment. He murmured a few words, "I'm sorry, I feel terrible," but his face said it all. He clearly wanted his son to know this was NOT the father he meant to be. Oba was never afraid of his own parents, and this was an inadvertent wound he had visited on his son.

Oba responded to that meeting by writing Anton a long letter, describing and apologizing for all the anxiety he caused as Anton was growing up. He talked about his own upbringing, some residual family trauma, his worries, which he now saw as excessive, and vowed to do better. Oba talked to me about the letter, knowing that he took a chance, and having no idea how Anton would respond, or if he would "forgive" him.

A couple of years have passed since that letter and Oba has his answer. Anton has since sent him Father's Day cards with "love" in the signature—a first—and has written him a heartfelt note for Oba's birthday. Anton is now in college near Oba's home. They get together for dinner when Anton is free, and much to his father's surprise, Anton sometimes unexpectedly stops by and stays for a few hours. Oba says, "We laugh. He lets me tease him. He told me about his new girlfriend, though he won't let me meet her yet. And now when I text, he texts me back!" For Oba, this is the greatest achievement of all. He earned it.

Each of these stories illustrates, in different ways, how depression is embedded in patterns in relationships. These adults knew they were depressed but couldn't understand it or do anything about it. Looking at depression in the context of their relationship offered each of these couples a new perspective, a new set of possibilities. Some couples, however, don't, can't, or won't respond to therapy, paving the way for continued misery, or divorce. There are some special ingredients with these kinds of couples. The next chapter shows you what this recipe looks like.

Questions for Reflection

In "The Problem of the Nice Boyfriend," Julie had no idea that David was depressed and lonely. She only saw his indifference, which she interpreted as meaning that he had no feelings for her. If your partner seems indifferent, it's probably a mask. What might be behind the mask? How could you find out?

In "The Woman Who Misplaced Her Voice," Paula developed a very cautious relationship with her husband, afraid to challenge him or speak out. This helped to foster depression in her. How else might she have handled her domineering husband? Have you ever found yourself continually avoiding conflict? What was the reason? What was the price?

In the story "The Man with the Stone-Faced Mask," the couple came to therapy too late to save their relationship. Since we know it takes (at least) two people to create a marriage, what did each partner contribute that made their relationship fail? Do you identify more with Francis or Oba?

Chapter 2

The Predivorce Couple

THE HUSBAND WHO CAN DO NO WRONG

For our first session, Mira showed up at my office alone. Barely one hundred pounds with lustrous long auburn hair, she exuded a cheerfulness that masked a desperation about the state of her life. Her wide brown eyes conveyed deep anxiety as she described chronic digestive issues that her doctor believed might be related to stress.

She said, "As soon as I told my doctor about my marriage, she said I should come see you. She thought my stress was affecting my stomach."

Mira described constant fighting, along with a coldness from her husband. "It's killing me," she said.

"Bring this gentleman in," I told her. "Let's see what's going on."

Mira's husband, Howard, came with her for our next session. You could feel the tension emanating from this couple from across the room. By the time they came to see me, Mira and Howard had burned through several other therapists, with no improvement. I learned that this was Mira's second marriage and Howard's first. Mira was very young when she married her first husband. That marriage ended with a whimper, not a bang. She said she and her first husband remained friends. "There were no hard feelings," she said. Howard had very little relationship experience before he got together with Mira. He had casually dated several women, but each relationship lasted no more than a couple of months. He was nearly forty when he met Mira. They both wanted children, and had almost given up, when they were unexpectedly blessed with the birth of their daughter, now four years old. According to them they always had "problems" in their relationship, but the conflict became more constant after the birth of their daughter. As I got to know these folks it sounded to me like they had had serious issues almost from the beginning. As a matter of fact, in the retelling of their history, Howard and Mira were not able to string together any memories of more than a month or two in their ten years as a couple where they felt happy with each other. For the majority of their marriage their connection was either neutral or rife with bickering and misunderstanding. You don't have to be a genius, or a family therapist, to know that this is a bad sign. Most couples, no matter how fraught their connection, can point to a period of time when they enjoyed each other. Sometimes it's before kids, or they can recall extended periods of time—not moments—being in love. Even if it feels like a distant memory, it's there. Love builds equity in the relationship for when times are hard. It's the foundation that helps keep the house from falling down.

So why did they marry? We can't really answer that question since our selection of a partner is a largely unconscious process. With this couple, it seemed like Mira's illness gave Howard a chance to be her knight in shining armor; something they both may have been craving. That sealed the deal.

Mira told it this way: "Howard and I had broken up for the second time, and it looked like we were finished. Then I got sick."

It turned out that Mira developed serious complications from pneumonia and had to be hospitalized for several weeks. She could have died.

Mira remembered, "Howard was wonderful. He was by my side the whole way. It was a really scary time. I was so grateful to him."

Mira's own parents, while caring, were unable to be there for her in the same way. They were immigrants, having left the Ukraine in their early twenties, settling in New York, where they raised Mira and her older brother. Both her parents now suffered from their own health problems, and I got the impression that Mira didn't expect, or ask for, much caretaking from them. She was more their parent, navigating the culture and helping to manage their finances. That was Mira's side of the story. What reason did Howard give for marrying Mira? "She's beautiful," he said. That summed it up for him. He alluded to that reason many times during our sessions, wondering if "I just fell for her because she's beautiful. I can't help it."

Howard seemed to flourish in his role as caretaker. He glowed when Mira recounted how "wonderful" he was during this difficult period of her illness. In fact, Howard seemed to thrive on being told he was "wonderful," which he learned from being treated as "the prince" in his own family. I saw this firsthand when I had his parents in for a session. Since the initial days of our therapy, a great deal of the couple's bickering centered on Howard's complaints about how Mira treated his family. He wanted to spend more time with them and take their daughter to visit his family more often than Mira was willing. I mostly supported Howard in his cause since I thought Mira was overcautious with their daughter. She closely controlled their daughter's time with the in-laws, an unnecessary monitoring that fueled tension between the couple. Because in-law dynamics figured so prominently in their fights, having both sets of parents in for a session was important. I wanted to see this battleground for myself, which I thought might open some new therapeutic opportunities for my work with this difficult couple.

Both of Howard's parents came, while only Mira's mother showed up. Her father had a number of chronic illnesses that made travel difficult. Both sets of parents enjoyed a cordial, though not especially close relationship with each other. Mira's mother was a lovely, dynamic woman who laid the blame for her daughter's troubled marriage at the feet of both partners.

"They are both stubborn," she said of her daughter and Howard. "I tell her to go easy on him, not to argue so much. But she gets mad. I can't do anything." She added, "I love my granddaughter. I will do anything to help them."

When I invite the parents of a couple into a session, I usually treat them as my cotherapists, asking them to weigh in with their observations. Of course, I am observing them as well.

When I asked Howard's parents about their son and his marriage, his mother's protectiveness toward her only child proved a striking contrast to Mira's mom.

"Howard is a wonderful husband," his mom said, "and he just loves his little daughter. I just wish we could see her more" (a dig at Mira).

I tried to push a little: "Don't you have any advice for your son? His marriage is in hot water," I said. Howard's mom shook her head. "Not really," she said.

I knew, from both Howard and Mira, that Howard was often verbally abusive toward his mother, yelling and belittling her. It sounded like his mother gave it right back, and they ended up fighting like lovers. Howard had talked about this in our sessions, always saying, "I feel bad when I talk to her like that. I shouldn't do it." Neither Howard nor his mother addressed this in our session. But Howard's mother apparently didn't mind. She couldn't come up with anything her baby could do differently. The father, a man of few words, an old-school kind of guy, offered little during the session. He operated mostly as a quiet, though friendly witness.

I continued to see this couple for more than a year, with no real change, except in Mira. In nearly every therapy with a couple, I treat both partners as players in the duet. Both contribute to the music they make, its dissonance and harmony. I spent many sessions challenging Mira in a variety of ways. After the surprise birth of her child rather late in life, Mira's protective mothering instincts led her to put their daughter's needs front and center, even when it wasn't necessary. Howard felt sidelined much of the time, a lonely place to be.

I said, "I think it's hard for Howard to break into your cozy bond," alluding to the overflow of attention she directed toward her daughter.

Mira also unknowingly patronized Howard, chiding him for parenting faux pas: "Honey," she'd say, "I need you to man up," when he failed to feed their daughter the "right" way. She also belittled his efforts in the romance department, calling him "cold" and "robotic." "He doesn't know how to turn me on," she'd say. When I challenged Mira about her patronizing attitude toward Howard, she would listen, respond, and try to understand. She openly reflected on her behavior and emotional responses. She was not defensive. Mira was interested in learning and growing. I enjoyed working with her. Our relationship felt dynamic.

Mira made efforts to change. She loosened up her "rules" for visiting Howard's parents, taking their daughter to visit more often, and making the effort to be closer to them. And, for her husband's fiftieth birthday she put on a display of affection worthy of a king. She arranged an elaborate party for all their friends, complete with an adoring, flattering slide show presentation, all about "wonderful" Howard.

Not so with Howard. He wouldn't let me tell him anything he didn't want to hear. Howard seemed like a man intent on propping up his brittle self-image. A successful managing director at an accounting firm, he harbored resentment that he hadn't made it as a part of the "boys club" in the finance world. That was his dream, thwarted when he failed to land a job on Wall Street. He was a guy with a chip on his shoulder. I tried everything I could think of with Howard, even seeing him a few times individually. During therapy the couple would experience a month or two of relative peace, usually because Mira had taken a "one down" position to Howard. She would praise him, cater to him, or otherwise feed him in the way he liked. But of course, no couple can sustain this fragile pattern, nor should they. Inevitably it falls apart. As long as Mira was loving toward Howard, the relationship rolled along with relative calm. But if she was upset with him, angry, or hurt, Howard shut her down, claiming, "She's crazy. I have tapes to prove it." Awful as this sounds, he apparently audiotaped her during their arguments at home.

During our year together, believe it or not, this couple came to sessions almost weekly. They showed up more regularly than most couples I see. I think this reflected Howard's compulsive nature: he liked things orderly and predictable, and our sessions became part of that. But this guy frustrated me; he lacked curiosity about himself, and he displayed no imagination. He showed a remarkable pseudo-innocence, a virgin-man, like someone who had not made mistakes in life and taken responsibility for them. More than that, he was unable—or unwilling—to hear Mira's pain in the relationship. He mocked her in our sessions or showed disdain for her viewpoint. He threw mini temper tantrums in the sessions when he felt "falsely accused" by Mira. Mostly, he remained stubbornly rigid, unable to look at himself honestly.

In order to get through to this guy with his ten-feet thick armor, I often bordered on therapeutic rudeness. "According to you, you're always the smartest guy in the room," I said. Or, "You're determined to remain blind, deaf, and dumb. You'll never be able to get the love you're hungry for." Whenever I challenged him in this way, attempting to expand his vision of himself that conflicted with his own idealized self-image, he shut it down. But he kept returning to therapy. I had no idea what, if anything, the guy was getting out of it.

Eventually I had enough. I felt like I was propping up a marriage rather than helping to create any meaningful change. And it's hard to capture the vitriol Howard projected toward his wife. As part of my therapy practice, I have family doctors, residents in training spend time with me in the office. I felt bad for them. Many of these doctors were women. They appeared mildly traumatized as they heard, and experienced, Howard's rancor toward Mira. They weren't used to such drama in their office setting. The catalyst for ending the therapy came when Howard mocked me one day. That was it for me. The couple came in as usual, at odds about some small thing.

I challenged Howard's reaction to something Mira said, and he shot back, his voice dripping with disdain," Oh, yeah, Mira knows everything. How come you don't believe me when I tell you this lady is crazy? How come you just don't get it?"

I was done. I knew I wasn't going to get through to this guy. I felt the contempt in his voice. He didn't respect me, much like he didn't respect Mira. Maybe it was a woman thing.

I didn't officially end the therapy that day, but I did see Howard alone the following week when Mira was out of town. I told him there was no point in continuing the therapy.

"I've done what I can do. I'm not a magician who can pull a rabbit out of the hat." I told him what was on my mind: "You clearly don't respect me. You're not really interested in what I have to say."

He of course protested and said, "No, no . . . I respect you!"

I went on. "I've given you the only kind of caring I know. I've tried to help you see yourself in new ways, that would make your life sweeter. I've tried to help you learn about your wife. I've listened to your worries, and your pain. But you don't let me in. Not really."

I continued in this vein for a while with some mild give-and-take with Howard. If he cared that I was ending the therapy, he didn't show it. He listened to what I had to say, but, as usual, didn't really hear. He continued to believe that his wife was "The Problem," and if only I would realize that, things would be better. We ended the session, stood up, and shook hands. I told him I would call Mira and tell her we wouldn't continue to meet. I wished him good luck.

During the course of our therapy both partners talked openly about divorce. At one point I referred them to a mediator, whom Mira contacted. She was mostly worried about the impact on their four-year-old. Howard made it clear that he would insist on joint custody, a prospect that worried Mira, since their daughter was so young, and very attached to her. She decided not to pursue divorce at that point; the idea that her daughter would be living with Howard half-time scared her. They both continued to make "lawyer" sounds, though they had not made any official moves when our therapy ended. It is only a matter of time.

Ouch! What a painful case. Why did I continue to see them for so long—over a year—you might ask? Part of it may be my incurable optimism, which I cannot really help. It's my nature. All of my baby pictures show me with a smile on my face, appearing to enjoy myself, no matter what else was going on. I also may have been seduced by the times when their relationship seemed improved. I, naively it turned out, thought it might be a turning point for the couple.

Looking back, I realize I was always holding my breath, waiting for the other shoe to drop. I also cared about these people. They were suffering—even if it was of their own making—and it's not easy to tell people to go away, especially when they keep wanting to come back. Maybe I must confess to unconscious hubris, a dangerous quality for a therapist. I do carry the conviction that I can help most people. This is borne out of my many years of experience where I've had the pleasure of helping all different kinds of folks who come to me for therapy. Mostly I can figure out a way to give patients what they need, even if it's not the way they want it. Translation: I am mostly able to help the folks who come to me for therapy. But not always, as this case attests.

I felt relieved, and just a touch guilty, after I stopped seeing them. I had no illusions that the results would have been different had I done this or that. The fact that my young family doctor students were borderline traumatized in their sessions with this couple reminded me that Mira and Howard were probably beyond repair, at least with me. Even though Howard irritated me, I did my very best to care about him. I looked for his soft spots, especially in his caring behavior with his daughter. I saw the family for a couple of sessions with their child, and Howard was a playful and attractive dad. He allowed himself to be a kid with her. It was the first time I saw any sweetness in him.

I told him at the time, "I like it when you're playful. You're much more attractive like that. I think Mira might be turned on if you showed her THAT soft guy."

He blew me off. His marriage was DEADLY SERIOUS to him. Ultimately, it was my failure to connect with Howard, and his failure to connect with me, that didn't allow for movement with this couple. He never really took in what I was saying, unless I was "siding" with him.

He could only see things from his perspective, and I could never break through. When they divorce, which I expect they will, I hope they don't continue this ugly battle and are able to find a measure of peace.

My long career as a family therapist has taught me a lot about couples and what contributes to marital misery. Most people come to my office believing that they can't change their partner. "My husband is the way he is," or "My wife is that way with everyone." They imagine their partner to be a fixed entity. They see themselves as primarily responding TO their partner, a one-way street filled with frustration. People fail to understand the most fundamental law of relationship physics: each partner changes and helps to create the other. The only question is, how? Having treated many couples over the years, I have ample evidence that each partner in the relationship changes the other—for better or worse. In fact, one of my favorite provocative questions is, "When did you stop trying to change your wife (or husband)?" Imbedded in this challenge is the idea that changing our partners is a natural phenomenon, part of a healthy dynamic. In fact, when one partner stops trying to "change" the other, the relationship tends to slip into a coma that can last for months, or years.

DELICATE FLOWER

I had begun seeing Nadine and Seth, a couple in their early forties with one child, after Nadine first came to my office on her own. She was referred by her family physician for depression, which she described as "a down, down feeling, like nothing will ever get better." She told me that she felt depressed much of the time and wondered if she needed medication. She had a job she enjoyed, though work demands at times overwhelmed her. When I asked about her marriage, she started to cry as she talked about her "cold" husband. She longed for more cuddling and physical expressiveness from Seth. She didn't hesitate when I extended an invitation for him to come for our next session.

At our first couple's session, Nadine didn't hold back. She recounted a list of the ways that Seth failed her, but what bothered her most was his lack of physical affection.

She said, "I literally have to beg him to touch me. He's so cold. I feel like I'm dying! I can't go on like this." She added, "And I've tried everything."

Seth listened, seeming attentive to Nadine; he didn't defend himself. He said, "She knows I've never been totally comfortable with open displays of affection. It's how I was raised. But I think I've gotten better?" he looked at her for affirmation.

Nadine was clearly the firecracker in the relationship: expressive, dramatic, opinionated, wearing her needs on her sleeve. Seth, by contrast, reacted slowly but thoughtfully. To me HE seemed depressed.

A bit more exploring revealed the nature of this duet doldrum: it's what can happen to a relationship when a partner quits trying to change the other.

Seth said, "Nadine has been complaining about my lack of affection since we first got together, more than ten years ago now. I took her seriously. I know it's not my strong suit; no one in my family is very demonstrative, so I come by it naturally. But I heard her. I read this awesome book about massage, and I tried some of these techniques on Nadine, but it wasn't what she wanted."

It soon became clear that his efforts were a big fat failure.

He said, "I always felt clumsy with her, that I couldn't please her no matter what I did. I guess I gave up."

The way he saw himself, he might as well have had "LOSER" plastered on his forehead.

It turned out that Nadine's notion of physical affection was pretty specific, although to be honest, I never could tell what exactly she wanted. My guess is that she was trying to fill a symbolic emptiness; she was seeking a feeling, a connection that would make her feel whole. Whatever she was looking for didn't include improvisations from her man. There was a "right way" and a "wrong way" to be close, and Seth's efforts were, apparently, wrong, wrong, wrong. This showed up in our sessions. It wasn't that Nadine was exactly cruel to Seth, but she treated his efforts with a kind of condescending resignation.

She said, "You never seem very into it. It seems like you can't wait for it to be over. That makes me tense. I feel like you're just going through the motions."

He denied it, saying, "I want to please you. I just wish I could."

Seth had obviously become very self-conscious with his wife. Nadine didn't realize how she was taking the wind out of her husband's sails. He was obviously ready, willing, and able to try to please her, but she had, inadvertently, created a husband who had lost confidence in his ability to please her. Seth was now more withdrawn and "colder" than ever.

My early work with this couple revolved around these patterns of which they, of course, were mostly unaware. I wondered how Seth had become so timid with Nadine. During the first months of therapy, I was impressed by his intelligence, his humor, and his sensitivity to Nadine. In response to my interest, he shared his fantasies about ways to connect with her, but her previous dismissal of his efforts discouraged him from persisting. I worried that Seth was TOO sensitive. As soon as Nadine got upset with him, he backed off. He couldn't tolerate upsetting her. If Nadine ever, heaven forbid, started to cry in our sessions, Seth would immediately stop whatever he was talking about and reach over to pat her. Her tears, her upset, had enormous power over him. He couldn't take it.

In the course of our work together, I never saw Seth be cruel to Nadine. If anything, he was too generous, too understanding, and buried his own needs and wants. And he seemed almost congenitally afraid of his own anger. Throughout the therapy we talked about his family. He described his dad as an "anger machine" who would explode unexpectedly at Seth, his older brother, and his mother. Seth's parents divorced when he was eighteen and both went on to remarry. Seth had a loving, though semidistant, relationship with his mother who now lived in Europe. He and Nadine saw his father regularly. "He's an awesome grandfather," he noted somewhat ruefully. Apparently, the "anger machine" had slowed down with age. But he gave "anger" a bad name with Seth, and he bent over backward to be sympathetic. According to the couple, Seth did occasionally erupt in anger, volcano-like, undoubtedly a result of his pent-up feelings. Seth was always remorseful after these short-lived episodes. Nadine counted these explosions as another strike against him.

Nadine was a powerhouse in the marriage and didn't know it. For many months during therapy I openly appreciated her vivacious nature. Nadine had a real comical streak, entertaining us (me) with a variety of facial expressions and voices. I knew she needed appreciation, and I enjoyed showing it to her. But her ideas about closeness and what she wanted from Seth were very particular. She covertly controlled how, when, and why she wanted things done. Most damaging from the perspective of the couple, she was incredibly thin-skinned when it came to what she called "criticism." There was little room for Seth, or me for that matter, to point out how she threw cold water on their relationship. At the slightest suggestion that she was doing something unlovely she got her back up or dissolved in tears.

I turned to Seth. "I think Nadine is great. She's a really charming, caring person. But I'm having trouble helping her see some of the ways she's a part of the distress in this marriage."

He said, "I don't know what to do. . . . I try, but then I get tired. She takes everything so personally. I can't get through."

I said, "Maybe if you could help Nadine to feel your pain, that might help her to change. But when you withdraw, she can't feel you."

I was thinking that Seth's kid-glove treatment of his wife made it difficult for her to realize the pain she was causing him. There wasn't enough sustained heat in the relationship for the marital fever to break.

Nadine's family background also became a part of our work—she even brought her mother in for therapy when she was in town for a visit. Nadine turned out to be a classic "parental child," one of those kids who ends up as the mother's or father's parent. In Nadine's story, she became responsible for her mother after her parents separated when she was seven years old. Nadine's mother, Angela, only twenty-five years old at the time, became overwhelmed after her husband left, and ended up scrambling to make ends meet. She also had a series of unfortunate boyfriends for several years, before she went back to nursing school, which gave her both income and self-esteem.

At the session in the office, Angela, a lovely, thoughtful woman, talked about how she believed Nadine "ended up watching over me, during that period when I wasn't too stable. She was a really good kid. Just a little bossy sometimes," she added with a smile. They had an open conversation, sharing reflections from that difficult period after the parents separated.

"I remember being very anxious," Nadine said. "I never knew if we'd have enough money, or if you'd end up getting engaged to a bum!"

Nadine laughed, but the pain in her voice showed through. She also talked about an open wound related to her father: he was the power center of the family, a businessman who went on to make a ton of money, remarry, and have a couple of kids, Nadine's half-brothers. Nadine thought what she called her "low self-esteem" stemmed from the relationship with her critical father. "I was never good enough for him," she said. They continue to see each other, vacationing as a family, with most of the past troubles swept under the rug.

At our next session Nadine said she was "grateful" for being able to have this kind of free conversation with her mother. "I think it helped us be more honest with each other," she said. "It brought us closer."

In addition to the turmoil in their marriage, Nadine and Seth expressed a lot of shared anguish over six-year-old daughter Mia. Nadine said, "I'm at my wit's end." Mia was apparently a handful, refusing to go to bed, not listening. By their report she sounded like quite a willful child. Family therapist that I am, I said, "Bring the little darling in for the next session."

What a child! This little girl kept me and her parents on their toes. Bright, hilariously funny, emotional, she was a mini version of her mom. She resented any instruction from her parents, especially when it came to minding her own business. Mia was in EVERYBODY's business. She had an opinion on everything. After we were playing for a while with my dollhouse, I asked Mia to tell me about her family.

She looked at her parents and with the eye of a sober judge said, "They fight all the time. I tell them to stop, and they don't listen to me." I said, "You sound like the doctor. They're not very good patients?" "Exactly!" she said. "They're terrible patients!"

Mia was so busy monitoring her parents and being at the center of their attention that she would not, literally, let them have a conversation in which she was not included. This is a phenomenon not uncommon with an only child, but Mia presented this version in exaggerated form.

I noticed, meanwhile, that Seth looked like a good dad. He enjoyed his daughter and her comic ways. She obviously delighted him. However, he wanted to be firm with her when needed. Seth said, "Hold on, little dude," as Mia tried to worm her way into a conversation between her parents. I watched as Nadine undercut him; Seth metaphorically closed the door, Nadine opened it. She acted like she didn't trust Seth, that she had to remain on duty with Mia.

I looked at the parents and suggested, "How about if the grown-ups have a few moments to finish their conversation and Mia can do some drawing?"

Boom. Mia went nuts. She started crying (not real tears), looking at her parents, complaining, "You don't love me," generally being a real pest. This child was obviously so used to having an open door to her parents, especially Mom, at all times. A closed door, even for a few minutes, felt like an insult, a betrayal. Mia repeated, "You don't love me," an obvious effort to get her parents to give in. I could see Nadine wavering—she allowed Mia to push her buttons even though Seth was there for support, trying to reassure Mia and still have a two-person conversation with his wife.

I said to these well-meaning parents, "Wow. Mia acts like you've just sent her to jail. Like she's being punished. This little smart child doesn't know that parents sometimes talk between themselves, without her." I looked at Mia, shrugging my shoulders, "It's crazy. The grownups even make decisions without consulting you!"

Mia soon settled down, plopping down on the floor with crayons and a large pad of drawing paper I keep in my office. As the grownups talked, Mia seemed happily engaged in her drawing, though she kept herself in the middle of the conversation by interjecting in a sing-song tone. She would mimic her mom or dad: "I feel like you're not listening to me," she sang or adding her own spicy comments. She WAS quite a pistol. We ignored her.

I sounded a small alarm as I looked at the couple: "Mia's having a hard time being a six-year-old. It's strange that she thinks she's in charge of what her parents do. And it's a burden for her."

As the session continued, we talked about Mia's intrusiveness and hypersensitivity to limit-setting. According to the parents, bedtime was a harrowing ordeal every night.

I told them, "You guys have to fight too hard for authority about small things. This may be semicute now, but you're not going to be having any fun when she's thirteen."

A pout crossed Nadine's face. "I'm a bad mom," she whined. She looked like she meant it.

I had a quick "aha" moment—this is where Mia learned it. Mom looked just like Mia, sad, pouty face, appearance of fragility, like I told her she was a bad mommy. And I was a mean therapist.

I looked at Nadine: "You're acting like I'm a meanie. When I'm talking to you about the problems you're having and what you might be doing to contribute to it, you look like you're going to collapse."

My next question was implied but not stated: "What's up with that?" I knew that Nadine was anything by fragile, had a good sense of humor and a well-developed sense of irony. She looked surprised. I brought Seth into the conversation.

I said, "I know where Mia gets it. She makes you feel like you're doing something bad to her, just by telling her to go to bed. Nadine just made me feel like I was treating her bad, telling her she was an awful mother. Of course, I didn't say that, and I don't feel that. I think Nadine's great."

Seth said, "I have the same problem with Nadine. She does not want to hear what I think, especially if it's at all critical, or different from what she thinks. So, I shut up."

This theme had emerged in previous sessions, with Seth complaining that Nadine is oversensitive to criticism and that she doesn't want to hear what she doesn't want to hear. Then he withdraws and remains on the sidelines in her battles with her daughter.

Mia appeared to be intent on her drawing, not saying anything, though I assumed she was listening. She knew all about what we were discussing. She felt these patterns acutely.

As the session finished, Nadine burst out, "You know, that 'collapsing' thing—that's something my mother used to do to me. It's obnoxious!"

We all laughed. That's what I liked about Nadine—her defensiveness seems permeable, open to transformation. She appeared willing to work on herself. But she couldn't do it on her own. Her husband needed to help her—REALLY help her, including being willing to fight, if necessary.

Nadine was an attractive woman, stylish, funny, and honest, but this was her Achilles' heel. She didn't like criticism and overly personalized any challenge as being a blow to her self-worth. We hadn't previously made the connection between her behavior and her daughter's, but now it was painfully obvious. When the family got up to say goodbye, Mia sidled over to me and gave me a hug. I thanked her, saying, "That was the best hug I've had all day." I think, maybe, that was Mia's way of showing appreciation; I saw what was going on in her family and I was trying to help.

Our next session continued with the same theme. Nadine apparently still wanted to take issue with me. "I felt very defensive in that meeting. Sometimes I feel like you're judging me." I asked what she meant, and she said, "I feel like you're telling me I'm a bad parent. When you say something is strange, I feel like I'm bad."

This was not, of course, the first time she'd mentioned this. I began to feel exhausted. I've heard Seth say he was "exhausted" and now I knew what he meant. I've showered Nadine with so much caring since we began meeting. I've talked about how smart and funny she is—she can be very attractively comical—I've showed appreciation for her in so many ways. But criticism or "rejection," as she calls it, is intolerable. I think that's why she had so much trouble learning new ways of operating. What a tough way to live—both for her and her family.

Seth again tried to duck out of this mess by wondering, in a joking tone, "Isn't there a drug for this?" I looked directly at him, saying, "Nadine's medicine is sitting next to her," meaning him. He said, "I've tried . . . but you can only do so much."

Months prior, we had several sessions that related to Seth's conflict-avoidance and the way his stepping away from problems made his wife feel "empty." Over the course of the next several months, I continued to press Seth to stop being so wimpy with his wife. I teased him, I cajoled him, I challenged him. I really liked this guy. He was superintuitive, smart, caring with a deeply ironic sensibility. He felt my respect for him, and he grew slightly more confident about his ability to change Nadine. He stopped withdrawing so much, came a bit more alive with his wife, and their relationship seemed to improve.

Is this a predivorce couple? Sadly, yes. Though things got better for a while, nothing really changed. They started fighting less and having sex more. Nadine accidentally got pregnant, and they had another daughter, which thrilled little Mia. She now had someone else to boss around. They moved to a nearby suburb and stopped therapy. I never felt that I had a meaningful breakthrough with Nadine. About four years after our last session, I got a call from Seth. Nadine wanted a divorce. She had a boyfriend. They wanted to come in to talk about how to tell their children they were separating.

I met with them a couple of times, but the first meeting was the most telling. At some point during the four years since they'd left therapy, things started deteriorating. Nadine said they saw a couple of therapists in their neighborhood—sessions that she described as "useless." She and Seth started talking seriously about separating, which was more Nadine's wish than Seth's.

As she told the story, "I was starved for affection. I couldn't take it. I proposed that, until we separated, we could have an open relationship. We could date, as long as we didn't tell the other person about it. I thought Seth was on board."

Then she met someone. Seth went ballistic.

He erupted, "I never agreed to that! We talked about it in theory, and you know I never liked the idea. I said we needed to wait until we actually separated to start dating. This is not okay with me!"

I had never seen this Seth before: angry, in a good way, passion flaring, demands front and center, non-negotiable. He looked amazing, attractive, alive. I couldn't help myself: "Wow. Where was this guy during the marriage?" I asked. It was a rhetorical question; the marriage was over. Nadine had supposedly fallen in love.

I cannot tell you how my heart sank when I heard Nadine say, "I was starved for affection." These were almost the exact words, and the exact sentiment, she expressed when I first met her nearly six years earlier. I couldn't help but sigh. Had her perspective not shifted one inch? Maybe it was part pride, part ego on my part, but a creeping, useless feeling crept over me. Had she not gotten anything out of our work together? Well, I can't say she didn't get ANYTHING out of it. They got a new baby, conceived when the couple enjoyed a period of harmony. But still . . . I had to make an internal adjustment not to try to talk them out of it. Although, of course, I didn't say so, I didn't like the idea of this divorce. I thought it was unnecessary. These people were not any more mismatched than any other couple. They had small kids who now had to deal with the rigors of growing up with divorced parents.

What stuck in my craw was Nadine's blindness to her own contribution to the marital woes. I wondered, in retrospect, if I had been too cautious with her. I may have inadvertently become like Seth, wary about any sustained challenge to her way of operating, unconsciously protecting her thin skin. Nadine still saw deprivation of affection as her lot in life with Seth, a fact of their marriage, not part of a dynamic between them. I may have agreed with her had Seth been a stiff, soul-less, uncaring guy. But he was none of that. He was smart and sexy, funny, and self-deprecating. He had more of an emotional range than he used in his marriage to Nadine. In his marriage he became "Shut Down Guy." The man who showed up at our last session, emotionally unleashed by his wife's affair, was the Seth I had been waiting to see. I believed he had it in him. But Nadine thought that a new relationship would fix her problem. I was far from convinced.

Both of these predivorce couples traveled through the world with what we think of as socially acceptable pathology. In other words, they functioned well as couples in society, socializing with other couples, showing up at their kids' school events, taking extending family vacations. Outside observers and friends, no doubt, noticed strains, but these couples didn't loudly announce themselves as predivorce. Let's look at a couple where that announcement was deafening.

WHEN BABY MAKES THREE

A couple, Bill and Giuliana, had been referred to me by their family physician, ostensibly because of their disputes over breastfeeding. Giuliana had been nursing their son for nearly two years, and Bill wanted her to stop. The couple came in wanting help resolving this impasse.

Bill and Giuliana had been together for around ten years. They had a two-year-old son, Paulo. Giuliana moved here from Brazil, though, according to them, not "officially" to be with Bill, whom she had met when he traveled there on work. Shortly after she moved here, however, they reconnected and soon began living together. Their early relationship sounded passionate and rocky, with Bill as "Big Daddy." He parted the waters for Giuliana, showing her the tools needed for living in New York, helping her navigate language and culture. It sounded to me like their relationship began as part marriage, part adoption.

Over time, however, the relationship balance shifted. Giuliana had developed a successful career as a Pilates instructor, sharing a busy office with several colleagues. And she became a mother, a transformation that profoundly shifted her sense of herself, giving her a sense of her own power. Bill, on the other hand, had seen his formerly thriving career as a graphic designer bite the dust. A number of factors went into what he called "my career catastrophe." He sounded depressed and bitter as he recounted his professional losses. Bill now had little work, which he attributed both to "the economy" and changing trends in his design specialty. He became a stay-at-home dad while Giuliana worked. This description of the contours of their relationship does not begin to do justice to the ugliness that emanated from Bill's mouth within the first five minutes of the first session. I realized that "breastfeeding" had little to do with it: the energy they radiated was highly toxic, mostly from Bill. It was relentless. Every time Giuliana spoke, which she did thoughtfully and without venom, Bill snapped that she was being "passive-aggressive," "dishonest," "infantile," and any other disqualification he could think of, rolling his eyes with frustration at his hopeless wife. Crazily enough, this guy showed zero self-awareness that he sounded and acted like a jerk.

The puzzle for me was that Bill was a smart guy, and a big-hearted person, in his own way. He showed the capacity to "take it"—at least from me. Since the first session, he let me call him out on how he bullied his wife. I didn't use the term "bully," but I'd been relentless about letting him know that "for a smart guy who thinks he's right, you're wrong most of the time." Though I found his behavior with his wife extremely off-putting, I also took great pains to try to understand him, and to respond positively when he allowed a moment of self-doubt to creep in. I invited him to talk about how awful it must feel to deal with such professional adversity.

I said, "You must feel like a shadow of your former self." He agreed.

Maybe because I genuinely cared about Bill, he had been surprisingly willing to let me therapeutically push him around. Occasionally, he worried out loud that Giuliana would weaponize our sessions.

"I think she's going to use what you're saying against me. She'll keep that in her mind to build her case," he said.

For Bill, if he's wrong, it means his wife gains power over him. It was all about control. Giuliana countered him. "I don't see it that way. I'm not trying to score points. I just want things to be better between us." She added, "I promise I won't use these sessions against you. I promise."

She looked like she meant it. As far as I know, she kept her promise.

We spent several months in therapy, to not much avail. Things improved slightly after a month or so. I helped to give voice to Bill's opposition to Giuliana's breastfeeding. I needed to take Bill's side on occasion if I was going to have any chance of helping them. It sounded to me like Giuliana used their son as a kind of shield against Bill, putting this little child between them to blunt her husband's constant animosity. Their child mostly slept with them, interfering with any possibility of a sex life.

I told them, "I hear Bill's distress at being shut out. It sounds like he wants to get closer to you, but he doesn't know how, with your son constantly between you."

I talked, as I often do, about how when a baby is born, the mommy "divorces" the daddy and "marries" the baby. This is a normal, healthy part of family development. The problem is that some couples have trouble "remarrying." This was such a couple, and more.

I saw that Giuliana did what she could in this marriage. She acknowledged Bill feeling "shut out," and she began weaning her son from breastfeeding. It wasn't as painful for her, or her son, as she'd expected. There was a slight uptick in good feeling between them for a minute, and they even had sex a couple of times, a new feature in their marriage. Sex had mostly stopped, buried beneath the hostilities. But pretty soon, despite Bill having gotten what he so-called wanted with his wife—no breastfeeding—business returned as usual. Bill's biting, demeaning, patronizing way of dealing with Giuliana resumed unabated. It was very painful to experience, both for me, and obviously, for Giuliana.

I didn't let up on Bill, but I wasn't really getting anywhere. I called him out, saying in every which way that he was driving his wife out the door. Bill's parents were quite involved in the couple's life, mostly as babysitters, but according to the couple, also offering loving support. Bill had two younger siblings who lived nearby and doted on Bill and Giuliana's little son. Bill sounded like he was in awe of his father, a larger-than-life character who was born in Egypt and came here as a child. His father built a successful career as an engineer, and I suspected that Bill worried he was a disappointment to his father. I invited Bill's parents to come in for a session and, somewhat to my surprise, Bill agreed to it. His parents readily accepted the invitation.

When these older folks showed up, they weren't at all what I expected. I thought that Bill's dad would be a formidable presence—even Giuliana characterized him as "a powerhouse." I didn't expect to see such a softy. When they came in, the father showed a lot more tenderness than I expected, both to Bill and to Giuliana. Both he and Bill's mom—astute, caring people—expressed enormous concern about the strife in Bill's marriage, especially because of their young grandson. They seemed inclined to want to protect Giuliana from Bill's emotionally rough treatment.

Bill's parents criticized their son with care, but neither parent sugar-coated his behavior, or their consternation.

Bill's father said, "It troubles me to see my son speak to Giuliana the way he does. He needs to show her more respect. She is a good woman, and the mother of his child."

Bill's mom, exchanging glances with Giuliana, commented, "We are very worried. Giuliana seems terribly unhappy. And we hate to see Paulo [the grandson] hearing all that language in the house." She added, "I wish Bill would realize the damage he's doing."

Bill mostly didn't react to their comments. He sat there, appearing to absorb his parents' admonition. I was wondering what he was thinking, and at our next session he let me know. "I felt like I was at an intervention," he said. I agreed. That's what it felt like: a last-ditch effort to persuade this guy to save himself—and his marriage.

We continued the therapy for another few months. Meaningful dialogue was nearly impossible with this couple. I realized that Bill was completely unwilling to learn anything from his wife. One session, I decided that words were not working. Anything I said bounced off Bill to no effect. I decided to go nonverbal. We began talking about music, especially bossa nova, one of Giuliana's favorite musical genres. She talked about how she loved to dance. I picked up my iPhone and selected one of my favorite bossa nova tracks, Flor de Lis, by the popular Brazilian singer Djavan. I looked at Giuliana and I nodded toward Bill. "Show him how to bossa nova." She said, "Now?" I nodded and pushed the play tab. Music filled the room.

Slowly, Giuliana got up on her feet but didn't seem to know how to cross the invisible barrier to reach Bill. I nodded again, encouragingly. She put her hand out and got him to his feet. They began to dance, awkwardly at first, then with a little more pizzazz. Bill didn't know much about dancing, but his wife, a smile on her face, responded gracefully to his clumsiness. When the tune ended, they returned to their seats, slightly breathless. Bill said, a slight smile crossing his lips, "We haven't had any fun like that in a long time." There was silence for a few minutes. Then, perhaps realizing that he just showed an ounce of vulnerability, Bill moved to reestablish his authority with some critical, patronizing comment toward his wife. I told him, "I think Giuliana's a fabulous teacher. I watched how she danced with you. I think she needs to teach you how to bossa nova. You should let her." We all recognized this as a metaphor. Bill said something to the effect that she didn't have the credentials to show him anything. I disagreed and said, "I just saw what a patient and sophisticated teacher she is. She knew just what you needed and led you there." I added, "Unless you let her teach you to dance, I don't think you're going to have a marriage." I repeated several variations to this theme, just to be sure he didn't miss it. And it was true. Giuliana would leave him unless she could feel like more of a person in their relationship. Not surprisingly, they had both made noises about separation during our meetings.

About six months after our first meeting, we all recognized the limitations of the therapy. I certainly felt like I had exhausted whatever creative powers I possessed. I couldn't get Bill to bend. He needed to be in charge. He needed to be the doctor in the relationship at all costs. But he had lost his patient. Giuliana had grown into a competent woman, a mother, a well-respected health instructor, a woman who knew her way around. Bill couldn't—or wouldn't—marry this woman. He could only be the husband to the woman he first met—the immigrant who needed him to show her the way. Any other arrangement proved intolerable to him and his ego.

We mutually decided to end our sessions and they thanked me. I later got an email from Bill with an additional thank-you saying they had "made more progress" in our work than with previous therapies. I'm not sure what he meant, but I accepted his seemingly heartfelt thanks. Several months later I heard from their family doctor that they separated. I had no further word from them.

I'm almost always sad when a couple who comes to see me ends up in divorce. Not so with this case. They had "divorce" written all over them when we first met. More than that, Bill's toxicity with Giuliana was unbearable. I knew she felt it, and I couldn't do anything to change it. In this case Giuliana grew up in front of her husband's eyes. She had more ownership of herself, as a mother, as a woman. Bill couldn't stand it. I believe Bill was depressed and, as is often true with men, depression presented as anger. He was depressed about his loss of status, both with his wife, and professionally. When he first met Giuliana, he was her knight in shining armor, her daddy. Giuliana outgrew him and he couldn't accept the new, and in my view improved, arrangement. His business failure ate into his identity as breadwinner and must have made him feel terrible about himself. But he wouldn't really pause long enough to consider these possibilities; he was too busy cruelly scapegoating his wife for all that was wrong.

In retrospect, I was mostly at peace with my work with this couple. I didn't argue too much with myself during the therapy or afterward. I gave it everything I had. I cared about both these people and didn't tiptoe around the issues as I saw them. Even though I was hard on Bill, I believe I got away with it because I maintained my respect for him. I'm pretty sure he felt it. I don't know what happened to them, but I hope they were able to create a more satisfying life separately than they were able to do together.

It is noteworthy that each of these predivorce couples came into therapy sideways. None came requesting couples therapy. For Mira, the ticket of admission was stress-related illness. In the case of Nadine, her depression prompted her to make the initial phone call. Bill and Giuliana wanted to figure out the whole breastfeeding conflict. In each case the misery of these couples was on dramatic display, crying out for attention.

For some couples, however, there is nothing subtle about their distress. Nothing focuses the concentration, like a bomb going off, more than the discovery of an affair. In the next chapter we see what affairs are made of, exploring the ingredients of this most painful of life's experiences. We watch to see how this betrayal can end in either disaster or triumph.

Questions for Reflection

In the story "The Husband Who Can Do No Wrong," the therapist ended up "firing" the couple. How do you feel about this? Is it ethical for a therapist to "fire" a client? Under what circumstances is this okay? In this case did the therapist give up too soon? Was there something she missed?

The case of "Delicate Flower"' told of a couple who didn't seem like they were going to end up divorcing. The therapist's disappointment was palpable, leading to some soul-searching at the end of the therapy. She wondered if she was too careful, not challenging enough with Nadine. Nadine typically cried or reacted with a sense of shame when she was challenged in the therapy. What do you think? Should the therapist have been stronger, more direct, with Nadine?

In "When Baby Makes Three" the husband showed himself to be an especially toxic character with his wife. He was top dog when they married and his loss of status in the relationship brought out his ugly side. In this case Bill's depression masqueraded as anger and meanness. This is not uncommon in men. Have you seen this? Do you know men like this? Has this happened to you?

Chapter 3

Affair Repair

I'D RATHER DIVORCE THAN FIGHT

Bill and Esther, a proper-looking couple in their early forties, came to see me after being referred by Bill's family doctor. Bill had recently confessed to his wife that he had been having an affair for the last several months with a woman he'd met at a local bar. When they came to see me, I noted to myself that a confession like Bill's was unusual. Most cheating guys wait until they are caught and are cornered into an admission. Even then they often deny it. But Bill said, "I couldn't live with myself. I love Esther and my kids." He added, "I can't stand the guilt."

Indeed, Bill looked pretty rattled when I first met them. He, in fact, looked much more distressed than Esther. While she admitted to being "shocked" by this betrayal, her tone and demeanor remained rather cool and controlled. She hadn't yet learned much about the affair, and strangely, didn't seem especially curious. It looked like she wanted to keep the affair at arm's length. But I was curious. I wanted to know what the affair was about for Bill, and what it had to do with his relationship with his wife.

Bill acknowledged that he had "fallen" for this young woman who had recently emigrated from Peru and worked as a nanny. He described their relationship as "tumultuous" (it sounded like he meant "passionate") and, though he said he ended it in order to work on his marriage, I could hear longing in his voice. He described his lover as "very demanding"—she didn't take the ending of the affair very well.

51

Esther seemed like the antithesis of the passionate, high-maintenance girlfriend. Esther was cool, calm, and collected, despite having her world shaken to what should have been to the core. In the initial therapy I knew I needed to help raise the temperature of this marriage. It looked like it had been cool for too long. "Cool" as in disengaged, polite, superficial. Since Esther seemed reluctant to show anger, or passion—positive or negative—I highlighted the damage Bill caused by the betrayal of his wife. I tried to make Bill sound like a real bastard so Esther could feel free to react.

I said to her, "Your husband cheated on you and lied to you for months. What kind of guy does this?" And, "He went through the motions of living a life with you, but his passion was somewhere else."

Strangely, Bill looked at Esther hopefully when I said this. He signaled he was ready for a lashing. He seemed to want it. I think he was begging for it, actually. He would have at least felt that Esther cared enough to retaliate or, at the very least, hold him accountable.

But Esther didn't oblige. Hmmm. This was a first for me in the therapy setting. As I got to know Esther over the next several sessions, I began to wonder about her emotional stoicism.

I said, "Esther, I've seen quite a few women in my office who've been betrayed by their husbands. Usually, they want to kick them in the shins, at the very least. You barely seem ruffled at all. What gives?"

She said, "Bill is a good man, a good father, and a good provider. He made a mistake. I think we can get over this." My heart sank. Esther seemed almost constitutionally unable to get angry.

Over the course of the next couple of weeks I began to find out about Esther's upbringing, which yielded some clues. She was the eldest child who grew up in a turbulent home. She said, "My parents bickered constantly. It was an unhappy home." Esther described how she became her parents' emotional caretaker, navigating their arguments, tending to their wounds. Now elderly, they still kept her in that role.

She said, "I'm constantly running over there to put out fires. My father is upset with my mother, my mother needs something and my father's not home. They're old now. They can't take it."

I said, "That sounds exhausting."

"Not really. I'm used to it. They need me."

Dutiful daughter. Good girl. I think Esther felt unable to escape, though I offered help and implored her to bring her folks in for a session, but she continually declined. I think she was afraid of rocking the boat. As if it hadn't been rocked!

I guessed that Esther, longtime family peacekeeper, never had the opportunity to have her own temper tantrums; she always had to be the grownup. I was not-so-secretly rooting for her to lose her cool. I mean really lose her cool. I knew it would be good for the marriage. And definitely good for her. I wondered, of course, if part of Esther's reluctance to confront her husband was part of their unconscious marital contract. Was the unspoken agreement that Esther would always remain the calm one, while Bill got to indulge his wild side? Did Esther worry that Bill couldn't handle a more emotional, demanding wife? Did she think he was too fragile or too rigid? Was this a chance to reset the marriage, to expand their roles to include more complexity and dynamism?

As I tried to shake up this dead status quo, I attempted to challenge Bill.

I said, "You opted for the cheap version of excitement. Instead of bringing some of your needs, your wants, your passions, to Esther, you chose to avoid her, not to ask anything of her."

Bill perked up a bit when I verbally pushed him around, but these conversations never gained any traction. He didn't defend himself. He wanted, and needed, a good fight. Esther wanted everything to be smooth, however. So even if I ruffled Bill's feathers, she would manage to deflect the tension. A couple of times when I pushed Bill to talk about his subterfuge, asking, "Why didn't you let your wife know you were so unhappy?" Esther would become quietly tearful, silently begging me not to be "mean" to her husband.

Bill shook his head, "I don't know," he said. "I guess I thought she had too much on her plate already."

I tried to get Esther and Bill to bring their kids in for a session. They had two daughters, ages twelve and fourteen. The couple declined.

Esther said, "I don't want to get them involved. They have enough to worry about with all their schoolwork and activities. I don't want to burden them with our troubles."

"I'm pretty sure your kids have some idea of the problems between you. They may not know about the affair, but I'm betting they feel the tension. It would give your kids a chance to talk about their family and any worries they might have. They might want to help," I answered.

I thought that having the kids in might give me a chance to stir up some helpful therapeutic trouble. Maybe one of the kids would offer something thought-provoking or challenging to the parents, something that would stir up new energy for the couple, or for Esther. I knew I wasn't having any luck getting anything going within this static, duty-bound marriage.

As we explored some of the preaffair dynamics of this couple, it became clear that they specialized in mutual avoidance. Esther said, "Bill was usually grouchy when he came home from the office. I left him alone. I knew he had a lot of work stress." They clearly never, ever, talked about their relationship and their lack of intimacy—sexual or otherwise. Bill said, referring to their sexual connection, "That's been over for a while. She's always tired, and I just got used to it." Of course, this couple never, ever fought. Heaven forbid. Mostly, their marriage was a contained, controlled duet. Bill played the role of dutiful husband and father but was dying inside. The affair was by far the biggest explosion of their relationship, and, despite Bill's hurtful, desperate effort to generate some heat in the marriage, nothing changed.

I wondered, during the course of the therapy, if Bill's longing for the other woman remained. I believe it did, though he denied it. He said, "She keeps calling me, and I finally had to block her from my phone." Esther barely seemed interested when Bill referred to his lover. That's what a marital coma looked like. Even though he cut off contact with this woman, I think something in Bill had been turned on, and he couldn't turn it off, didn't want to turn it off.

In the therapy both he and I tried in different ways to coax some intensity of feeling from Esther, but she remained closed. Bill was longing for passion—sexual and emotional. He seemed to need to know that he mattered, that he was wanted. These desires came alive for him with the girlfriend. There was no putting the genie back in the bottle.

We met for nearly half a year. Nothing moved. The marriage ended with a whimper, not a bang. Bill decided to separate. The marriage had clearly been dead for a while, probably years before the affair. As the therapist I wondered what I could have done differently. Perhaps I should have insisted that Bill and Esther bring in their kids. Or that Esther bring in her parents. Usually, expanding the number of people in the therapy setting helps get a "stuck" therapy moving. But I think

I came to feel like Bill: I couldn't get through to Esther, whose closed, predictable world traded aliveness for safety.

I haven't heard from them since they separated. I have wondered if Bill reunited with his girlfriend, and, if so, how things worked out. Or if Esther remained single, comfortable in her primary identity as a mother and daughter. In any case, I hope these good people have found a way to secure some morsels of happiness.

Bill and Esther are an example of a couple who failed that most difficult marital stress test: an affair. In thinking about the handful of cases from my office where the couple does not recover from an affair, when they split up despite coming for therapy, I have seen what distinguishes these couples from those who stay together and gain from the experience. Several different scenarios emerge: Occasionally, the problem is that the affair has lasted too long. Too much damage done, too much deception over too long a period. Or the guy who cheated balks at severing the connection with his lover. In other words, the affair is still (semi) going on. He doesn't want to let it go. No healing can begin while the intruder hangs around. Sometimes, when it's the woman who has the affair, the man's pride is injured; his hurt and anger don't allow him to consider that HE might have had something to do with the sorry state of the marriage preaffair.

The pretext for affairs varies as much as the couples themselves. But one theme stands out: these couples specialize in conflict avoidance. Out of the many couples I've seen who have been through an affair, in each and every case the couple's relationship is marked by tensions that get chronically covered up. Both people, on some level, cooperate in avoiding conflict. They may go through the motions of fighting, but it's more like bickering. They never get to the pain. Nothing gets resolved. Then the affair, like a bomb going off, blows the cover off these tensions, exposing hurt and anger in the relationship that was simmering beneath the surface. If the couple is smart, and brave, they will use this explosion to get at what has been hidden, not talked about or acknowledged, often for years. Usually, the couple did not know how to get at these tensions any other way. That's when I think, and sometimes (gingerly) say, the affair is the best thing that could have happened to the marriage.

I think of "affair repair," with its powerful dissonances and harmonies, much like a piece of music, a symphony with two movements: the first and second.

The first movement, which sets the stage for the therapy, is the apology. The apology involves, but is not limited to, the offending partner's full, honest, thorough, no-holds-barred, admission of guilt. And it can't be the "you made me do it" kind of apology. It's got to be a full-throated acceptance of complete responsibility. Because, no matter how you slice it, an affair is the coward's way out. The damage is done. It's also true that couples—especially the person on the receiving end of the betrayal—often don't know if they want to stay together. This period of confusion means that all bets are off for the moment.

The high-quality apology also means giving the injured party (almost) carte blanche for whatever they need in order to heal. This often means talking about the details of the affair, sometimes again and again. It is common for the injured person to fixate on what happened as a way to gain a measure of control. When your world has collapsed, human tendency wants to make sense of the pain. Sometimes the person on the receiving end of the betrayal wants to confront the "enemy," the person who invaded the marriage. I've never seen this backfire. It usually removes one more layer of deception.

Healing involves the proverbial "one step forward, two steps back" thing, because often the injured person needs to continually return to the scene of the crime, until they are ready to move on. This is a kind of PTSD. The good news is that, if both partners are willing, they can work together to help heal the wound. In my office the vast majority of these postaffair couples involve a husband's adultery. I have found that when the woman insists on "the truth, the whole truth, and nothing but the truth," the couple enters a new level of honesty that works in their favor on many levels.

The second movement is where the affair becomes the "best thing that could have happened." The crisis of the affair has a way of stripping people of their usual ways of seeing and doing things. The usual patterns are up for grabs. Sometimes people have to give up cherished illusions about themselves. The tricky part of this movement is that it means looking at the marriage preaffair—the whole marriage, which involves the role the wife plays if, for example, the cheater is the husband. During this movement the wife gives up clinging to a version of herself as victim and begins to look at ways she inadvertently contributed to the state of the marriage before the betrayal. The wife loses any residual innocence. Both people are, ultimately, responsible, though only one person is guilty of the betrayal. This is where the marriage enters into a more mature, honest, more complex, deeper, and richer relationship. And ultimately more satisfying.

Affair repair is not for the fainthearted. But of course, neither is marriage. I often observe the affair and recovery process as a "death/rebirth" experience for the couple, both as a duet and as individuals. As they discard the "dead" parts of the marriage, unexpected avenues of connection can come alive. It's not unlike the sense of renewed appreciation for living that people often feel after the trauma of a life-threatening illness.

In my experience the repair process for a couple looks slightly different when the woman is the transgressor. Most of the cases I've seen involve male infidelity, and I think there is a reason for this. Women, in general, are most often willing to explore difficult emotional terrain. Women tend to be more inclined, almost wired, to be tuned into their relationship and its nuances. Further, women tend to be better in the apology/forgiveness departments. A telling example occurred during the US presidential debates in December 2019. All the candidates were asked a final question: they could choose to ask forgiveness from one of their rivals onstage or offer a gift. The seven men onstage chose to offer a gift. The two women asked for forgiveness, either for getting "worked up" or being "blunt."

Forgiveness was far from the mind of a man who called me after discovering his wife's affair. When Richard called for a first therapy appointment, his voice sounded tight as he said, "My wife cheated on me. I'm not sure what to do about it. Maybe you can help?" We set up an appointment for the following week. "Have your wife come with you," I said.

THE POLITE BETRAYAL

When Amanda and Richard showed up for their first therapy appointment, you would not have immediately known anything was amiss. Richard, a well-pressed, muscular man in his late thirties, presented himself as exceedingly controlled and polite. Even his clothes were polite: perfectly creased jeans, white shirt impeccably fitted and sparkling clean. It was as if he wanted to make a statement: "Nothing is wrong with me." Only when he began to shake as he talked did he give himself away. He was traumatized.

"I just found out Amanda is having an affair. I found her texts last week. She apparently fell in love with some guy. I'm not sure I can stay in this relationship."

Amanda, quietly tense, listened as he spoke. A raven-haired beauty with green eyes, she was the picture of fragility. Slim, with pale skin, she looked like she wanted to disappear into the couch.

She said, "I feel terrible. I don't know what happened. But I told Richard the affair is over. I'm not going to see him again."

As I got to know the couple during this first session, I saw the seeds of what eventually grew into an affair. The couple had met in Toronto where they were both raised, had married five years earlier, and shortly afterward moved together to New York where Richard got a high-powered job in finance. Richard, the eldest of three siblings, stood out as the powerhouse of the couple. Despite being shaken to his core, he tried to project an image of authority.

"I never knew Amanda was unhappy, or unhappy with me. I'm pretty sure I would have known if something was wrong. I can't believe she did this to me. To us."

Amanda revealed early on in our meetings that she was used to deferring to Richard. She seemed hesitant in her own voice, and now, guilty as charged, she sounded halting as she tried to explain her version of events. She had recently landed a new job—a dream job—as a writer for a popular women's magazine. She was on assignment in Spain when she met Tomas. They apparently spent the week together in Barcelona and had been sending torrid text messages since her return, with plans to meet again. Amanda said, "I must have lost my mind. I know I've hurt Richard terribly. Maybe beyond repair."

Richard started to weep, softly at first, then let himself go. This was a strange sight. My guess is that this carefully controlled man had barely, if ever, let himself cry. I took this as a good sign. I didn't have to do much. I just tried to hold his pain in the silence. He needed to know that such a display of emotion was safe, that he wouldn't be exposed. Amanda looked at him with tenderness. I guessed that she had never seen this "master of the universe" husband fall apart. I said some encouraging words to them, to the effect that it seemed like this may allow for a new kind of openness in their relationship.

The couple returned to my office the following week, and we continued to meet for about ten sessions over the next five months. The first couple of sessions were devoted to Richard's grief and anger, which he began to express more openly. Amanda did what she could to provide comfort.

"This is completely my fault, my responsibility. I'll do whatever it takes to fix it." Slowly Richard began to soften, and it was time to explore the roots of the affair.

At my invitation, Amanda began to talk about her marriage, and what was going on for her prior to getting involved with her Spanish lover. In earlier sessions she had alluded a few times in passing that "Richard didn't really know me" or "I never felt really heard." In one session I asked her about this recurring theme.

"Richard is used to being in charge. This was part of the reason I married him. He seemed so strong, so capable. I knew I could lean on him. But for the last few years, especially since he's been working so much, I never felt that he took the time to listen to me." Amanda sounded almost apologetic as she expressed her pain.

She was clearly not used to making a stink about any demands she might have. The youngest of three, Amanda talked about feeling "invisible" growing up. Her parents were working-class folks who spent much of their time trying to keep food on the table. She said, "And my older brother was a handful. He was always getting into trouble, so I tried to give my parents as little to worry about as possible." Richard listened intently as Amanda told her story. I think he was getting to know her in a new way, as someone with needs and wants, and little practice in asking for much for herself.

Of course, this couple hardly ever fought. This is true of most of the couples who come to see me postaffair. In general, these affair-laden relationships are cool, characterized by not much outward drama, which usually takes place underground. With Richard and Amanda, they both entered the relationship with not much experience with conflict and seemed to have made an unconscious pact not to fight. Inwardly I thought, "How Canadian of them." But of course, there was more to it than that. I asked Richard about where he thought his aversion to conflict came from. He answered immediately, "My father." "Please explain," I said.

Richard began to talk about his upbringing, which revolved around his father's role, as he put it, as the "king of the castle." Richard's father was a successful builder—a self-made millionaire who enjoyed the perks of power, which he wielded benevolently.

"My mother adored him and catered to him, night and day. We all pretty much did the same." While Richard said, "Of course, I felt loved," it was clear that he could never, ever challenge his father, and mostly had to go along with whatever his father wanted—big and small. "He picked my university for me, and I knew I had no choice." He added, "He always had the final word."

As Richard talked, he began to openly reflect on himself.

"As much as I resented him in some ways, I may be rather like my father." Amanda was all ears. I directed them to talk together in the session. I watched as Amanda turned to Richard.

"You know I love your father. But yes, you are like him. I always feel like everything has to be on your timetable. You design the program, and you just want to plug me in." She softly added, "Even when it comes to having a baby."

Apparently, Amanda had been yearning for a child for the last couple of years, and Richard kept putting it off. Methodical guy that he was, he needed all of his ducks in a row before doing something so bold as having a baby.

Their relationship was opening before my eyes. Richard, to his great credit, showed an impressive degree of honesty and self-searching. He didn't remain a victim but used the bombshell of the affair to examine his shortcomings, and his contribution to the affair. We continued to meet for several more sessions. The therapy came to an end, rather unceremoniously, when the couple became engrossed in their new project—renovating their apartment. They were adding another bedroom to make room for a baby.

It might sound like affair repair is a long, drawn-out ordeal, but it isn't always, as we saw with Amanda and Richard. The first steps toward healing often begin as soon as the couple comes together to deal with what happened. The two people are propelled into an unknown world, stripped bare, nothing to lose, exposed to each other in totally new ways. During my years of practice, I've seen a number of couples whom I consider to be models of affair repair. They showed me how it's done. The following story is such a couple.

WHEN POETRY BECOMES PROSE

Ella made the initial phone call. "I just found out my husband has been cheating on me. I think we need help." We scheduled a time to meet the following week. I never know what to expect when a couple comes to therapy postaffair, the wound still open. Usually, however, the fact that they're looking for therapy means that they are hoping for some healing in whatever form that takes.

Tall, elegant in her flowing loose pants and shirt, Ella looked like the artist that she was. Christopher projected the kind of rumpled casualness of an academic; he had spent the last twenty years on the faculty at a prominent local university. Ella had recently found out that Christopher had been carrying on an infatuation with an office colleague. Though he claimed that they didn't actually sleep together, the relationship became sexy and intimate. It lasted for almost two years. Ella found out about her husband's "cheating" when she came across Christopher's email intended for the girlfriend.

This couple handled the first movement—right after the bomb drops—very impressively. I wish I could take credit as the therapist, but frankly, I mostly got out of the way as Ella did her thing. I supported and encouraged her as she revealed herself to be one of the healthy responders: she kicked the stuffing out of her husband—symbolically, of course. She was furious! Fury, in Ella, emerged quietly, insistently, without compromise. This woman knew how to wield power, in a good way. Soft-spoken and subtly elegant, she aimed her fury at Christopher.

"You will not return to our bedroom until you tell me everything that happened. I want to know how you could lie to me, how you could betray me for these past two years. Right now, I don't even know who you are."

Christopher did not even try to escape her rage. He couldn't, of course, if he wanted to stay in the marriage, which he said, unequivocally, he did. He looked at her.

"I love you. I've always loved you. I love our family. Nothing will change that for me. I have no excuse, except that I may be the biggest idiot who ever lived."

But more than not avoiding Ella, Christopher seemed open, if not eager, to talk about his affair. It looked to me like he felt some relief that he was busted.

The first several sessions of our work involved Ella's lacerating Christopher for his transgression, and Christopher offering many versions of what felt like genuine remorse. I didn't have to encourage Ella, though I looked on admiringly while she carried on. This kind of bravado seemed out of character for this woman, who struck me as quiet and introspective. A professional poet, she laced her speech with metaphor, which, to my ears, sounded like music. Even when she was laying her husband out, her word choice was beautiful. I said, "Sometimes I forget to pay attention to the content of what you're saying. I get lost in the music." She smiled, accepting my appreciation.

In one session they recounted their conversations from the previous week. Christopher said, "We've had an emotional roller coaster these last few days." Ella said, "I'm tired of secrets. Secrets are poison." She then began recounting some new bits of information she got from her husband about the affair. In our sessions Christopher spoke with hesitation, clumsily trying to fill in any details about the relationship with the other woman, but he didn't back away or try to cover anything up. I think he admired Ella's unapologetic boldness. "I've never seen her like this," he said. She responded, "I've never seen me like this either." Painful as it was, I think they both semienjoyed her full-throttled expressiveness on display.

Ella opened one session saying, "Just so you don't think I see myself as an innocent victim, I know I've made mistakes in this marriage. I'm not fully aware of where I went wrong, but we will need to get to the bottom of it if we're going to heal."

But she, and they, couldn't move on until Ella's questions were put to rest. Week after week Ella continued to insist that Christopher divulge every detail of his relationship with this woman. She didn't let up. Then, she did what I consider the coup de grâce of being on the receiving end of this kind of betrayal: she went to the office and confronted "the other woman." Ella did not hold back. She came into our session describing what happened.

"It wasn't a bloodbath, don't worry. But I wanted her to see my face. I wanted her to know what she did to me, to our family. I wanted her to be accountable. I wanted her to be ashamed."

Christopher, ashen faced, looked on. There was nothing he could say. His guilt and shame spoke volumes.

"I didn't know the two of you before the affair, but I'm wondering, Ella. Were you always this fearless?" I asked.

By their description, and my observation of this soft-spoken woman, I believed Ella historically tended to retreat from conflict. Now, her take-no-prisoners approach looked to me like a refreshing change. I also openly appreciated how, in our initial sessions, Ella seemed intent on acknowledging that she, as she put it, "made mistakes" in their marriage. She wasn't merely interested in holding her husband to account: she was in pain, and curious about, as she said, "where I went wrong."

The first movement in this therapy subtly ended. As may be obvious, I wholeheartedly sided with Ella these first sessions. Experience has taught me that in order to set the stage for the second movement, the exploration of the preaffair relationship, the betrayal needs to be thoroughly acknowledged and addressed. The husband, in this case, needs to stay in the doghouse for as long as it takes. He needs to be there, since no matter what his wife "did," he took the coward's way out. Whatever suffering the marriage engendered in him—and it always does—he took a damaging shortcut. For this he deserves the responsibility that comes with it. Most important, he needs to fully acknowledge his breach of faith. This is a tricky process, but once he fully comes clean and commits to repairing the damage, he's got his ticket out. At the least he's got his reservation.

But the second movement . . . a different story. After several months, Ella seemed to have accepted her husband's acknowledgment/apology for his betrayal: his full commitment to repairing the damage healed her wound some. The conversations in our session shifted to exploring the underpinnings of their marriage, what their marriage looked like and felt like to each of them, before "the other woman" entered the scene. As we began this exploration, I understood, more clearly than ever, how Ella helped to create the conditions for the affair.

The telling event revolved around the children. One session, as they walked into my office, Christopher muttered, "We had a difficult weekend." This particular conflict centered on their two young daughters, nine-year-old Maya and eleven-year-old Sarah, which highlighted the couple's differences in parenting.

Ella and Christopher told their versions like this: Christopher said, "You're always too hard on Maya," as Ella retorted, "You give her a free pass."

This played itself out in an ugly way around this child's birthday, where Ella ended up storming out of the house, feeling like Christopher preferred the company of his children to her. She felt invisible.

As we began to explore these parental dynamics, Christopher suddenly changed his tone. I saw a different version of this man.

He said, "The kids are sensitive to the family hierarchy." I asked him what that meant. He said, "I'm low man on the totem pole."

He talked about what he saw as a pattern of having to ask Ella for "permission" with their kids.

I asked, "If the kids were here, who would they say is the boss?"

He looked to Ella for her response; his feelings were clear. She equivocated. Christopher had no doubt. According to her husband, Ella was the clear-cut boss with the kids, he just worked for her. (And not happily.)

I began to see a different Christopher. Throughout our therapy thus far, he presented himself as soft-spoken, open, worried about his wife, and guilty. He had never so much as raised an objection about anything she said or did. Now, for the first time, I saw more of him, and their marriage. He talked about how even when he was with the kids, she would call to him from the other room to monitor his parenting.

He said, "I always have to do it her way."

It was hard to miss the simmering resentment and pain coming from this guy.

Christopher elaborated on his feelings of being marginalized in the home. Ella listened, interrupted to dispute his rendition of their family, but I signaled for Christopher to continue. Something new was happening and I wanted to encourage it.

"You totally lock me out of even buying Christmas gifts for the kids. You take their list and have everything bought by Thanksgiving. I can't even participate in buying gifts for our kids!"

Ella didn't like the way this session was going. I had, until now, mostly supported her while maintaining a good connection with her husband. But clearly, without being aware of it, Ella helped to create this imbalance where Christopher lacked his own voice in the parenting department. Ella became defensive and started to throw in the kitchen sink, especially the affair.

"Now you tell me what's bothering you! You're always too busy or too distracted. Now, now, you want to tell me these things? And, by the way, where were you when you were having your cozy lunches with Rebecca?"

"You're throwing up a smoke screen. This is important for us to talk about. Ever since we had kids, I've never found a way to talk to you about how shut out I feel." He added quietly, "It's been bothering me all these years." I nodded in agreement.

Ella turned to me, saying, "I'm not just talking about the affair. I'm talking about how he always disappeared." I said softly, "He's not disappearing now."

Though still tender toward her, Christopher took the risk by telling Ella how she made him feel marginalized in his own family. He hadn't dared to talk about this before. He'd been afraid to make her the least bit uncomfortable. He was searching for some new notes in their duet.

The session was getting ready to end. Ella looked clearly upset. She was frantically reaching into her purse for something. I asked her what she was looking for. She showed me. She was clutching a bottle of gummies designed to calm nerves in a crisis. She didn't smile. She was rattled. She was used to a cautious, more distant husband. She wasn't used to this guy. She wasn't sure she liked him.

I thought to myself, "*Wow!* Here is a husband who is really used to tiptoeing around his wife. And she is used to him being away, not altogether emotionally present, not always reliable—and now add 'cheating' to the list." But, for the first time, I understood how Christopher learned to become cautious with his wife. Now he spoke strongly, but with care, about his experience of exclusion. These new notes in their duet clearly rattled Ella and she looked like she would fall apart.

Our therapy lasted for several more months. The young daughters were included for a few sessions. Initially, I observed that Christopher was mostly right, Ella was the parental powerhouse. I noticed each time I asked a child a question, they would look at their mother before answering. She was the switchboard through which all communication passed. Both children were tentative at first, but slowly Sarah, the eleven-year-old, began to open up.

"My mom always does everything for us. Sometimes I feel sorry for my dad. He seems kind of lonely." She looked at him. "I'm sorry Daddy. I hope I'm not hurting your feelings."

These were lovely, caring children who, like all kids, were attuned to the subtle tensions between their parents.

The parents felt the tenderness coming from both their daughters. In our sessions with the kids, I made sure to affirm Christopher in the eyes of the kids. He was an outsider dying to get in. I said to Maya, the youngest, as Christopher commented on a recent school prize she received, "That's cool. I see your dad is your biggest fan."

These sessions gave Ella and Christopher an opportunity to explore some of their unspoken tensions around parenting. The balance of power between the parents began to shift, with Christopher gaining more of an autonomous voice with their kids. He clearly wanted to be involved in family life and now he had his chance. Ella, after some initial discomfort, seemed to welcome this change.

She said, only semijoking, "Less work for me with the kids."

She now had a real partner. After about six months, the couple decided they were doing well and gave the usual farewell: "We'll call you if we need you."

About a year after our last session, I got a call from Ella. She wanted to bring in her parents who lived in a nearby state. I knew she had a difficult relationship with both parents, especially her mother. They were visiting for a week, and Ella thought it might be a good chance to see if she could work things through with them. She felt bad about her strained relationship with her own parents; she wanted her daughters to have a closer relationship with their grandparents.

We scheduled a session, which turned out to be our only consultation. Ella's younger sister Leah attended as well. Leah was single, in her early thirties, and living with the parents. This single session didn't allow me to get to know her folks well, but I met with them long enough to see what Ella meant. Her mother didn't seem to like her much. It was hard for me to detect much warmth flowing from Ella's mom to her oldest daughter. I wasn't sure what was going on, except that Ella's mother seemed like a very compromised person.

Ella had mentioned that her mother was on a lot of medication, and she did indeed seem to be emotionally fragile, brittle with some underlying anger peeking out. Ella's father seemed like a thoughtful guy who appeared to welcome our session and the chance to talk about his wish that "our beautiful daughter Ella were closer to us." I got a chance to talk about my admiration for Ella, which pleased the father (I'm not sure about the mother). I saw that Ella's sister had become very protective of the mom, solicitous, often finishing the mother's sentences for her.

The father wanted to schedule a second visit, but Ella declined. I wasn't sure why, but I was disappointed. I thought there was enough good will, at least on the part of the father, to make some headway in the family impasse, especially between Ella and her mother. Then, two years after that visit, I got a call from Christopher.

He said, "Ella and I want to come for a checkup."

I didn't know what to expect, but as it turned out, it was nothing dramatic. They were doing mostly well, though Christopher worried, "We're not talking as much as we used to." He was, fundamentally, a talker, a communication guy, and he sounded like he was feeling lonely. We met for two sessions where they shook the dust off their marriage. Connection restored. That was about three years ago. I've had no contact with them since.

Ella and Christopher stand as an example of folks who get the most out of a relationship crisis. To her credit, Ella didn't hang on to her privileged position as the wounded one in the dyad. She showed a lot of courage in her willingness to look at her unintended contribution to the marital tensions that preceded the affair. And Christopher did not attempt to shortcut or minimize the wounding nature of his betrayal, and, through work, fully owned his shortcomings in his relationship to his wife. When we said goodbye, it looked to me like this couple had succeeded in creating a much-improved second marriage. A long marriage is many marriages, and in Christopher and Ella's case, the first one died, as it needed to. This new marriage emerged with greater honesty, integrity, and freedom. I think they'd agree that, despite the enormous pain, it was worth it.

Our stories and clinical experience challenge the conventional wisdom that suggests that extramarital affairs produce irreversible damage to marriage. We see how, if the couple genuinely engages in a therapeutic experience, they can develop a deeper, more authentic connection than they'd previously known. Usually, they couldn't figure out how to get at these issues any other way. As a therapist, I can't exactly say it's exhilarating, but "affair repair" therapy is often very impressive. I have the opportunity to guide these vulnerable people on a journey toward a new, more alive, more authentic partnership than they had thought possible before.

But where is sex in all this? As we've seen with our couples, the affairs, in fact, had little to do with sex: the betrayals had more to do with an avoidance of conflict that inhibited a sense of aliveness and connection. Sexual intimacy is a part of that. Sometimes, however, couples do come into therapy complaining about the quality of their sex life. We'll see in the next chapter if sex is, in fact, about sex at all.

Questions for Reflection

In the first case of Bill and Esther in "I'd Rather Divorce Than Fight," do you think there is anything else the therapist could have done to get them unstuck? What do you think happened to them after they separated?

In "The Polite Betrayal," the story of Amanda and Richard was an example of a woman having an affair. What differences do you notice compared to a man's affair? What did this couple do that contributed to their ability to heal?

The case of Christopher and Ella, "When Poetry Becomes Prose," showed what an optimal postaffair therapy looks like. What were the ingredients in their recipe? What would each of them have had to do differently for them to fail this marital stress test?

Chapter 4

The Couples Where
Sex Went to Die

THE SEXUALLY BORING HUSBAND

Sarah called me at the suggestion of her family doctor. She was suc-
cinct: "Everything is fine except for our sex life." She hinted that she
thought the lack of sexual connection between she and her husband
might turn out to be incurable. Though she didn't say so directly, it
sounded like Sarah thought that if the problem didn't improve, they
could end up divorced.

At their first therapy appointment, Sarah—casually dressed in baggy
pants and a sweater—exuded a kind of confidence that said, "I don't have
to please anyone but myself." Alan, tall and reed-thin, with wire-framed
glasses, carried himself in a proper, professorial kind of way. Based on
the description of their marriage, Alan and Sarah functioned smoothly
in most aspects of their life together. Intelligent, sophisticated people,
they painted a picture of a couple who got along fine.

"He's my best friend," Sarah said, looking at Alan. She added, "Our
problem is sex." She paused. "We don't have it."

For Sarah, their sexual disconnection was an open wound. She said
she felt "turned off" to Alan. She described his romantic overtures:
"Whenever he tries to get something going sexually, he always seems
half-hearted. He doesn't show any oomph." She sighed, "I'm incredibly
frustrated." She looked at Alan apologetically, adding, "And bored."

This was a familiar scenario in my office. Over the years I've seen many couples whose presenting complaint revolved around sex. Usually, it was because of infrequent sex, too lackluster, or the male partner suffered some kind of sexual dysfunction (I've only seen one case where the complaint was too much sex!).

Sarah and Alan had been married about fifteen years and had three kids. They met while visiting mutual friends in Europe. Alan was born in Belgium where his mother and sister still lived. Alan's perfect English was elegantly punctuated with a French accent. He presented himself as an intellectual, meticulous in his grooming, but with a soft, tender quality. He worked at a prominent, progressive architectural firm, which he said afforded him the opportunity to indulge in what he called his "artistic inclinations."

Sarah's parents were born in Russia, but they moved to the United States shortly before she was born. Sarah, the oldest of three sisters, had a Bohemian air about her, with vibrant, slightly unkempt hair. She had a natural and appealing sexiness about her: she wore no makeup and didn't appear to care about clothes or what she might have called "girly" things. She was a partner at a highly demanding investment banking firm. She characterized it as "a real boys' club."

I listened to Sarah bemoan the lack of sexual connection with Alan.

"It's embarrassing to say this, but we hardly ever have sex! And Alan just seems like he's not into it. I wait for him to initiate it, and weeks and weeks go by. Then I mention it, and he tries, but it just seems like he's going through the motions. It's always the same routine. I can't go on like this."

Sara looked rather sheepish as she spoke, clearly not wanting to hurt Alan's feelings. Their sexual connection did, indeed, sound constricted. Sexual deadness or dysfunction is almost always symbolic of a broader inhibition in the couple's relationship. With Sarah and Alan, I could see the inhibition as soon as I met them. Alan seemed scared of his wife, but not the kind that's easily detectable. He spoke with what seemed like confidence, but in a controlled manner, cautious and correct in his responses to Sarah; he appeared careful not to upset her or challenge her perceptions. He absorbed Sarah's criticisms without blinking.

Sarah came across as bold and opinionated, but she also had great humor and conveyed an openness and willingness to look at EVERYTHING—herself included.

She smiled, saying, "I know I come across as large and in charge," as she described Alan's shortcomings in the bedroom. I took Sarah's self-acknowledged control issues as a good sign. Most people who are genuine control freaks don't identify themselves that way. For them, the problem is mostly other people. But Sarah didn't seem brittle. She had questions about herself. This is perhaps the most important ingredient in assessing a person's health. Are they willing to become a patient? Are they willing to learn something about themselves they don't already know? I saw an opening for the couple.

The therapy continued semiregularly for about nine months. I approached their unhappy sexual duet in a couple of ways. One thing was certain: I knew I needed to tap into, and loosen up, what I had observed as Alan's carefulness with his wife. After a few low-stress, getting-to-know-you sessions, I began to zero in on Alan, in an open-ended, conversational way. I saw how he had become too uptight, too controlled with Sarah. The couple had unfortunately dedicated themselves to trying to "get somewhere" in their sex life, with a kind of explicit goal-directed-ness that interferes with aliveness in a relationship. Sarah had assigned a few instructional books on sex for Alan to read, which he, of course, dutifully did. He seemed to have signed on to this project of "How to Have a Better Sex Life in Ten Steps or Less."

I needed to help Alan get out of his "good boy" box. I suspected this made him boring to Sarah, though she didn't say so explicitly, and maybe didn't fully realize. Alan seemed compelled to follow his wife's prescriptions to cure their ailing sex life.

"I've read everything she's given me about how we can have a better sex life. I even checked out the Tantric sex book she gave me. Sarah's done a lot of research, and I'd like to do what I can to make things better."

It seemed like Alan had overtly dedicated himself to pleasing Sarah, to doing what she asked of him. But where was his own voice, his own desires?

Alan needed more confidence and freedom, both sexually and otherwise, which doesn't come from a prescription. In one session, I invited Alan into a symbolic dance, where we had a wide-ranging conversation about his artistic vision, about jazz, not trying to get anywhere. I openly enjoyed the way he talked, the way he thought, and I let him know.

I said, "I'm liking the way you express your ideas about what creativity is made of. You're an original, a real freethinker."

He was. I wasn't just buttering him up. Alan showed himself to be highly intelligent and imaginative. Alan seemed emboldened by my appreciation.

He responded, "I love to talk about music, art, life. I don't get much of a chance to do it at home, we're always so busy."

Our conversation confirmed my suspicion that this guy had a more dynamic range of personality than his overly correct version of himself allowed.

I kept my eye on Sarah as Alan and I batted the metaphorical ball around.

When I asked Sarah what she was thinking as Alan and I were talking she responded, smiling, "I like this guy I'm seeing here. I want to take THIS guy home with me, not the boring one I usually have at home."

We all laughed, but I felt the underlying meaning of her comment. She wanted, and needed, Alan to be freer with her. This kind of reaction happens a lot. A wife or husband will see a side of their partner in the office that they don't usually see, and it can be both pleasing and disorienting. Sometimes a woman will be resentful that her husband is charming, funny, thoughtful in the office, while he's a louse at home.

We are all contextual beings, expressing different aspects of ourselves according to the interpersonal dynamics of each situation. Sarah's idea of "Two Alans" reflects what happens when the therapist disturbs the (unconscious) balance in a relationship. To understand how Sarah ended up with such a careful husband, we invoke our law of relationship physics: couples create each other. This mysterious process of cocreation in intimate relationships is not easily visible to the naked eye. It takes place over time, in a subtle duet, where partners shape and change each other, mostly without knowing it. Most of us cannot see what we are doing when we're in it. As a husband in my office commented, "A relationship looks different from the inside out than from the outside in."

In the case of Alan and Sarah, the couple had inadvertently become trapped in rigid, stereotypic ways of being with each other. Alan's constricted self was an unfortunate and unintended by-product of the couple's relationship. Their relationship now looked narrow and robotic. My relationship with Alan in the therapy setting was an effort to stimulate Alan's more playful self, which could then slowly work its way into the relationship with his wife.

After nearly two months of therapy, Sarah got to see a side of Alan usually denied to her. Sarah's open enjoyment of this new, looser husband in the therapy office gave him confidence to take a few more risks with her at home. They reportedly had sex slightly more often with, according to Sarah, slightly more enjoyment. Their sexual connection was not yet perfect, but better. However, they were not yet out of the woods.

You might wonder how Alan ended up being so cautious with Sarah. Was it his nature to be cautious, or was it something in their relationship that engendered his caution? The answer is, of course, both. Our session revealed how he was open to playing, able to be less uptight, when he stepped away from his relationship with his wife. He had a broader range, a more expansive repertoire as a human being than he expressed in his role as husband and lover. I saw how Alan adjusted himself to subtle, mostly unconscious signals from his wife.

Again, we wonder how they helped to create each other. Why has Alan been so cautious with Sarah? Why has he seemed so worried about upsetting her? How did he become so emotionally overprotective? These signals are sent back and forth at such a low-grade frequency that they can be easy to miss.

As the therapy progressed, I wondered openly about Alan's emotional overprotection of Sarah, his apparent worry about upsetting her. During one session, when the time seemed right, I looked at the couple and asked, "What's Alan's cautious thing about? It looks like he's afraid to make a mistake. How did this happen in your relationship?"

Instead of reacting defensively, Sarah began ruminating about herself, and how she was with Alan. Part of Sarah's charm was her candor when it came to herself and her own shortcomings. A self-described control freak, Sarah now admitted to being overly vigilant and controlling when it came to sex.

"You know, I'm always criticizing everything Alan does in bed. Everything he does annoys me. I don't usually say it out loud, but I'm pretty sure he feels it. I don't know why I'm so judgmental!"

Sarah had built a wall around her when it came to her sexual connection to Alan. At the same time, she had fantasies about how other people must be having what she called "wild sex." She compared herself and

Alan to these imaginary people and felt mortified that they fell so short. Sarah was also afraid to apply these fantasies of "wild sex" to herself and her husband, since as she said, "I'm sure we'll fail." I wondered to myself why Sarah needed to diminish the power of the couple's sexuality. Sarah seemed to crave being "wild" and feared it at the same time. As I began to explore Sarah's family background, a striking pattern emerged. Her father, a well-known painter, was apparently a demanding, tempestuous kind of guy. Sarah described how her mother catered to him in a way that looked demeaning to Sarah.

"My sisters and I have talked to our mom about not being such a doormat. But she claims she loves doing things for my father and doesn't think it's a problem. But I can't stand to see it."

Sarah's parents had (and apparently still had, after many years) a passionate relationship, occasionally engaging in boisterous sex within earshot of Sarah and her sisters, horrifying them and leaving Sarah feeling "disgusted" and "dirty." When I asked Sarah if her mother knew that her daughters had been exposed to their parents' sexual escapades, Sarah said, "I've always been too embarrassed to talk to her about it."

But wild, passionate sex became psychologically charged for Sarah, associations that related to being overly exposed to her parents' sexual relationship, and what she felt was her mother's subservience to her father.

Though Alan knew Sarah's history, his alert stillness in the office made it seem like he was hearing this story for the first time. Sarah clearly came into this marriage tormented by, and attracted to, the idea of "wild" sex. Passion became associated with being out of control, not in a good way, where someone could get hurt. On some level, she associated the noisy sex of her parents with what she perceived to be her mother's exploitation by her father.

Though he didn't say so directly, I believed that Alan had picked up on Sarah's fear early in their marriage, which helped shape his cautious approach to his wife sexually. Sarah's unconscious anxiety, especially about being exploited, now stood in the way of her openly enjoying herself as a sexual being, with full responsibility and free of coercion. Alan's tentative gestures made her more tense, more critical of every move he made. Sarah knew she didn't make it easy for her husband. As she said at the end of one session, "It's not easy being me," meaning always in control.

Alan's second-guessing himself with his wife reinforced her control in the relationship, which over time interfered with their freedom as a couple. In addition, Alan's status as an immigrant, not always being sure of cultural rules, operated covertly but powerfully in reinforcing a sense of insecurity in himself. It contributed to an ongoing, subtle power imbalance in the couple.

In the course of therapy, I discovered that Alan would run his emails by Sarah before he sent them out. Since his English was excellent, I took this to be an artifact of their caution/control duet, where he was giving her unnecessary control over his voice.

I teased Alan when I learned about this. I said, "Are you kidding? You're an incredibly smart guy. And your English is better than mine!"

I knew that for the couple's sex life to come alive, Alan needed to unleash his own energy and be free from worrying too much about getting it wrong. He couldn't do this if he constantly kept seeking Sarah's approval.

After about nine months of semiregular therapy sessions, Sarah talked about how much better their relationship felt, sexually and otherwise. During this time, I had also seen them with their kids a couple of times to get a sense of how they operated as a family. It's important because a couple with children is not a couple in a vacuum. Kids put pressure on the couple in unexpected ways.

Sarah and Alan's children, two boys and a girl, were great kids, with their own diverse opinions about their family. The oldest child, a fourteen-year-old girl, got straight to the point, as only adolescents can do, about her mom's "controlling" style. But she said this with care, calling out her mother, but with affection. Sarah nodded her head knowingly when her daughter spoke and said with a smile, "I'm working on it." The daughter also used our sessions to try to gain some more freedoms for herself; she was only partly successful.

The two boys, one bold and charmingly sassy, the other reserved and quiet, also offered some advice to their parents: "Mom, you need to stop working so much" and "Dad, you need to have more fun." Kids, indeed, see everything. Sarah expressed concern about her younger son's "sensitivity," and the session offered him a chance to talk about some of his worries related to school and friends. These sessions with the family revealed a robust, messy, and healthy relationship between parents and children; caring and respect were firmly in place, and I openly shared my appreciation for their lovely little family.

As the therapy began winding down, Sarah reflected on what had been meaningful for her.

"It really helped when you said it has nothing to do with chemistry," she said.

When I initially saw them, Sarah was convinced that the problem was "lack of chemistry" between her and Alan. Chemistry, of course, though it sounds immutable, is a purely subjective response. The "it's not about chemistry" perspective reframed the problem, introducing a dynamic, relationship-oriented perspective. As the great philosopher Epictetus said, "It is not the things themselves which trouble us, but the opinions we have about these things."[1]

It's probably obvious that I enjoyed working with these people. I was impressed by their commitment and courage in being willing to learn a new story about their marriage, different than the one they came in with. In reflecting on these sessions, I believe that rejecting the "chemistry" explanation for their comatose sexual relationship helped to create a different mind-set around what change looked like. Change wouldn't come through divorce, getting a new husband, or a prescription for "low T." The problem wasn't Alan, or the fact that Sarah had married the wrong person.

Contrary to how many couples feel, the psychological radar that we use in our selection of partners is uncannily accurate. Most people choose the right partner for them, no matter how it looks. This selection process occurs, of course, on an unconscious level. The family therapist Carl Whitaker wrote about this unconscious selection process: "We assume that marital partners have chosen each other with great wisdom . . . [with the] unconscious awareness of how they complement each other's person." He goes on, "If you accept this kind of assumption, new things appear in the framework of your conviction that these two people are good for each other." Whitaker adds that this is not new information: "Voltaire said that each person gets the thing he wants. The only problem is that you don't know what you wanted until after you get it. Then, we insist it wasn't really what we wanted at all."[2]

Indeed, it's what happens AFTER the marriage that brings a couple into therapy.

With Sarah and Alan, the therapy was aimed at loosening their rigid patterns with each other, to interrupt the sexual/emotional constriction in the marriage, to give them more freedom to play. Alan needed to be less scared of Sarah. They entered couples therapy cautious and polarized, under the symbolic heading of "Sexual Dysfunction." Sarah had decided Alan was sexually boring and inept, which I saw as being an artifact of their cocreated relationship rather than qualities possessed by Alan. Alan, in fact, had much more to offer, but his overprotectiveness toward Sarah prevented him being more himself with his wife.

It's a credit to this couple that they got so much out of the therapy in a relatively short period of time. Two things made this possible. First, they were ready—meaning desperate—for change. Misery can act as a huge motivator. As most often happens, the wife led the way in this effort. She refused to cover over, compromise, or medicate her unhappiness. She owned her unhappiness and she wanted to do something about it. Her take-charge personality helped to get, and keep, the ball rolling. But no change would have been possible unless Sarah had been open to looking at herself and her own power in the relationship, how her chronic disapproval contributed to Alan's constriction with her. Sarah was not thin-skinned; she could handle push back from me, and from Alan. Sara really, really wanted a new and different marriage, and she preferred to have it with Alan, if possible.

Alan presented more of a challenge. Sarah's liveliness was easy for me to relate to; Alan's cautious, controlled presence felt more difficult. I knew I needed him to connect with his emotional side if he were to address, and ultimately let go of, his fear of his wife. This fear needed to go if the relationship was going to come alive. I wasn't sure Alan was willing to talk directly about his feelings, so I took the indirect route, engaging him in playful, improvised conversation. I wanted to see if he had a greater emotional range than he let on. He passed with flying colors, showing that he enjoyed our freewheeling discussions, which were like a symbolic stroll in the park. Alan took some risks, exposing both thoughts and feelings that were new to Sarah. When Alan felt that Sarah liked this new, less careful guy, it gave him courage to take some risks with her. Both partners in this relationship ended up exposing some of their previously shielded vulnerabilities, making room for a greater freedom between them, sexually and otherwise.

Sarah and Alan came into therapy looking for help with their discouraging sex life, which, for Sarah, threatened the very existence of their marriage. She thought it was a question of sexual chemistry, a problem of lack of desire. What they discovered, however, is that sexual chemistry was buried beneath the hidden dynamics in their relationship. They found out what prevented them from turning each other on, both in bed and out. As Alan grew bolder, less approval-seeking, and less worried about upsetting his wife, Sarah's trust and respect for him grew. She began to lean on him, sexually and otherwise. This was a different kind of sexual liberation, a whole-person freedom that could, with any luck, develop and grow over the course of a lifetime.

Looking at libido through the lens of the relationship changes the way we think and talk about sexual desire. Many people, like Sarah, often think of sex drive as something either you have, or you don't. If you've got it, great. If not, time to worry. But, as we've learned, it's not that simple.

When someone is one part of a couple, libido is a dynamic concept, part of their dance, an integral part of the aliveness of the partnership. When sex dies, or goes into a coma, it often signals a deeper trouble in the relationship, trouble that might be covered over, shielded from the naked eye. Sometimes, in a relationship, sex doesn't just die. It is killed.

MY WIFE HATES SEX

Mike and Sandra came to see me for therapy following a brief flirtation Mike had while on a business trip. Sandra discovered the incriminating text on Mike's phone, confronted him about it, and he came clean. While Mike stopped short of sexually hooking up with the other woman, he acknowledged that his texting/flirting qualified as a betrayal, and he said he was angry at himself for letting it happen.

According to the couple, who had two daughters, aged five and three, this was the first time anything like this had happened in their ten-year marriage. Sandra was devastated. The stress of this textual infidelity motivated them to look at what had happened and to try to understand it. In our first session the couple appeared to handle the issue of the other woman relatively well, although maybe a bit too expediently. Mike claimed he understood how harmful his behavior was to Sandra, and to them as a couple. I observed that Sandra seemed like a kind of low-maintenance spouse. She quickly accepted her husband's remorse as a well-meaning attempt to bind the wound. Since we were meeting for the first time, I wasn't sure if her easygoing nature indicated a healthy self-esteem on Sandra's part, or perhaps signaled a lack of self-confidence. If they returned for therapy, I would be able to gauge the meaning of Sandra's relative ease in forgiving Mike.

The couple did return. We spent the next couple of sessions exploring the miniaffair and its impact, though, again, Sandra's requirements in terms of accountability from Mike seemed rather easily met. I noticed myself wanting her to hang on a bit to her distress over the infidelity, to expect more from her husband. I wanted to say to her, "Don't let him off the hook so easily." By the third session, however, Mike moved from "apologetic husband" to "angry husband" and the true colors of the marriage began to show.

"I'm sorry to say it, but I've been telling Sandra over and over how unhappy I am. There is no passion in this relationship. I've done what I could. She just doesn't get it."

When I asked him what he meant, he said, "She's incredibly uptight. She rarely wants to have sex, and when she does, she doesn't really seem like she's into it." He fumed, "I don't know how I can go on like this."

Sandra said she'd heard this from Mike before—many times.

She said in her small voice, "I really blame myself. I haven't had much of a sex drive for the last few years. I may be having a hormonal problem. I will get it checked out. And I know I'm uptight. I don't know why. I'm working on it." She turned to Mike, "Please have patience with me."

I listened as Sandra painfully described her shortcomings—painful to the therapist, that is. Sandra was apparently used to feeling the distress of falling short, of being the object of her husband's disappointment and thinly veiled ridicule. I found this all the more striking since, in the brief time we'd been meeting, Sandra struck me as a thoughtful, articulate, and sensitive soul. Her expressiveness came across as attractive and appealing. Sandra had a way of downplaying her attributes, though, which showed in the way she dressed and carried herself. Her plain, almost drab, style said, "Don't look at me." Or rather, "I don't deserve to be looked at."

On the surface, this couple talked to each other calmly and respect-fully, looking at each other, appearing to listen intently to their partner. Despite their politeness with one another, I observed a not-so-subtle power dynamic at play. I saw that Sandra lacked confidence with her husband, not just sexually, but as a woman, as a person. In their duet, her husband, a high-powered tech guy, often left his wife with the feel-ing that she was letting him down. He wasn't overtly mean about it, but his aggression was wrapped in an abundance of confidence in the correctness of his opinion. I noted Mike's subtle way of making Sandra feel inadequate, saying things like, "You know how many times we've talked about this," like Sandra couldn't get up to speed.

Though she didn't say so directly, it was obvious to me that Sandra became convinced she was incapable of pleasing Mike. While his social persona said, "good guy," Mike had a sophisticated way of one-upping his wife, which left her looking small. In this duet, both partners accepted the myth that Mike was the victim of Sandra's "coldness" and "of course" Mike would feel frustrated.

The passion in this relationship had indeed been shut down, but it wasn't primarily sexual. Passion needs to show up in the relationship OUTSIDE the bedroom; the sex IN the bedroom is an expression of the relationship outside it. With Mike and Sandra, Sandra had begun to feel cautious and inadequate with her husband. These were intelligent, articulate people—good people—and seemingly self-aware. But this dance was quiet, subtle, repetitive, and toxic.

By the time they came to see me, they had internalized the story of "poor Mike" who had to "tolerate" Sandra's lack of interest in sex. Neither partner realized how Sandra's spirit—her voice, her perspec-tive—had been inadvertently reduced in this relationship. Actually, Sandra undoubtedly felt a lot of pain at the way Mike talked to her, but she had, for some reason, acclimated herself to being portrayed as wrong, lacking, unsubstantial. That pattern, which persisted and gath-ered steam, over time, quashed the liveliness that came with two full, distinct, slightly unpredictable voices. Wife depressed. Passion stymied. Relationship stasis.

Mike and Sandra were clearly lousy fighters. I saw that Sandra felt outmatched by her quick-witted, self-assured husband. I didn't know what their relationship looked like in the early days, what their uncon-scious contract was made of. Did they covertly agree that Mike would be the expert, with Sandra deferring to his wisdom? The dynamic of a couple in therapy usually reflects a variation on their early unconscious arrangement, only magnified, for good or evil. Now Mike and Sandra were in "relationship hell," with real, productive conflict shut down. The only thing they appeared to share was disdain for Sandra.

During the brief course of therapy, these hidden tensions began to be exposed, which challenged the static, stuck quality of their marriage. Both Sandra and Mike were taken aback that I didn't share their view that Sandra was the only patient in the relationship. I repeatedly admired Sandra, saying, "Where have you been hiding your intuitive gifts?" Or "I'm impressed by your astute observations about your marriage." Sandra seriously outclassed her husband in her intuitive, observational skills. I wanted Mike, the "doctor" in the relationship, to become the patient.

I began to slowly comment, sometimes with pointed humor, about Mike's semidisguised belief in his own superiority, and his unfortunate talent in shutting down his wife. I'd say to Mike after one of his typical displays of self-assurance, "Wow, it sounds like you've got it all figured out, huh?"

This wasn't what they came for, but that's an uncomfortable, though necessary part of the therapeutic process. We are professional disrupters, respectful of the people who come to us for help, but at times disrespectful of the unhealthy dynamics they have unwittingly created.

With Mike and Sandra, I needed to help them move past their destructive story that Mike was the "frustrated sex doctor" with an incurable patient. I wanted Mike to understand how he had inadvertently "created" Sandra, a wife who now believed she had little to offer him. It felt tricky; it's never easy to move against the family script, the unconscious narrative created by the couple, because it adds tension to the therapy session. How the couple or family respond to this challenge says something about their health and willingness to change.

The early sessions exposed Sandra's tendency to emotionally collapse with Mike. Sandra usually couched her pain in language like, "I know I'm a big part of the problem" or "I know I don't make it easy for Mike." It was not easy to get Sandra to complain about Mike's treatment of her without her issuing a qualification. I was repeatedly struck by how, as soon as tensions emerged, Sandra dropped out. She had become convinced that she couldn't win in an argument with Mike, that he was too strong for her. Mike, despite his stated goodwill, didn't like to be wrong, and he had a really sophisticated way of putting Sandra down. Not one to use brute force, his suave, articulate, hipster language conveyed a subtle disdain for her opinions. I noticed how he was, like most people, completely unaware of this.

By the fifth session the conversation in the therapy room had begun to shift. Part of the challenge was that Mike, like many people who come for couples therapy, came with a static story, one in which he had a starring role as a superior, and thwarted, lover. In his script, his wife was cold, not interested in, or perhaps even capable of, meeting his sexual needs. On some level he may have hoped I would feel sorry for him, as his friends did.

I should note that, in many ways, Mike was a likeable guy. With his hipster casual appearance, intelligence, and polite manners, Mike made an initial impression as an affable, articulate, and caring young man. An only child, Mike's mother emigrated to New York from Italy in her early twenties, when she met Mike's dad. They now lived in the suburbs near Mike and Sandra. I gleaned from the story that Mike was a classic "parental child," a kind of little grownup. Since about age twelve, when his parents met with financial adversity, Mike felt he had to step in by finding work after school to help out. Mike was critical of both his parents for their "poor choices." He described their relationship as "solid," but marred by constant bickering with no outward physical affection. It seemed that Mike had functioned as a care-taking "doctor" in his family for many years, and now he helped to support them financially.

I recognized Mike. I had seen many people like him in my office, the kind of person who begins parental caretaking early on. A child can be thrust into this role for a variety of reasons. Sometimes, as a family of new immigrants, the child becomes the bridge between the parents and the outside world, inadvertently becoming an authority on the new culture. In other cases, a parent may be ill, physically or mentally, and the burden for care may fall on the child. Perhaps an early parental death or major family dysfunction can thrust a child into an unnatural position of authority in the family.

Equally common, but more problematically, the parents have a dysfunctional relationship, and the child becomes an emotional doctor for one or both parents. In any case, if the child takes on parenting functions in a way that is not explicit—perhaps the parents don't even realize it—this pattern can set up this child for an overdeveloped sense of responsibility in the future. I've seen many cases where these "parental children" go through life taking care of everything, sometimes making it difficult for them in intimate relationships in which they need to accept care/criticism from their partners. It's often hard for them to be a patient. Mike was such a guy.

My challenges to Mike's superiority complex with his wife were subtle. I wanted him to stay with the therapy, and I was careful—probably too careful—not to alienate him. In other words, I was very nice to him, even as I questioned his air of certainty.

In one session I remarked, "Mike, you have a bright, intuitive woman at your side, but you don't let her help you. You don't even seem to understand her, like you're tuned to a different channel. That's a real buzz kill."

Mike, at first surprised—and defensive—about his role as "passion slayer" with his wife, soon took the therapy to heart. Mike was like an A+ student, and once he got used to the idea that he "created" his wife, he took up this challenge with zeal. He began to search for ways to encourage Sandra to open up to him. However, as Mike began his open soul-searching, Sandra remained cautious. Most of her comments maintained the same self-deprecatory quality. Unfortunately for her, she clearly had learned her role as "failed wife" too well.

Sandra, in fact, had abundant credentials as an accomplished person. It wasn't until several sessions into the therapy that I learned that she was a rather brilliant artist who specialized in collage. Though she had begun to garner some national recognition for her work, she put her career aside after the birth of their daughters, and had, at least on the surface, accepted the idea that her career would be on a partial hold while Mike built his business. It looked to me like Sandra had too much experience hiding her light under a bushel. I wanted to help her bring it out.

During one therapy session, after Sandra again deferred to Mike, I turned to her and said, "I am continually struck by your almost reflexive swallowing of your own voice. I don't get it. You are a smart, capable, intuitive woman. What's that about?"

Sandra began opening up about her own family, whom she described wryly as "your typical American family," meaning that her mom stayed at home while her father went to work as a manager of a furniture store.

Sandra believed that while her parents got along on the surface, her mother harbored some resentment at not having what Sandra called "more of a life." Sandra characterized her mother as always supportive of her father, but believed she was lonely and frustrated in what Sandra indicated as a too-narrow "woman's role."

"My parents were never very happy that I became an artist. They thought it was selfish. My mom, especially, thought I should put being a wife and mother first. I don't think she really felt a woman should have her own voice. Come to think of it, I don't think she had one herself. Maybe that's why she didn't want me to have one."

I wondered aloud if perhaps Sandra's mom harbored some jealousy of Sandra's talent and early ambition.

The therapy lasted for eight sessions over a three-month period. I did my best to shift the interpersonal, energetic balance in the relationship, hoping to get Mike off his pedestal to make room for Sandra to come alive with her husband. The fact that Sandra turned out to be intelligent and highly attuned to the dynamics in their marriage made it easy for me to invite HER to be a doctor for the relationship.

Slowly, and through faint movements in the therapy, Sandra began to find her voice with Mike. He reacted first with ambivalence, then with greater openness toward his slightly more assertive, and present, wife. This process felt painful for both of them, though it was certainly less painful than what they'd been experiencing prior to therapy. That is probably a good way of characterizing a productive therapy experience: you trade an unproductive pain for a productive one, exchanging the torment of repeatedly fighting the same futile emotional battles for the semiarduous work that comes with hard-won self-knowledge and responsibility.

Mike and Sandra showed some courage in taking a candid look at their relationship and themselves. It was, of course, especially difficult for Mike, since it involved shedding some of his "good guy" self-image. As therapists, we often frustrate our patients' view of themselves and their situation, but our challenges are not personal in the usual sense. We want to show our patients that we see the game and the rules they have unconsciously constructed that govern their relationship. The game that they are playing is not life-giving, and we try to help them change it. We are always moving against the story that the couple or family want us to see. Psychotherapy is probably the only profession where the customer is always wrong.

Even as I challenged Mike, sometimes tentatively, I was rooting for him, and I believed he felt it. I believed that Mike's current way of operating constricted him, not just his marriage. I thought he would be more fully alive with a little more vulnerability, a little less self-assurance. By the eighth, and what turned out to be the final, therapy session, Sandra and Mike appeared to be on their way to developing some new patterns in their duet. Sandra grew slightly less cautious with Mike but it wasn't yet clear to me if Mike liked this bolder version of his wife.

In that session Mike spoke about something new that happened the previous week.

"I must tell you I was shocked. Sandra came on to me this week. She never, ever does that." He added, "I don't remember the last time she did that."

His last comment sounded like a jab, like he wanted to use something good his wife did as an opportunity to school her.

"It sounds like you got what you wanted and you're not happy about it. Sometimes it's hard to take 'yes' for an answer," I teased. "No, no, it was good," he protested, but I wasn't sure I believed him.

The couple started fighting more, too, both at home and in the sessions. Nothing too crazy, but it seemed like Sandra didn't immediately swallow her resentment if Mike performed his standard put-down move. Soon, their relationship music had slightly more dissonance AND more harmony. This new, tentative, low-grade sexual heat felt precious, perhaps evolving into a newfound freedom for Sandra and Mike.

I thought of this new heat as an early sign of change, still fragile, but an important beginning for the couple. This would set the stage for the subsequent therapy, hopefully to further explore and solidify these new patterns. But Mike called before the ninth session to say they were "fine" for now and would call if needed. I didn't really feel that they were at all "fine"; their long-standing patterns had just begun to loosen, and I wondered what would happen to them. I found out, unfortunately, nearly three years later when Sandra contacted me. They wanted to come in. Sandra said that Mike wanted a divorce.

The couple returned for therapy and, indeed, Mike decided he "wanted out." He was "fed up" with feeling stifled, sexually and otherwise, in the marriage. During the last year Sandra had developed all sorts of physical symptoms, especially problems with her digestion, accompanied by debilitating body aches. Doctors had been unable to diagnose her illness, but Sandra was clearly suffering. I thought to myself, "This is what can happen when you swallow garbage for too long." Of course, I didn't say that. I just filed it away under the heading of "Psychosomatic Illness."

I also smelled the presence of an outside girlfriend. From my therapy experience it's uncommon for a man to want to leave a marriage without another woman waiting in the wings. While Mike denied it at first, it turned out that yes, there was a woman who had "caught his interest," as he said, though he denied being "involved" with her. He reiterated that he had no hope of improving his marriage, or his wife. "Nothing will change," he said. Meaning Sandra. He was cool.

I saw this couple for several months as they worked through their separation, including having several sessions with their daughters. Mike impressed me as a good dad, committed and loving with his children, doing his best to ease the pain of separation for them. But he remained steadfast that his marriage, for him, was "over." During the course of this postseparation therapy, it became clearer that Mike had indeed fallen in love with another woman. Too bad. He was leaving the marriage without really having learned anything about himself.

What a troubling ending to a difficult case. I remembered Sandra and Mike well when they called me for the second round of therapy, this time a preseparation therapy, three years after our first meeting. I recalled how shut down and timid Sandra was with Mike and how, through the therapy, they had begun to inch toward something new, more dynamic. I wondered when I saw them again if I could have done something differently. Maybe I should have been more challenging toward Mike? I remember, at the time, stepping around him a bit gingerly. I was aware of trying not to alienate him, and this may have made me more cautious than I should have been. Perhaps I was afraid to upset him just like Sandra was?

When they returned to therapy to discuss separation, Mike said that the reason he didn't want to return after our last therapy session was that he felt that change wasn't happening "fast enough," meaning that Sandra wasn't changing fast enough. SHE was still, in his eyes, the patient.

It might sound strange, but, despite everything, I liked Mike. He was a good person who seemed to have a congenital impatience, a man with significant emotional blind spots who wasn't curious enough about himself and his power in his marriage. This became clear as I worked to help them navigate the separation. I had to deal with my own inward frustration with Mike when we met again; I felt he was taking the easy way out, opting to switch one relationship for another, without really caring to understand his impact on Sandra. But it was not my marriage. I'm not really in the business of saving marriages, though I sure prefer it when couples stay together in a healthier way. I am in the business of doing what I can to help troubled couples, by challenging them to go beyond their comfort zone, to look at themselves in the context of the relationship, to become more creative and as fully and genuinely expressive as possible. I (almost) always carry the conviction that people can change. That's a vote of confidence that runs through every therapy session.

Sandra seemed to want, and need, these postmarriage sessions. She was clinging to Mike, and I didn't blame her. The marriage didn't really need to end, in my opinion. Mike, obviously feeling guilty, tried to be friendly and accommodating in our sessions, but seemed anxious to end them. Finally, he announced in one session that this would be our last meeting. We said goodbye, and I assured them they could reach out to me if I could be helpful in the future.

These two very different cases shed some light on how therapy with couples with sexual dysfunction can play out. Despite different outcomes, the themes were similar, in that we explored the dynamics that contributed to the stuck, static quality of each couple. Both couples thought the problem was sex, not enough or the wrong kind. What emerged was how each couple unconsciously, partly through inherited family patterns, shaped each other in ways they did not know. Both Sarah and Alan and Mike and Sandra had no control over these patterns. They couldn't see them and/or didn't know about them, so they were helpless to do anything different. One couple showed the imagination, humility, and commitment necessary for transformation of their partnership. The other, sadly, did not.

What we saw in these stories was how each couple was battling openly, but without success. But sometimes a couple avoids open conflict with each other and instead the battleground shifts to the children, or a specific child who has become a problem. In this case the issues between the couple are disguised, but no less potent. Let's see how this happens, and how it offers the possibility for healing.

Questions for Reflection

In the first case, "The Sexually Boring Husband," we refer to the law of relationship physics. How did Sarah and Alan create each other? Sarah and Alan were successful in addressing the issue of their sex life, which Sarah initially saw as doomed. What did they each do that contributed to this successful outcome?

In the story of Sandra and Mike, "My Wife Hates Sex," they both initially agreed that Sandra was the problem. How did that happen? How did both partners participate in that myth? Why does this stand in the way of healing? What happened in the therapy that began to shift this idea for the couple?

What would you say is the main reason this couple ended up separating?

Chapter 5

Little Kids Behaving Badly

THE BIPOLAR THREE-YEAR-OLD

Frederick, a fortyish, handsome man with an erect bearing, walked into the office carrying his little son, Jonathan. His wife, Brandy, a fresh-faced, attractively casual woman came in behind them. Frederick had called me the week before at the suggestion of his family physician. He told his doctor that he worried that his three-year-old son was bipolar.

As we seated ourselves, Frederick, with his crisp British accent on display, told his son to "shake her hand" (meaning me). This little old man, disguised as a three year old, might as well have been wearing a tux as he came up to me and shook my hand very properly.

The father beamed, but I noticed the mother did not look especially happy by this cultivated display of "manners." I was careful not to show I was impressed by this show, since it looked to me that this kid was already being groomed for perfection. I just imagined the pressure this child experienced. I then spent a few minutes connecting with their little son: I showed him my dollhouse and took out some little figurines of people for him to look at. He appeared to be a rather serious child, very carefully groomed and dressed, but with a sweet expression. He was attentive as I took him on a short tour of the dollhouse. I wanted to be sure I treated him like he was three, not thirty.

"How can I help?" I asked Frederick and Brandy.

Frederick answered immediately. "I'm worried that my son is bipolar."

"Of course he's bipolar. He's three," I thought. But I remained dead-pan as the father described how every few days his son would have "meltdowns" where he would cry and throw himself on the ground. Little Jonathan was inconsolable during these episodes. What troubled Frederick most was that these episodes tended to occur in public.

I guessed that for this "correct" father, these wild tantrums in front of others would be particularly mortifying. I must admit that my heart went out to this father. He seemed like a good man. In our few brief moments together, however, I observed a kind of emotional rigidity, a brittleness that I assumed he developed as part of his own upbringing. Frederick seemed like the kind of guy who wanted to have fun but didn't know how.

After listening to Frederick's description of his concerns, I turned to Brandy and asked, "What's your idea about what's going on with your little boy?"

I was immediately struck by the difference between the parents. The mother was soft, in a good way. She had an easygoing way about herself.

She took a deep breath and said, "I never considered the thought that Jonathan might be bipolar. He's only three, and I know that this is part of the terrible twos. But I do worry because he seems so unhappy during these episodes."

As I observed Brandy, I was struck by the hesitancy in her voice. She looked at her husband as she spoke, like she was worried about his disapproval. I guessed (inwardly) that Brandy was not used to being an authority on her son and that husband Frederick carried more expert weight in the relationship.

The parents and I spoke for about twenty minutes, during which time I watched as Jonathan traveled back and forth between the dollhouse and his parents. He was quite a self-contained child, not a cuddly baby-type, more a budding grownup. I imagined that his temper tantrums might be a way of letting off steam.

As we talked, and I observed Frederick and Brandy with their son, I was struck by Frederick's fear of emotions—not only his, but his son's and wife's as well. It seemed like he wanted everyone to be in control. Though Frederick appeared to be a caring person, his language had a kind of repressed quality, like he wanted to be sure he was precise, that he didn't make a mistake. It also seemed as if he felt like he needed to be the in charge, head-of-household kind of guy. He reeked of dutifulness.

The poor guy. I felt the pressure he was carrying. I also think Frederick was afraid that, underneath his cultivated, correct exterior, he might just be as wild as his little son was during his meltdowns. I used this as a chance to weave this idea into our conversation. I thought some well-placed teasing might help.

"You know, no matter what we pretend, we're all a little mad," I said. "Dad, what do you think you might look like if you went off the deep end?"

I asked this question with the utmost respect. I think of "madness," which we all have, as part of our intuitive, unconscious, nonlogical selves; the part that allows us to fall in love, get carried away by a piece of music, or take a leap of faith. It's our fear or dislike of this part of ourselves that causes difficulty.

When I posed this question to Frederick, he just stared at me, obviously taken aback. But the lighthearted tone I used disarmed him, and he slowly appeared to enjoy this kind of question.

A smile crossed his face and he said, "No one has ever asked me this before. I guess I never had much room to lose control, or to act out. I was sent to boarding school when I was eight, and I pretty much have had to toe the line since then." I could tell Frederick wasn't one for self-pity, but his voice contained a tone of sadness, of loss, that was hard to miss.

Brandy looked at him, then looked at me, and nodded.

I smiled and said, "Maybe your son's trying to show you how to let loose. Sometimes that's the job of a bipolar three-year-old. Anyway, all three-year-olds are bipolar."

I wanted to normalize their son's outbursts since I could see that little Jonathan was programmed to be impeccably behaved. He mostly succeeded, playing quietly with the toys in my dollhouse, occasionally navigating his way toward his mom to help him adjust a doll's clothes. The session continued in this playful spirit, but there was a message in my undertone. I was indirectly addressing what I thought this child was unconsciously reacting against—the overcorrect orientation of a repressed, though caring, dad.

The session had a seemingly freewheeling quality to it, with the three so-called grownups sitting on the floor and the child playing in the dollhouse. The deliberately playful quality of the session was a strategic attempt on my part to invite Frederick to enjoy the feeling of regression, to let go of control, to taste the freedom of what it feels like to be a kid (which he never really got a chance to do), so I could help free up his son from his father's overrigid demands.

During our floor-sitting session, Brandy kept an eye on her son, talking to him in a way that projected warmth and care.

I looked at Brandy and asked, "I'm impressed by how you are with your little guy. How did you get to be such a good mom?"

She looked taken aback, like she wasn't used to words of appreciation.

She said, "I was an only child, and I always wanted a baby brother or sister. I babysat since the time I was nine, and I always felt like I was born to be a mom."

I wanted to affirm Brandy's looser, more intuitive approach to parenting, which I believed would help this little child. The hour went by quickly. As the session ended, we got up off the floor, I dusted myself off, and the parents thanked me for my time. Frederick looked rather bewildered, however.

He said, "I'm not sure what happened, but I think this was helpful." I assured them that they could call me anytime.

I didn't hear from them again.

According to the family doctor who referred them, the parents didn't bring up concerns about their child's behavior, and as far as I know, the bipolar issue did not come up again. My guess is that Frederick and Brandy could benefit by some therapy in the future to address some of these underlying patterns that I observed. But, meanwhile, I believe our session offered them a chance to experience themselves in slightly different ways, opening up the opportunity for alternative ways of responding to each other, and their child. What they did with that experience is, of course, up to them.

This session reveals how parents are often unknowingly reinforcing the problem in their attempt to help. I watched as Frederick, the father/authority inadvertently put pressure on his child to "behave," meaning to act like a grownup, while the mom, Brandy, appeared to back off, perhaps afraid to upset her husband with her freer, more intuitive parenting style. These patterns were subtle, but they repeated themselves often in a short, one-hour session.

I was mostly concerned that the dad, Frederick, didn't know how to play, and his need for control didn't allow him to let his wife or his child show him how. I imagined that being shipped off early to a strict British boarding school probably put the kibosh on his freedom to play, and this trickled down to his son. I guessed that little Jonathan had unconsciously picked up on his dad's anxiety about play and freedom and was trying to reassure him with his contained, pseudo-adult demeanor. I knew that in order to help this little guy, I had to open up the sense of possibility for the family, to help them experience what a less duty-bound life felt like. Mere words wouldn't have helped; we needed to sit on the floor and play, to enjoy the fantasy of going wild, knowing that it posed no danger. I believe that's what Frederick found helpful. He looked about ten years younger when he left.

I also went out of my way to treat three-year-old Jonathan like the little child he was. Small kids who end up in a therapist's or psychiatrist's office are just that—little children. These kids—three-, four-, and five-year-olds—do not have any real power on their own. They are not autonomous beings, capable of rational thought or independent decision-making. Without the development of much language, children become very creative in how they tell their stories. Without access to complex words, they are at the mercy of their bodies and their moods to try to convey what they need, what they worry about. And, no matter how it feels to the parents, these little children are not in charge. Their language is simple, not able to encompass their complex experience of being a child in a family. We know it is easy, and understandable, for parents to feel helpless in the face of their child's behavior, but that is really a problem for the parents, for the family, not the child. Making a small child a "patient" in the mental health sense increases the burden on this little person, who is already trying to navigate the challenging, and perhaps stressful, terrain that they call their world.

It may seem obvious to think of kids as having not much power, that they are at the mercy of their families. In fact, it is not. This perspective has lost traction in the contemporary world, where the medical model of human distress holds sway. To treat children as "patients," as having an individual mental disorder, is not merely a difference of therapeutic framework, however. It has a profound effect on what happens to families, and on the kids themselves, when a family seeks help for their kid's troubled, and troubling, behavior.

A haunting example of what can happen to a child who is treated as an individual, separate from the family, and given a serious psychiatric diagnosis, took place in 2006. The child was Rebecca Riley.

THE LITTLEST VICTIM

Little Rebecca Riley was born into a family under stress. A brief review of the reports showed a chaotic household pressured by economic strain, violence, and dysfunction. The family had been living in public housing up until a month before four-year-old Rebecca died. Michael, Rebecca's father, was not living with the family. He had been banned from public housing after his thirteen-year-old stepdaughter accused him of sexual assault. Michael described himself as suffering from "intermittent rage disorder" and "bipolar disorder" (though it's not clear where he got these diagnoses). When Rebecca's parents were together, their home life appeared to be characterized by periodic violence: Carolyn Riley, Rebecca's mother, once obtained a restraining order against her husband after claiming he grabbed their son by the neck and banged his head against the back window of a pickup truck, a claim Michael denied. The family left public housing on November 14, 2006, almost a month before Rebecca's death, and moved into a new home with Carolyn's half-brother and fiancé Kelly. Michael joined the family by the end of the month, two weeks before Rebecca died. This incredibly brief, minuscule, tip-of-the-iceberg snapshot of a family in chronic trouble creates a context where we can begin to understand little Rebecca's anxiety, her trouble sleeping, her "hyperactivity," and her mother's limited ability to cope.

An account in *The Boston Globe* describes that fateful evening: "On the night Rebecca received her fatal overdose, her father, who had been prone to violent outbursts, became irate about the child's pleas to be with her mother. Rebecca had been battling a respiratory illness for days, and that night, according to housemates, Rebecca kept trying to enter her parents' bedroom, moaning, 'Mommy, Mommy.' That night, the state said, Carolyn Riley gave the coughing and feverish child as much as twice the girl's daily dosage of clonidine at once, the equivalent of seven tablets of .1 milligram each."[1] It seems the mother was attempting to quiet the child so as not to arouse the violent anger of her husband.

Little Rebecca Riley was four years old when she died from a prescription drug overdose on December 13, 2006. At the time of her death, she was being "treated" with three medications: Seroquel, an antipsychotic, Depakote, an antiseizure drug (she did not have seizures), and

Clonidine, a blood pressure medication, all prescribed by a psychiatrist at Tufts–New England Medical Center. None of these medications had been approved by the FDA for use on children. Rebecca was just two years old when she was diagnosed with "bipolar disorder," a diagnosis made by the psychiatrist after several visits over an eight-month span. In a 2007 interview with Katie Couric on *60 Minutes*, Carolyn Riley said she brought her daughter to the psychiatrist because of her concern that Rebecca was "hyperactive" and had trouble sleeping. Ms. Riley knew this psychiatrist, Dr. Kayoko Kifuji, because she had already "diagnosed" Rebecca's seven-year-old sister and ten-year-old brother with bipolar disorder, both also at the age of two. Incredible as it may sound, this Tufts University Medical Center psychiatrist diagnosed three children, each only two years old, with bipolar disorder, a serious, and formerly rare, condition. Carolyn herself was taking Paxil for anxiety and depression.

A glimpse into a copy of Rebecca's medical records obtained by *60 Minutes* quotes Dr. Kifuji as describing an "increased risk of mental illness" because of her family history, a "family history" designed, in part, by Dr. Kifuji herself. The psychiatrist diagnosed two-year-old Rebecca as "bipolar" based on Carolyn's statement that she was "driving me crazy" and that she also had fluctuating moods that would switch from minute to minute. Little Rebecca, in her stroller, often slept right through her visits with Dr. Kifuji, very possibly as a result of being overmedicated. Asked by Couric if Rebecca's behavior couldn't have been "normal" for a two-year-old, Carolyn responded, "The psychiatrist said that she thought it was more than just normal." And when pressed by Couric about the use of multiple medications, Carolyn said, "I trusted the doctor." Again, these decisions were made, with the full weight of seeming medical authority, based on the mother's narrative. A diagnosis was made, and multiple heavy-duty drugs were given to a child with no meaningful direct observation of the child or of the child's family. A sleeping three-year-old, plus an overwhelmed mother, apparently were enough to convince this psychiatrist that Rebecca was mentally ill.[2]

Small children like Rebecca Riley often look like little storms as they express (often buried) pressures in the family. Children sense, and feel in their bodies, conflict and tension, particularly between parents and/or important adult figures. This is felt most painfully for kids when those conflicts are chronic, often unacknowledged, and unresolved. Kids carry this stress in their still-developing nervous systems, and as children grow, they often, usually unconsciously, try to help repair these family wounds. Children perceive these stresses as unspoken, energetic imbalances in the family that permeate the home front. This instability can feel dangerous for children, particularly when they detect depression in a parent or are subjected to intense conflict or violence. This is powerful stuff for little kids, and they respond with their bodies, their feelings, their distress.

In response to an inquiry from *60 Minutes* Tufts–New England Medical Center issued a statement: "The care we provided was appropriate and within responsible professional standards." In fact, they were right. This represented a "professional standard." Dr. Kifuji described her work as being influenced by research conducted by Dr. Joseph Biederman, chief of the Clinical and Research Programs in Pediatric Psychopharmacology and Adult ADHD at Massachusetts General Hospital and professor of psychiatry at Harvard Medical School. Biederman, a highly decorated psychiatrist, epitomized the authoritative declarations of psychiatry regarding "psychiatric problems" in children. He is widely credited with popularizing the "juvenile bipolar" diagnosis. Katie Couric interviewed Biederman as part of the *60 Minutes* inquiry into Rebecca Riley's death and posed this question to him: "Previous studies that were conducted in the seventies and eighties determined it was very, very rare for a child to have bipolar disorder. And now you're saying up to a million children are running around with this? Why such a sea change?" "The idea is rare if you define it in very strict ways," Dr. Biederman explained. "Our contribution has been to describe the many ways that this condition may emerge in children that may make it a little bit more diagnosable and less rare than people have thought about it."

The Rebecca Riley case eventually went to court, and Biederman testified. As part of his deposition, he noted that psychiatric diagnoses are "subjective in children and adults." In other words, diagnosis is in the eye of the beholder. Biederman acknowledged the rebranding of earlier psychiatric diagnoses: "These children have been called in the past conduct-disorder, oppositional-defiant disorder." He went on to say that these newly labeled "bipolar" children existed "under different names," but now these "conditions" have been "reconceptualized" as juvenile bipolar disorder. Perhaps more than any other figure, Biederman helped to usher in an age where it became "standard of care" where psychiatrists began to prescribe antipsychotics, as well as other non-FDA approved psychiatric medications, to children as young as two years old. The bipolar diagnosis in children, once considered "temper tantrums" or later, in psychiatric parlance, "oppositional defiant disorder," increased forty times thanks to his work.

Not surprisingly a Senate hearing in 2008 revealed that Dr. Biederman had received $1.6 million in speaking and consulting fees from various pharmaceutical-industry giants who manufactured antipsychotic medications for use on children thought to have bipolar disorder. He was found to be on the payroll at AstraZeneca, the makers of Seroquel, which is among the most frequently prescribed drugs for kids with bipolar disorder. Rebecca Riley was taking Seroquel when she died at age four.

In 2010, three years after Rebecca's death, her parents went on trial for murder. Carolyn Riley was charged with second-degree murder. She was sentenced to life in prison where she would be eligible for parole in fifteen years. Michael was charged with first-degree murder. He received life without parole. Dr. Kifuji was exonerated. She continues to practice as a child psychiatrist.

This is where we put on our metaphorical "Question Authority" T-shirts. The pathologizing of adults, and of children, has crept into our culture to the extent that, now, we barely notice it. We've adopted a language that is replete with static, seemingly objective diagnoses to describe behavior and moods of all kinds. It is common to hear people throw around the label "bipolar" as if it were as frequent as the common cold. With adults, that's one thing. Adults are, theoretically at least, capable of critical thinking and making choices about what treatment is best for them. But our children are sitting ducks, at the mercy of the grownups in their world to look out for their best interests. In modern psychotherapy culture, led by the biological model in psychiatry and adopted by most of the psychotherapy community, the behavior of a child is separated from the family. It's as if a child's mood or behavior has nothing to do with context, that most vital influence on a young child's life—the family. Little attention is paid to the powerful ecosystem in which the child lives, and which lives in the child.

We do not say this as part of a parental "blame game." As parents, we know intimately the complex and, at times, painful, experience of raising kids. We have had our share of run-ins and hair-raising episodes with our own children. But blame is different from responsibility. When we engage the whole family in therapy, we offer parents a chance to tell the story of their efforts to help their kids, of their own personal struggles from their childhood, including trauma. Tensions in the marital relationship emerge from the shadows, where, in a caring, therapeutic relationship, adults can explore the intractability in their own intimate partnerships. The parents' disappointments, frustrations, fears, unmet needs are given value and meaning in the therapy setting. Everyone becomes a patient. There is unexpected power in that: everyone becomes a part of the healing process. That's a very different experience for parents than standing on the sidelines waiting for the doctor to "fix" the child.

As family therapists, when families come to us for help, we often feel like an intrepid Sherlock Holmes, using our training and experience to examine these family relationship patterns for clues. The next case shows what happens when desperate parents, at the end of their rope, seek help for their five-year-old.

THE CASE OF THE FIVE-YEAR-OLD BOSS

Teresa and Mel were referred by their family doctor who wasn't inclined to start their child on medications, as the parents requested. She suggested a family consultation instead. At the initial phone call, the parents asked to come in alone for the first visit to tell (warn) me about their son's behavior. I agreed.

This stressed-out-looking couple in their late thirties came to see me for help with their five-year-old son Robbie's temper tantrums. They reported little Robbie as "out of control." At times, his defiance included hitting his parents and kicking. Once, he swung his arm hard enough that it broke his father's glasses. Armed with a video of Robbie in full temper tantrum mode, Teresa and Mel backed up their claims by a visual presentation. With reluctance, I briefly looked at the video; my heart went out to this child. He looked utterly beside himself, out of his little mind, jumping on the table, screaming, tears streaming down his cheeks. He looked completely tied up in knots and didn't know how to reverse himself. We scheduled an appointment for the following week with their son.

The parents made it clear that they felt defeated by their little Hercules, so it was funny to see them walk into the next visit with this cherubic-looking five-year-old in tow. This tousle-haired guy was as polite as could be as he played with the toys in my office. But I knew that in order to be helpful I needed to see him in action.

I said, "It looks to me like Robbie knows how to behave pretty well when he wants to. What would typically make this young man act up?"

The parents thought for a moment, then Teresa decided to ask Robbie to relinquish the Batman toy he was playing with. He refused. She insisted. And on it went. A game between them ensued. He then began to hit and kick. What a little bruiser this guy was! I watched as Teresa struggled helplessly for a minute or two. Mel mostly remained on the sidelines.

I said calmly, a slight smile on my face, "Dad, it's obvious that Robbie's own brakes aren't working too well. Can you help him?" What followed told me what I needed to know: the strange phenomenon of a five-year-old overtaking two grownups.

Mel showed a real aptitude for taking control of his son. With my encouragement, he held him, not too hard, just firm, and caring. Robbie screamed bloody murder: "You're choking me!" as he kept trying to kick and bite. Mel held fast.

As I praised the father, I glanced at Teresa and asked, "Mom, what's happening for you now?" She looked ashen, face tense, clutching the arms of the chair like she was holding on to her seat for dear life.

She said through clenched jaw, "I worry that's he's going to hurt him" (meaning that her husband was going to hurt Robbie).

I looked at her quizzically and said, "Actually, he's giving this child just what he needs."

Brief verbal check-ins with the couple as this took place assured me that father had never lost control of his son. Not even close. Teresa and I continued to watch as Mel held firm. I said things to Robbie like, "Wow, you're so lucky that your daddy cares about you so much. What a lucky boy you are." Etc., etc. I think my praise helped, since Mel became increasingly relaxed in his custodial role, even making a few jokes that made his son laugh.

Mel kept asking his son, "Are you done yet? Can I take my hands away?" But this kid was tough—he didn't quit. He had a lot of fight left in him.

Meanwhile, as Mel held Robbie, I turned to Teresa. It soon became clear to me why this problem persisted.

"Sometimes Mel makes that face," she said, mimicking an angry, scary, face, which told me that she felt she had to monitor her husband's parenting skills, that he couldn't be trusted.

Mel said, "Why do you keep saying that?" He was annoyed that his wife kept disqualifying his efforts, painting him as a near lunatic.

"Sometimes you get so angry. I can see it in your face." She mimicked him again. Now Mel was clearly annoyed, though quietly so.

He said, "I get angry when I feel like I'm fighting both of you!" Bingo. Family systems lesson 101. Words from one of my professors echoed in my ears: "When a child is taller than one parent, [they're] sitting on the other parent's shoulders."

Teresa's obvious anxiety as she watched Mel with her son helped to create a strong mixed message about what was expected from this child. It looked to me like she was trying to disarm her husband with her eyes. And what's a five-year-old to do? Should he obey Daddy? Fight to the death for Mommy? Pretty confusing for everyone.

I ruminated out loud. "It looks like Robbie doesn't know if he's supposed to surrender or keep up the battle with the old man. That's a tall order for a five-year-old."

Meanwhile, I continued to admire Mel's loving firmness with his son. Slowly, Teresa joined in.

She told Robbie, "Daddy cares about you."

Her tone was softer. I think she started to worry less. Without explicitly stating it, it had become obvious that when Mel felt his wife's support, everything and everyone became calmer. Even little Robbie. He soon gave up the fight. As Mel released his arms, Robbie put his own little arms around his daddy and climbed onto his lap. They remained holding each other for a few minutes. Teresa stared incredulously.

"Robbie has never, ever done that!" she said.

"That's because of what you did," I said, nodding to her and her husband. I credited her for the change in her son; Teresa's affirmation of her husband allowed their son to surrender and be glad about it.

The session was now coming to an end. I didn't want to talk too much about what happened: this family experienced something new in terms of their usual way of operating and I wanted it to resonate for a bit. Mel felt empowered to take care of his son, to give this child what he so desperately needed—a firm, calm, parental hand. And this time, for the first time, Teresa joined in. These folks got what they came for, though, as usual, not in the way they'd envisioned. Teresa made it clear when they initially came to see me that they might only come for one or two sessions. She had recently decided to leave her administrative job and was hoping to develop her own business as an interior design consultant. She said she needed to focus on getting her new career off the ground. I didn't see them in person after that visit.

I did get a call from Teresa the following week. She said that "things are much better" and asked if I would talk to Robbie's teacher, who had expressed concerns about his meltdowns in class. When I spoke to the teacher, she said Robbie would "dissolve in tears" if another child did better than he did at something, and she was concerned about his sensitivity. I shared my observations from our session and said, among other things, that little Robbie needed to learn to lose. I told her that his parents made a good start in this direction, and I hoped they'd keep it up. The teacher thanked me, and we did not speak after that.

I must confess, when the parents first told me about the struggles with their son, I wondered if I could help them. I almost always wonder that. When people present their stories, before I meet everyone involved, it almost always sounds dire, perhaps incurable. Then, when the family shows up at the office, I typically breathe a sigh of relief. For some reason, when actual human beings show up with actual human problems, things rarely feel insurmountable.

That was certainly true with this case, more so because Robbie was a little boy. How much real power can a five-year-old have, especially with two educated, reasonably intelligent adult parents? They were not overly stressed by issues of poverty or homelessness, immigration problems, or recent trauma. The issues were emotional/relational. These good people were caught in a cycle of anxiety, unable to see themselves, unable to get out. But because they were relatively healthy, able to be curious about themselves and willing to learn, they responded well to my intrusions into their family patterns.

I'm pretty sure that what turned the session, and the family dynamic, around was my unequivocal support for Mel. I interrupted the subtle message that Teresa had been sending to her son, "Daddy is not to be trusted. He's too strong with you." I could not have given my wholehearted support to Mel had he seemed rough, angry, or brutish in any way. But both Teresa's confirmation that Mel didn't have "anger issues" and my observation of him and the couple allowed me to shake up their unhealthy arrangement. Not only that, but both in my visit with the couple alone and with their son, Mel struck me as a thoughtful, reflective, though somewhat depressed man. Teresa didn't seem afraid of him or appear to be worried about stepping on his toes.

Little Robbie clearly had too much power in his family, and he was miserable because of it. Young children relax when they can trust the grownups in their world, when they don't have to second-guess their parents. Being expected to comply feels good as well as normal to little kids. With this family, Mom's ambivalence about using both her and her husband's authority with their child was troubling. Why was Teresa afraid of using her natural strength as a parent? What was her anxious relationship to authority, male or otherwise? These are questions that occurred to me during our visit, but that I didn't have a chance to explore with them.

I imagine that these issues relate both to Teresa and Mel's personal histories, as well as their relationship as a couple. In our first visit with them alone I detected some quiet resentment between them, and not just about their child. Mel seemed unsatisfied in his demanding career as a lawyer, and it sounded like he wanted some emotional support from his wife. Teresa, while not saying it directly, indicated that she, too, might be feeling let down by Mel. His slightly depressed countenance contrasted with her sunnier disposition. I wondered about the nature of the stresses between them. I never found out because, as promised, they came for a single consultation.

Teresa and Mel showed some courage in our sessions, but most likely they'll need some more help. My guess is that their responses to Robbie have partial roots in Teresa's and Mel's own lives. It's not uncommon to see a woman who has grown up in a house with a violent or unpredictable father to worry a lot about that trait showing up in her husband. Or there may be some repressed or unaddressed conflicts between the parents themselves. In my experience, it's useful, at some point in the therapy, to meet with the parents alone to air/resolve any unfinished grievances. This is perhaps the best way, ultimately, for parents to care for their children.

How might the case of Robbie and his temper tantrums have gone if he had been seen in therapy alone, or if his mother had merely reported his behavior to a psychiatrist or therapist? Robbie could have easily acquired the label of being "ADHD" or, because he appeared so difficult to control, of having "juvenile bipolar disorder." This case would have turned out differently if it had been assumed that Robbie had a mental illness, and we adopted a straightforward, linear, solution-focused "fix" based on his symptoms.

What are "symptoms" anyway? Symptoms are what we see on the surface, an outward expression of an underlying disturbance, a symbolic expression of a problem, but not the problem itself. When a child develops a pattern of difficult behavior like a temper tantrum, we pay attention to the context of relationship patterns in the family—those stubborn, repetitive, and mostly unconscious ways family members relate to each other. Though difficult to know from the inside, these dynamics exert powerful influence over our children. After all, our kids depend on the adults in their lives, and they need these adults to be well. It's the adult's business to figure the children out, and to try to help them if possible. We grownups are much, much more powerful in the eyes of our children than most of us realize.

As Leo Tolstoy wrote in *Anna Karenina*: "Happy families are all alike: every unhappy family is unhappy in its own way."[3] That wise observation, from one of the world's greatest literary psychotherapists, captures a truth that we see in our offices. We learn from the folks who seek our help that unhappy families come in many varieties. But certain themes run through their stories.

This next case chronicles a couple, Judy and Jim, who first came to therapy to deal with their terrible marriage. After about six months of rather painful sessions, things had improved considerably. The pain of these sessions was shared: this couple, with the wife's high drama yelling and the husband's cold, stiff rebuffs made these sessions, at times, exhausting for me. They left therapy in a much better place but called about eight months later saying they were in trouble again. After several sessions, harmony had been restored, although the wife voiced concern about their four-year-old daughter, who'd been having temper tantrums on a nearly daily basis, often before bedtime. The parents were perplexed about how to handle it.

THE LITTLE PRINCE AND THE WAIF

I got a distress call from Judy: "I need to see you immediately. We've relapsed." I had worked with Judy and her husband, Jim, in therapy for nearly six months—they went from having what I thought of as "end-stage marital disease" to enjoying a relatively healthy and harmonious balance. The work was difficult (for all of us), but the couple was committed to learning about themselves and each other and responded well to the therapy. It had been about eight months since I last met with them when Judy's anguished call came.

As soon as I saw them, their appearance confirmed their dismal state: crying, depressed wife ranting at her husband. Withdrawn, coldly pissed-off husband, withholding his love and care toward his wife. Fortunately, we had been down this road therapeutically before and the couple had done some excellent work. I reminded them of this as I tried to make them feel both proud of their past great work and a bit embarrassed that they allowed themselves to fall back into these unlovely patterns.

We only needed two sessions to help this duet restore the vibrancy in their relationship. The first session involved me reconnecting with Jim. I reminded him, "You forget that I know about your secret desire to be loved and admired by your wife." He smiled rather sheepishly. Jim seemed relieved at being "busted." In our first go-round of therapy, he specialized in a cruel indifference toward his wife—his method of disguising his need for her love and approval. He rose to the occasion when he had a chance to talk about his vulnerability.

With my support, Jim turned to Judy and showed her a bit of his heart: "You know I want to be a good husband to you. I feel like shit when I'm failing. I need you to know I'm trying."

Needless to say, this went over much better with Judy than Jim's cold indifference.

The second session centered on me putting some pressure on Judy and her unattractive tendency to continually rake her husband over the coals. Though she first resisted this challenge, she showed her pride by saying, "You know I take what you say seriously. And you know I can do whatever I set my mind to do!"

Judy's self-image as an "achiever" kicked in and she accepted my challenge. She openly (almost) apologized for her belittling of Jim as her poorly chosen way to get his attention. These sessions proved helpful because at our third session, Judy had become a lot softer with Jim, and he in turn became more available to her, giving her more of the husband and partner she wanted.

In this session they talked about their concern about their four-year-old daughter Lucy's temper tantrums. They had brought their two kids to a session during our first phase of therapy, but Lucy had fallen asleep in the stroller, and I didn't get to meet her. Now, it seemed like her behavior had become more of an issue. The couple described her as "impossible . . . she doesn't listen" and was, according to them, "out of control," especially when they asked her to do something she didn't want to do, like go to bed. These problems mostly showed up at home. Her teachers had no complaints as Judy reported that they loved this little child.

Judy commented that Lucy had a significant speech delay, which she thought might be contributing to her daughter's outbursts. Judy hoped to bring Lucy in alone, but I know that in order to understand a child's behavior, it's best to have the other siblings there as well because they can be very helpful. We ended the session with my suggestion to "bring the little cherubs in!"

As the quartet walked through my door for the next session, my first impression of Lucy was that she looked like a wild child. Her hair was unkempt, her clothes, though cute and pink, were disheveled. Her brother, Darien, by contrast, was the picture of a well-kept kid, neatly put together with his spiffy glasses and dapper clothes. The kids eyed my dollhouse, games, and Lego sets, and I gave the green light that they could start to play. I watched as they made a beeline for their preferred toys. After making some lighthearted connections with the kids, I gave them space to play so I could begin to observe. Slowly, as we watched, the parents and I began to talk about the kids. Lucy and Darien were told that they came to my office for a "family checkup."

As I listened to Judy and Jim, it sounded like six-year-old Darien could do no wrong. He was their "little prince." And there was, I knew, an underlying reason: Darien had been diagnosed with Crohn's disease at age four. Since then, this child had been through the medical mill with an onslaught of doctors and treatments, all of which had taken an emotional toll on everyone. His health was good now, but the parents had acquired a state of ongoing vigilance toward him.

I got on the floor and started playing with Lucy and Darien. I wanted them to feel comfortable with me before I started asking them about their family. When the atmosphere felt calm, I looked at the kids and asked casually, "How is your family doing?" After a bit of chitchat, I picked up the glittery magic wand I keep in the office and giving it to each child, asked, "What would you change about your family if you could?" Without hesitation they both mentioned that they wished Daddy "wouldn't go to the gym so much" and wanted Mommy to "scream less." Despite these requests, the kids didn't seem overly anxious about their folks. They played easily with their dad, who had by now joined me on the floor, and went back and forth between the parents as they played with the toys. Meanwhile, I was paying attention to the interaction between all family members.

I was struck by a couple of things: Lucy did indeed have a significant speech delay, so much so that it was often difficult to understand her. And though she had a really sweet quality, she had trouble getting much softness from her parents. They didn't seem to enjoy her much and reserved most of their interest, attention, and praise for Darien. When he boldly snatched Lucy's sticker from her wrist, the parents didn't admonish their son. I decided to praise little Lucy—it looked to me like she needed some appreciation.

I asked Judy to give her a couple of instructions; I just wanted to test the question of compliance, since the parents complained that she "didn't listen." Judy asked her to do a couple of things—put this toy away, don't touch the picture, etc.—and the little girl responded without a problem. Clearly little Lucy wanted to be good. She seemed eager to please. As I began to point out all the great things about Lucy such as, "See what a good mommy she is with my doll" and "Lucy is such a caring little sister," I watched as the family became somewhat uncomfortable. This was unfamiliar territory and went against the unconscious family patterns, their acquired homeostasis. They were not used to hearing loving and caring words about Lucy said out loud. Lucy lit up, wanting to show us all the good things she was doing with the baby doll in my office. She became gooder than good. Darien began to whine and demand more attention.

Judy was sitting on my couch, and I asked her to call her daughter over for a cuddle.

"Lucy is a special girl," I said.

Lucy plopped on the couch next to her mom and they both looked a bit awkward, though they appeared to enjoy this apparently unfamiliar closeness. Darien didn't like it one bit. He acted like he'd been robbed! He continued whining to his dad, accusing him of "not helping" him with the Lego house. Darien didn't cry but continued to pout despite Jim's assurances of help.

Darien groused, "I have to go to the bathroom," his way of expressing displeasure with this unexpected turn of events, an unfamiliar family script where he had to share the limelight.

As he left the room, Lucy jumped up to follow him. The parents were in the middle of crying "No!" to Lucy as she darted out of the room. Jim looked at me as if to say, "See?" I told him to go get her.

"She's easy," I said.

Jim brought her back, no problem. Lucy returned to the serious business of taking care of her baby doll.

I said, "She's easy to turn around."

And she was. I watched as she responded to commands and requests, showing that she was malleable. They had painted her as a two-ton giant, and I wanted to leave them with a different diagnosis, one that offered them a different, more dynamic view of their daughter.

By now our conversation had taken on a strong theme, one that subtly connected Lucy's temper tantrums with the ongoing, inadvertent parental neglect. This child needed attention; she was running a deficit of attention—not attention deficit—which showed up both in her behavior and in her speech delay. As a little child, Lucy couldn't express her distress in words. I must admit, I felt inwardly annoyed at Judy and Jim for their rather dramatic preferential treatment toward their son. But I had seen this before. It's not uncommon in families where one child has a chronic or life-threatening illness. The other kids are often overlooked in the mix, either becoming caretakers or overdeveloping a self-sufficiency that can become both a source of strength and problematic for them as adults. Of course, I did my best not to show my irritation toward Judy and Jim. Instead, I said that Darien has been "special" for a long time, and Lucy needs to be "special" too. The parents clearly saw how Lucy flourished during the session in response to her "special" treatment. It was unmistakable how good this little child really was and wanted to be. We talked about some things they might do, like develop some special bedtime rituals with Lucy. Mom also said she was going to plan some "mother-daughter" time, something she rarely did. We agreed to meet in a month or so. After they left I reflected on what just happened. I didn't expect that outcome. From the parents' description I expected to see a disobedient four-year-old who was being triggered by parental tensions and was busy pushing buttons. Instead, by seeing this child in her natural habitat—her family—I was able to observe patterns that are otherwise unknowable.

I called the family doctor who had referred the couple to me. I knew he was also the kids' doctor. I told him about the session and what I had learned about little Lucy and her behavior. He knew the family, but of course had never seen them together in the way that I did. He said the mother had recently reached out to him about Lucy, and he said he had given her the "usual temper tantrum advice." He thanked me for this added information, which was outside his scope of vision. He said he would recommend some "mother-daughter bonding time," in line with my observations. I continued to see Judy and Jim off and on for the next several months, before they moved out of state, where they addressed some of their residual issues as a couple. They didn't mention Lucy or her behavior again, except to comment briefly, "Things are better."

This case reminded me that you can never prejudge what you will see. I expected to see a defiant four-year-old reacting to the tensions between the parents, which I knew so well from my therapy with them. Instead, I saw unintentional neglect. Since this small daughter had already earned the reputation as Lucy the Incorrigible, I paid special attention to ways I could help Lucy lose this unfortunate label, offering new possibilities for the family. When I tested Lucy's ability to comply, and her obvious desire to please the most important people in her life, I knew this was the opening I needed to create some change. Luckily, I already had equity in the therapeutic relationship from my work with the couple. They knew me and, though I occasionally made life unpleasant for them with my challenges, the couple trusted me.

We bring our stories from the family therapy front to show the inner workings of three different families troubled by the behavior of their young children. As parents, of course, the challenge becomes how to decipher these hieroglyphics, how to speak "Child," a language most grownups left behind long ago, and may scarcely remember. These mysterious moods and behaviors of little kids often feel out of reach for parents, engendering feelings of helplessness and worry. "Am I being a bad parent?" "Am I too strict?" "Too soft?" "What if their meltdowns never end?" "What if they're a sign of something serious?" These questions are common sources of anguish for parents of young children. Anguish is a feature of all parenting; it's how we get our PhD in becoming a person. The introductory course might be called "Guilt 101."

One theme that connects these cases is that little children are malleable, and highly responsive to changes in the parenting dynamic. Though every human is born with a predisposition and a temperament, for little kids nothing is fixed. They are at the mercy of those towering figures in their lives, their parents. One helpful question for parents to ask themselves is, "What am I doing that may be reinforcing the problem with my child?" We saw how, in "The Bipolar Three-Year-Old," Frederick, the father, expected his child, Jonathan, to be a rational being, which was way beyond the child's developmental capability. The father, who had led a duty-bound life, was afraid to play. His personal demons created a cauldron of pressure for his son. Little children are imagination machines, powered by fantasy, not tethered to reality. They offer us, especially those who have carried too many burdens from childhood, a chance to escape into play. Children are great therapists for those who never got a chance to experience the freedom that play offers.

In "The Five-Year-Old Boss," we met Teresa, who worried about male aggression. Though she clearly wasn't afraid of her husband, she continually softened or undercut his efforts to firmly manage Robbie, their five-year-old. We've seen this dynamic fairly frequently, where the mother routinely positions herself between the child and the father, anxiously standing guard. Most often this reflects the wife's anxiety about male figures, which she may unconsciously project onto her husband, or even a son. This type of projective identification is often a reflection of her own history of family trauma. Somewhere, at some point, there may have been a father who was frightening or untrustworthy, which can leave lingering scars on the family nervous system. This acquired hypervigilance can show up in the woman's relationships in subsequent generations. With Teresa and Mel, we saw what happened when Mel was "allowed" to be strong and firm with his child: this can be powerful anxiety-reducing medicine for little kids.

In the story of "The Little Prince and the Waif," Judy and Jim were conscientious parents, but they couldn't see what their young daughter was trying to tell them. Most of their diligence, and worry, had been directed at their ill son, who flourished under their care. The other child, however, got sacrificed in the process. The family got stuck with the idea that Darien was perfect, and Lucy was trouble. This "good child/bad child" dichotomy always deserves rethinking on the part of the family. In the session, this little girl absolutely glowed when grownups paid attention to all the things that were lovely about her. That's good practice for parents of little children, especially unhappy children. Spend a day, or two days, or three, just observing and appreciating all the wonderful uniqueness of your child. Little children bloom when they please their parents. You may be rewarded.

There is a lot to the saying "Little kids, little problems; big kids, big problems." For the most part, problems of preschool or kindergarten kids can be resolved relatively quickly in therapy when the family is included. As children grow, their problems, and the challenges for the family, increase in complexity. In the next chapter we tell the stories of three families struggling with the behavior—sometimes outlandish behavior—of their children. We reveal a secret that was first discovered by the early family therapists. Understanding this secret may change your life.

Questions for Reflection

In "The Case of the Bipolar Three-Year-Old," the therapist didn't really respond directly to Frederick's concern about his son's being "bipolar." Instead, after observing the family, she decided the father needed to allow himself to play. Do you think this was a good choice? Have you ever worried about mental illness in your own children? Has this story affected how you think now?

The tragic story of "The Littlest Victim" made headlines when it occurred. What do you think of Dr. Biederman, the celebrated Harvard psychiatrist, in this story? If you brought your child to this doctor, do you think you would be able to question their recommendations?

In "The Case of the Five-Year-Old Boss," the little son could indeed be a ferociously strong-willed child. This session revealed the family dynamics behind his temper tantrums. Why do you think the mother was so afraid that the father would get too angry with their son, though the father gave no evidence of that? Do you have any hypotheses about why she felt the need to "protect" the son from the father? Have you seen this dynamic in yourself or others?

In the story "The Little Prince and the Waif," little Lucy had become the family scapegoat. Have you seen families, your own or others, where there is a "good" child and a "bad" child? Does this story help you see these dynamics in a new way?

Chapter 6

It's a Tough Job Raising Parents

THE CASE OF THE NINE-YEAR-OLD DOCTOR

"Who's this whore from New York City? Why should I go to see her? Why doesn't she mind her own business?" That was how I first encountered Eric; a child considered so incorrigible that he had to be placed in residential treatment for a couple of weeks to give his parents a break.

I was meeting his family for the first time in my role as a consultant for a child guidance clinic in Upstate New York. The family, parents Philip and Darlene, and their only child, Eric, were presented to me by the child's therapist as a notorious case of an uncontrollable nine-year-old boy. The therapist for this case said he needed my help desperately. He felt defeated by this family and their child's out-of-control behavior.

As I seated myself for the interview, I heard the therapist from the treatment center struggling in the hallway, trying to get young Eric to go into the interview room. The parents were already seated. Soon I heard this high-pitched voice, a baby voice really, trying to sound menacing. I burst out laughing. Here is this little kid, practicing throwing his weight around, doing his best to be a tough guy.

I wiped the smile off my face and turned to the parents: "What would you like to do?" I asked. After some equivocation on their part, I suggested, "Why don't you see if you can get him to come in?" I thought this would give me a chance to get a first glimpse of the family operating system. First his dad tried, then his mom. I could hear some ineffective yelling. Both parents returned to the interview room, defeated.

I proposed that we begin the interview without their son. In my mind, I didn't want the kid to hold his parents hostage. I guessed that this happened too much already. These grownups seemed to feel powerless with their own child.

As we settled ourselves in the interview room I turned to the parents. "Tell me, what brought you here?"

Darlene began by talking about the "impossible" behavior of their only child, who sounded like he had become an expert in pushing his parents' buttons. Eric's mom sounded utterly exasperated.

"He curses, he throws things, he refuses to obey," though, according to her, he was mostly well behaved at school.

As always, I assumed Eric's provocative behavior was embedded in the family operating system. I listened as Darlene began complaining about her husband's relative absence from the mayhem at home. She described how Philip's job as a health-care administrator meant that he had long days, in addition to his lengthy commute.

"He works all the time," she said. "He's exhausted by the time he gets home."

Darlene also complained bitterly about her own mother's overly intrusive behavior in the family. Her mother apparently couldn't stand Darlene's husband, and colluded with her grandson to raise hell against his father. Though Darlene and her mother spent quite a bit of time together, Darlene expressed her vitriol toward her mother.

"She's always been very critical and judgmental toward me."

Darlene harbored a lot of resentment toward her mom, and it sounded like this contributed to the tensions in the home.

Philip mostly concurred with his wife, both about the crazy behavior of their only child and the resentment they both held toward his meddlesome mother-in-law.

"And Darlene is right that I'm not around much. My job takes a big chunk out of my life. I wish I could change it, but someone's got to support the family!"

If you could have seen the thought bubble above my head, here's what you would have read:

It sounds like Darlene and her mother are a couple and Philip is an outsider. Maybe he doesn't know how to get in? Philip seemed like a cautious, timid kind of guy. Maybe he wasn't lively enough for his wife? Was Darlene trying to divorce her own mother and marry her husband? It sounded like she longed for Philip but couldn't reach him. Was Darlene's mother trying to get rid of Philip so she could have her daughter to herself? Why was Darlene's husband so absent—physically and emotionally? Was he escaping from the conflict at home? Was the young son (unconsciously) trying to bring his father home by being such a handful that his dad HAD to step in?

Darlene looked frustrated and depressed to me. Both parents, in fact, though obviously well-meaning people, appeared sadly isolated from each other.

"You look like two lonely people," I said.

I observed barely perceptible nods from each of them. We were in the heat of conversation about the tense family dynamics when their young son walked in. I pulled up a chair for Eric and he sat quietly by my side, listening. I purposely ignored him, since I believed he was already too powerful, and I didn't want to reestablish his position of eminence. Besides, there was a bit of a spell cast in the session: the parents were talking quietly about matters that were quite painful for them, perhaps for the first time. Some of the fissures in their relationship were being exposed, and to their credit, they didn't want to lose the moment. I think they felt rather relieved to be able to unburden themselves to a nonjudgmental professional, someone with an expertise in families.

As the session continued, I turned to Eric and said, "So what do you think about what your parents are saying?"

He seemed fascinated by the discussion in the room. Eric commented quietly, adding his own take on his family troubles. He sat by my side comfortably, like my cotherapist. Not surprisingly, he knew a lot about his parents' pain. That's generally true with kids—they feel the subtle tension in the family and worry about it. Eric weighed in.

"Granny hates my dad. She gives me money to be on her side. She counts on me to help her out."

He sounded like he felt a lot of pressure from "Granny." He talked about how his father was never home, and how he worried about his mom, who was often left alone with only Grandma as her companion.

His worry about the difficult triangular relationship between his parents and grandmother was clearly central in his mind. He knew all about it. He talked about his home life like he had made a study of his folks and their dilemma very carefully. I believe that in his own little way, he was trying to help his family with their suffering. I wondered if his "impossible" behavior represented an attempt to reengage his dad, to bring him home, to help rescue his mother. It must have felt to him that his parents were emotionally divorced, and it was his job to help them remarry.

His troublesome behavior did bring his dad home, at least temporarily. I think Eric was also perhaps trying to show his father how to stand up for himself, not to be so conflict avoid-y, something Philip needed to learn to do with his mother-in-law, and possibly with his wife. The father presented himself as a Casper Milquetoast, a timid soul who projected helplessness, especially in the face of his son's behavior and his mother-in-law's criticism. Little Eric was the self-appointed family therapist. I wanted him to know I saw this.

"Boy, I feel your worry for your folks. You see that your dad isn't home much and he's kind of an avoider. And it's obvious your mom is lonely. I'm guessing you're trying to help them out of this mess. You're a good observer. It looks like you've been working overtime to try to help. You've been the family doctor for a while, huh?"

Eric held my gaze. His somber expression told me that he understood. He must have realized that, in fact, he was too little, too powerless, to really do anything about his family's pain. The parents listened, and took it in. I kept it up.

"You know what, I think this job must feel heavy for you. I know you're doing your best to help, but there's not much you can do. You don't have any real power. But the good news is that your parents are starting to ask some questions about what they can do differently. That's an improvement."

Eric, still holding my gaze, quietly nodded.

This was not the kid I was led to expect. I don't think this was the kid who usually showed up. The session soon drew to a close. I would not be seeing the family again, as I was the consultant on the case. But the therapists for the child and family were observing the session on the other side of the one-way mirror and I let the parents know that I would remain as a consultant to their therapist. I told the parents how much I'd been impressed by their courage and wished them good luck. The room had a stillness to it. I shook hands with the parents and got up to leave.

As we walked out, and I headed to the other room, little Eric came up and put his arms around my waist and hugged me. At first, I was caught off guard. Here's this would-be tough guy, now looking like the little kid that he was. He didn't say anything, just hugged. I found this very touching. He seemed like a little nine-year-old boy, exhausted from trying to help his folks, and relieved to be off duty. He inadvertently transferred his job to a qualified professional, a grownup who could listen to his parents with understanding, without anxiety, someone who understood and talked about the bind they were in. This job was way beyond his pay grade.

In our postinterview follow-up, the therapists were stunned to see Eric like this—a softy, a little boy. I told them about the hug. I said that I thought Eric was showing appreciation for me and my willingness to address the suffering of his folks. His parents, through the subtleties of conversation, went from seeing Eric as a crazy kid to understanding his desperation at seeing his parents so stuck, so unhappy. This boy was very attuned to the undercurrents of their unresolved tensions. This little guy, a former terror, was now rebranded as the "family doctor."

Of course, nothing is simple. The child was released from residential treatment and the family began seeing one the clinic therapists. Therapy was rocky, with Eric continuing to act defiant from time to time, but with less intensity. At my last session as a consultant, the therapist described the progress of the therapy, as Philip and Darlene continued to slowly address some of their underlying tensions, gradually easing the pressure on the child. The family was slowly getting better.

In looking back on this case, I think my casual approach to "Eric the Terrible," the decision to start the session without him, and then to ignore him when he walked in, set the tone for what happened during the rest of the hour. The fact that I laughed out loud in the session when I heard his baby voice, attempting to sound threatening, sent a message to the parents that I wasn't afraid of this kid. How powerful can a nine-year-old be? Eric was used to having too much sway in the family. That was lousy for everyone, and if I treated him with kid gloves I would have helped maintain his power. As is often the case, patterns get set at some point in a family's life and then it's hard to escape.

I was quite surprised, however, that Eric was such a sweetheart. Nowhere, in any of the discussions with the therapists or the parents, did that come up. I think we got to see that side of him when he was relieved of responsibility, when he got a chance to be nine years old. As I got to know Darlene and Philip, it was clear that they had profoundly disconnected from each other and didn't know how to get back. The toxic role of the grandmother, Darlene's mother, who recruited her nine-year-old grandson in a war against her son-in-law, sounded particularly troubling. This was a dynamic the whole family agreed upon but hadn't been able to do anything about. If I were continuing to see this family in therapy, I would want the grandmother to join the sessions. This is not the first time I've experienced such a shift in a single session. No, the problems were not solved, and Eric was not cured. However, my teasing out of these latent tensions calmly, with caring, neither minimizing their distress nor adopting an urgent fix-it attitude, seemed to take some of the pressure off Eric and the family. As the consultant for the case, I didn't see these folks again and only followed their progress as reported to me by the therapist. By the time I left my role as consultant, the family was having a mildly easier time, and Eric had not been readmitted to the treatment center.

We hope that our readers don't think of this case as a mystery, or an anomaly. It, in fact, reflects one of the best-kept secrets—a "secret" known well to the early family therapists, and to us. But, like buried treasure, this secret remains hidden from the culture at large. The secret is this: our children's symptomatic behavior, embedded in the patterns of the family, is often an expression of, and an attempt to remedy, family tensions, especially when those tensions remain below the surface. Our children are masters at detecting trouble. Though too young to fully articulate what they see and experience, kids certainly feel these family tensions in spades. And they try to help, no matter how it looks. This remains true even with troubled behavior, which may get labeled as bipolar disorder or ADHD. Since children often experience their anxiety about their parents without full awareness, and without a language to go with it, their behavior emerges as a symbolic expression of their worry, their fear, and their attempt to help.

In telling these stories that illuminate the subtle, nearly invisible intimate dynamics between children and their parents, we are drawing not only on our own experience, but on many years of solid research and clinical study. This wisdom was gleaned over a period of many years, from the late 1950s through the 1980s, a very lively period in psychiatry and psychotherapy. During this period, clinical investigations were taking place across the country and worldwide about how family relationship patterns contributed to a child's mood or behavior. These pioneers, professionals from diverse disciplines, including linguistics and cybernetics, were guided by their seemingly limitless curiosity about how symptoms developed and how the family contributed to them. This relationship-based treatment approach has never been discredited or found to be in error; rather, the understanding of symptoms as an interpersonal phenomenon became eclipsed by the biological model of mental health.

As a result of the enormous body of work from this time, the idea that problems in children are related to interpersonal, particularly family, dynamics, became built into the DNA of family therapy. One of the fascinating early groundbreaking works was the book *Leaving Home* by therapist Jay Haley. First published in 1980, Haley and his colleagues developed a counterintuitive way of working with young people who became psychotic in early adulthood just as they were getting ready to leave home. The researchers hypothesized that these disturbed young people were anxious about their parents and were receiving covert, mixed messages from them about leaving home. Their psychotic symptoms were the result of the powerful (unconscious) double bind the young person was in: How do I leave home when I'm not sure my parents want me to go and I'm not sure they can make it on their own, as a couple, without me? In these families, dysfunction between the parents was mostly buried, unacknowledged, but their sensitive child felt their distress and unconsciously tried to help.

Haley's idea was that the young person was in a nearly impossible, though unspoken, bind about the prospect of leaving the parents alone. From these observations, he and his colleagues developed an unexpected therapy where the therapists instructed the parents to run away from home and not tell their child where they were going. This strange method proved stunningly effective. The clinicians discovered that these young people often pulled themselves together and their psychotic symptoms subsided. The researchers/therapists concluded that this "running away" by the parents sent an unconscious signal to their child that they were okay and there was nothing to worry about. The child could go.

Haley's work, one of many family therapy models, attracted a great deal of attention among therapists in the United States. It soon spread to Europe, where a group of prominent Italian psychotherapists developed a treatment approach based on his work. At the same time, pioneers in family therapy across the United States were developing methods of treating families with anorectic children, with teenage delinquents, with young adult schizophrenics, as well as more garden variety problems of anxiety, depression, and psychosomatic illness in children and adults.

We mention this not to take a trip down memory lane, or out of a nostalgic sentimentality, but to say that all of these fascinating, effective therapies had one thing in common: they stressed the powerful psychological interconnection between parents and children. These early clinicians perceived correctly that children worried about their parents, however unconsciously, and felt responsible for them. They understood that a child's symptoms were often an expression of, and an attempt to repair, family distress. Our stories show the various ways in which children, labeled as disturbed or destructive, are in fact carrying on a stealth-like attempt to help the people they care about most in the world, their parents.

As we uncover the dynamics in our therapy sessions, we see that, while each family brings its own flavor, style, and story, aspects of their relationship patterns are universal. A little-known truth about family life is this: our kids are minidoctors. They closely observe the grownups in their lives, feel the spoken and unspoken distress, and try to help. These young magical thinkers seem to believe in their power to effect change; they take their responsibilities seriously. Of course, lacking any real power, their efforts usually backfire. But recognizing their cry for help is often a useful beginning. In our next story, we see how a raging teenager went on a one-woman crusade to change her family.

A CRAZY TEENAGER SAVES THE DAY

The Wilson family was referred to me after the mother, Ayla, complained to her family doctor about her pitched battles with her teenage daughter, Jasmine. For the past five years, Ayla had been struggling with lupus, an autoimmune disease that tends to be exacerbated by stress, and the doctor thought it would be a good idea for the family to seek consultation.

When Ayla first called to make the appointment, she said, "Our home has become a battleground." She sounded really distressed and quietly furious, like she was on the losing end of these fights with her daughter.

She asked to come in with her daughter. I told her I needed to have the family come in if I was to be helpful. She agreed.

Ayla and her husband, Frank, had been married for nearly fifteen years. They had two kids: Jasmine, thirteen, and William, eleven. Frank, a well-respected English professor at a local university came across as Mr. Nice Guy. According to Ayla, Frank was the object of adoration from everyone: colleagues, staff, and students.

"Everyone loves him," she said with pride mixed with a hint of irony. He was the one people came to for help, the guy who could smooth over anyone's ruffled feathers. Frank acknowledged his role with a slight smile. "I hate conflict," he said.

"How did you two meet?" I asked. Ayla described how she had emigrated from Turkey nearly twenty years earlier, coming to New York to study. They met at the university where Frank was finishing his PhD. Ayla currently worked as a part-time translator but spent most of her time raising the kids. Most of her family remained in Turkey, except for one brother.

Ayla said, "Of course I miss my family, but my mother and I talk pretty much every day. She's difficult and demanding, my mother. But I understand her. She's had a hard life."

The first session, which included the parents and the two children, turned out to be pivotal. The family dance was on full, unattractive, display. Ayla and her daughter, Jasmine, did indeed go at it. Wow. Sparks flew. These battles looked well practiced, repetitive, painful for everyone, and unending. This was what being stuck in a family impasse looked like. Ayla treated her daughter like an adversary, responding to every trigger by going into battle mode. It was almost as if she couldn't wait to prove Jasmine wrong. Ayla, who seemed like an otherwise mature person, regressed to the level of a thirteen-year-old when arguing with her daughter. She stopped just short of name-calling. Ayla hissed, her eyes nearly bugging out of her head, "How dare you?" in response to some inflammatory comment from her daughter.

Jasmine, indeed, had become a real expert in button-pushing. She was certainly a handful: she rudely mocked her mother right in the session, scornfully belittling her demands.

"My mother is a crazy woman. She doesn't know what she's talking about," she sniffed dismissively.

This minidrama was disturbing to observe. Jasmine was right out of central casting, playing the role of "Terrible Teenager." William, a thoughtful-appearing eleven-year-old, maintained an air of anxious stillness while the battle raged. I guessed he had seen this play out many times.

Beneath all this drama, however, I could sense that Jasmine was clearly longing for her mother's love. At times, this young girl would let a bit of vulnerability show in her speech or glance toward her mother; after all, she was only thirteen, she still very much needed a mother's love. Ayla, for her part, seemed to have painted herself into a corner, not allowing herself to "give in" as long as her daughter treated her rudely. She talked about how she was raised in a traditional Turkish home, where, she said, children showed respect to their parents, no matter what.

Part of my standard repertoire in an initial meeting with families is to ask the kids what they worry about in regard to their parents. I have heard some very poignant comments from children as young as five. While sometimes reluctant to respond, the effect on the kids usually appears to be one of relief, that someone knows about their worry and is taking them seriously. And the effect on parents is typically one of surprise, which is often followed by a therapeutic moment where they absorb their child's anxious observations.

At my invitation Jasmine spoke openly about how she saw her parents' marriage. That's the good thing about having adolescents in the therapy setting: they are usually fantastic observers of the marital dynamic, have sharp radar when it comes to parental hypocrisy, and don't usually mince words. Jasmine seemed like she couldn't wait to weigh in.

"My parents are both wrong and they don't know it. It's horrible to watch. My mother is always picking on my father, and he doesn't say anything! It makes me sick." She paused. "I do worry about them though. My mother seems really lonely. And my father is a terrible fighter." She paused again. "And I worry about my mother's health. I want to see her get better."

I wondered out loud, rhetorically, not expecting an answer, "I wonder if you're trying to show your father how to fight?" Though she didn't say anything, I could tell that Jasmine heard me. These were subtle tensions, not part of this couples' social persona. They maintained the outward appearance of calm.

Looking at Jasmine, her father countered, "We've got a good marriage. In fact, we're the envy of all our friends," he said with a self-satisfied smile.

But, in fact, the parental battleground had instead shifted from the couple to mother and daughter. As we soon discovered, the daughter was a proxy in the underground war between the parents.

Where was the father, Frank, you might ask, when Ayla and Jasmine were slugging it out? Frank saw himself as a bystander, a self-appointed referee between his wife and daughter. But truth be told, he mostly sided with his daughter. He did this indirectly by not correcting his daughter's over-the-top rudeness or by openly admonishing his wife for her behavior toward their daughter.

"Calm down, dear," he said, laying his hand on his wife's arm.

I watched as Ayla stiffened at her husband's rebuke.

Frank, intelligent as he was, was blind to his own contribution to this ongoing, antagonizing conflict in his family. His self-image as a good guy, a peacemaker, kept him from seeing what family therapist and teacher Betty Carter used to say in our classes: the peacemaker is the cause of the war. The session ended with my framing the problem as part of "the family operating system" rather than a problem with Jasmine and her behavior. The family, in distress and eager for help, seemed to be okay with this formulation. I believe they felt my caring during the session and saw that I was tuned in to the dynamics of this difficult family dance. The couple said they'd like to come in alone, without the kids, for the next session. I wasn't sure what they had in mind, but I agreed.

Frank and Ayla came in on their own nearly two months later. Ayla's precarious health and the various family schedules made it difficult for them to come in more often, or with any regularity. In this second session, the tensions between the couple began to emerge. Ayla and Frank, in response to my probing, began to explore the long-standing—and unresolved—tensions between them. Though Frank claimed, "We stopped fighting years ago," the tensions simmered, spilling over into their parenting.

Frank presented his view: "My wife is too rigid with the kids. I can't stand to see it. It's my job to provide some flexibility for them. They need breathing room."

But what really bothered him, as it unfolded during that therapy hour, was what he perceived to be his wife's rigidity with him. He described what felt, to him, like her unwillingness to compromise. Frank cited one memorable example, which apparently still ate at him: "Ayla used to be too hard on my mother. It bothered the hell out of me."

Early in their marriage, Ayla apparently picked some battles with Frank's mother that Ayla felt her husband should be fighting.

Ayla chimed in: "Frank was a doormat with his mother," she said. "He never stood up for himself, or me."

During these skirmishes, Frank took his mother's side. He felt Ayla was too harsh in her judgments toward her. Sound familiar? These early mother-in-law battles helped set the stage for future (subterranean) warfare.

Ayla listened intently to Frank's version of his distress in their marriage. It was, I believe, the first time they had spoken openly about these (not fully buried) resentments. Ayla showed little defensiveness in response to what she termed Frank's "complaints" about her. In fact, she looked like she welcomed this opening up of tensions that had been accumulating over the years. This session felt to me like an hors d'oeuvre, an opening to a meal. I wondered what the next course would bring.

They scheduled a follow-up session two weeks later. When they returned, there was a powerful silence in the room as they walked in and seated themselves on the couch.

Ayla said, "I've had an epiphany." I waited. "I've just realized that a lot of the anger that I've directed toward my daughter was meant for this guy here," nodding toward Frank.

She sounded almost triumphant. Indeed, that was impressive stuff. Ayla, pleased with her new revelation, opened up about her troubles in her marriage.

She described how she had, for a long time, felt that Frank wasn't parental enough with the kids. It angered her that he avoided conflict with them, just as he did with her. That's apparently what really bugged her. He wouldn't fight with her, even when needed. Frank was a professional conflict avoider, which he apparently first learned in his relationship with his mother.

"Frank always smooths everything over. If I'm upset, or angry, I always feel like he wants to run away. And sometimes he does run away," she added.

Ayla was opening some painful wounds: feeling uncared for, unheard, and unseen. She clearly needed more warmth from Frank, both in the form of an occasional heated quarrel as well as the warmth of his desire. Frank tended to disappear, emotionally, and sometimes physically. Ayla said she felt jealous of the passion that he poured into his work.

She said, "He reserves the best of himself for his projects, and his students. Especially his young female students."

Ouch. I'm quite sure Frank felt the jab. I know I did.

As usual, both sides contained important truths. The crisis with their daughter provided an opening to explore these semiburied tensions in their marriage. This couple took on the challenge, showing courage in how they took an honest look at themselves and their relationship. While these conversations became painful at times, Ayla and Frank felt rewarded by feeling more connected to each other and the calmer atmosphere in their home. Ayla got a chance to air her grievances to Frank, without him running away.

To his credit, Frank signaled to Ayla that he understood what she needed from him.

He said, "My mom was a very powerful woman. She never let me talk back or even argue, really. I think I always saw conflict as something bad, to be avoided at all costs. Now I can see the price we're paying. I never knew." He looked at Ayla with genuine tenderness and said, "I promise I'll try to do better."

For her part, I think Ayla was so happy to finally be having a real conversation about their marriage that she didn't even get defensive when Frank talked about wanting her to be "softer." I believed that this was something she also wanted for herself. She just needed to be let off the hook. Having Frank's full attention, seeing and feeling that he wanted to make things better between them, acted as a powerful and long overdue medicine for her.

The healing process began. This couple came intermittently for therapy for nearly a year, about six sessions in all and, according to Frank and Ayla, the family atmosphere improved greatly. I wanted to see the kids again, but the couple seemed to want to use these sessions for themselves. According to Ayla, her relationship with her daughter grew easier, less stressful.

"Jasmine is a teenager, and she can still be difficult, but we don't fight so much anymore. And when we do, it doesn't get crazy. I feel more respected." She added, "Now Frank will correct Jasmine if she takes a mean tone with me. That's huge."

For this family, exposing the conflicts that had remained hidden—or ignored—for many years allowed the couple to unlock these destructive patterns in a relatively short period of time. This was a family of good people who, when I first met them, were definitely not their best selves. Their more mature, less reactive selves were lurking just beneath the surface, but they couldn't get at it. With this family, I had to be satisfied to meet with them whenever they could make time and whenever Ayla was feeling well enough to come to the office. At times this was difficult for me, especially since I worried about Ayla's health and the effect that the family stress had on her. When I first met her, Ayla seemed quite fragile physically and I worried that she might have a full-blown medical crisis. I worried that she could die. Because of her apparent fragility I might have felt a greater sense of urgency with this family than with some others, but I don't think the family sensed this. I did my best to isolate my anxiety from the work with them.

My initial framework of the mother-daughter battles as part of the "family operating system" set the stage for movement and change. It took some of the heat away from this two-person fight and enlarged the focus to include Frank. I wasn't worried that Jasmine's terrible behavior with her mother was somehow a sign of bad character or a mental disorder. Jasmine showed that she was in pain regarding her parents' relationship. She worried about her mother and her health, and she agonized about what she called her "wimp" of a father, who didn't know how to stand up for himself or use his own voice. I was pretty convinced that Jasmine was trying to show Frank how to do that, but in her one-woman crusade she was hurting herself in the process. Jasmine's thoughtful observations about her parents and their marriage helped to shift the lens away from the proxy war of mother and daughter.

The success of any case begins when the family lets me mess with their script. This family allowed me to help them, to see things differently than they did. It's a balancing act between respecting the family and not doing what they want me to do. In this case, I didn't do what the father wanted me to do, which was call out the mother or criticize her for her harsh treatment of their daughter. Neither did I react to Jasmine's provocative behavior with her mother. Both parents let me challenge them in different ways—Frank for his unhelpful avoidance and Ayla for her initially rigid stance with their daughter. But, as usual, whatever I did or did not do, the credit goes to them. These people used our sessions to do great work. They abandoned whatever false pride they might have had and looked honestly at themselves, understanding how they unwittingly got trapped in these destructive patterns. They reaped the rewards for their unflinching efforts.

In the cases we've just seen, the children in the family were trying to help their families through their "bad" behavior. Sometimes, however, a child tries to help by being too good. This is another form of parental caretaking, and while quieter than those we've already covered, equally troubling for the family. Why would a parent complain about a child being too good, you might ask? The answer is, they don't. Instead, these children will show up with anxiety, sometimes quite a lot of it. Or they may be depressed, sometimes even suicidal. Or sometimes they may develop other symptoms, stomachaches, eating disorders, or self-harming behaviors. Their anxiety and worry turn inward, rather than being directed outward toward the parents.

THE TOO-PERFECT KID

When Janet called saying she and husband Larry wanted to bring their nine-year-old son Henry in for a "check-in," I wasn't too surprised. I had worked with these good people for several sessions earlier that year. Some of our work revolved around the behavior of their only child, Henry, an adorable, almost too-good kid. This time, however, Janet said, "I'm worried that Henry might be thinking of hurting himself."

Henry had always been under the microscope, partly because of his single-child status, and partly because his parents were primed toward overprotectiveness related to their own childhood experiences. Larry was diagnosed as a type 1 diabetic at age seven.

"When I think about it, I spent a lot of my childhood in the kitchen next to my mom," he said in a semijoking voice, but his mom's anxiety-based parenting clearly restricted his sense of freedom and normal risk-taking. Larry attributed his mom's extreme protectiveness to what he described as "her constant fears about something going wrong because of my health." Larry said he was "mostly grateful" for his mom's love and care, but he also felt it handicapped him.

"I grew up thinking I was fragile, and I still have some of that with me today." Larry, a thoughtful, self-aware kind of guy, said, "I think this held me back, personally, and professionally. I'm still working it out."

Janet's childhood had a markedly different quality, characterized more by neglect. According to her, her folks "worked all the time," she said, still sounding resentful.

"They never, ever attended one of my events." She added, "I knew they loved me, but they left my younger brother and me to pretty much raise ourselves."

To this day Janet remembered this absentee parenting as painful, though she now enjoyed a mostly warm relationship with her elderly parents. Janet vowed not to pass this neglect that marred her own childhood on to her son. In some of our earlier sessions Janet also talked quite a bit about her parents' contentious relationship.

"They bickered constantly, mostly about money. It made our home not a very pleasant place to live," she said. It sounded like she was reliving the pain of her difficult family life.

Janet originally came to see me with her husband because, as she said, "I think we need an overall checkup as a family. I want to be sure I'm being a good mom." Then, glancing at Larry, she added, "And my husband seems like he wants nothing to do with me."

Janet began our first session by listing what she saw as her husband's priorities: "First, it's work. Then our son. I'm a distant third."

While that sounded like a dire characterization, it turned out that their marriage was, at its core, quite healthy. I saw that almost immediately in the way Larry responded to Janet's tale of woe. He acknowledged that he had been pretty remote as of late and began to talk about some of his work stresses, which he didn't feel he could share with Janet. Larry was the manager of high-end sporting goods store that had come under new ownership six months earlier. Apparently, this new owner turned out to be a combination of demanding and hypercritical, and Larry had to swallow a lot of anger related to his new boss. He worried that he might be fired. Larry said, "I'm scared that if I tell Janet what's going on she'll start to worry, and I don't want to lay that on her."

This confirmed my initial impression of Larry: he came across as a protective kind of man who's first impulse is to make sure everyone is okay. But now his stress operated like a wall in his marriage. Then to make matters worse, Janet responded to her shut-down husband by being critical, or as she said, "Downright mean."

I looked at Larry. "It looks like she's trying to reach you, but it feels to her like you moved to Siberia."

As Larry began to talk about his stress, Janet started to relax. She needed to see her husband, to feel him, to know what was going on inside him. They had a history of sharing intimate stories, and this felt like a cold chill in their marriage. Janet acknowledged that she may have helped drive him away.

"I've been kind of a pain these last few months, probably not that easy to live with." She turned to Larry, "I'm sorry." He took her hand.

They used our sessions to open these submerged tensions and were able to forgive each other. That's what health looks like. We met a few more times, and the couple brought their nine-year-old son for a couple of sessions. He was a wonderful kid: sweet, funny, and caring. The parents' concerns about him were pretty normal—mostly related to homework and academics. I saw, however, that this child got a lot of attention from his folks, probably too much. It looked like their world revolved around this little man, and I thought that might be a lot of pressure for him, especially as he moved toward adolescence. Then, later that year, I got a call from Janet—she was worried about Henry. She thought he might harm himself.

As the family walked into my office for the check-in, young Henry, as usual, brought a smile to my lips. I always enjoyed seeing this child. He was unusually cute and sweet in every way. A good and dedicated athlete, Henry always came to the office regaled in some kind of sports outfit. That day he came fully decked out in soccer gear. As they settled themselves on the couch, Janet opened up with the most recent concern. Then she invited Henry to tell his side.

Briefly, it sounded like Henry got himself embroiled in some relatively normal, though bruising, childhood politics. He appeared a bit more subdued than I'd seen him before.

He said, "I'm really bummed. Now I'm on the outs with William. He used to be my friend. We hung out a lot."

Janet looked on anxiously, adding, "Henry and William are the best athletes in the school, and they competed in everything."

I knew Henry was a popular kid and had other friends to play with, but he apparently became really upset at being rebuffed by William. After hearing the various versions of fifth-grade politics, I realized that both Janet and Larry gave too much weight to these normal squabbles and bruised egos. Their worry was palpable. Perhaps this was the first time their child had experienced painful rejection, which is part and parcel of every childhood. They found, as all parents eventually do, that they cannot protect Henry from emotional bruising. Janet's anxious look of "Help!" made Henry's wound appear dire, not merely part of the rough and tumble of childhood.

The parents' emotional weight about Henry's "rejection" by his friend looked to me like it landed squarely on their son. In fact, Henry had begun feeling so badly about this incident that Janet revealed that "he said he doesn't want to go to school."

And, more worrisome, Janet added, "He talked about wanting to die."

I naturally paid close attention to this remark. Every therapist does. It's extremely important never to take any expression of suicidal thinking lightly, and it's important to talk about it openly. I naturally followed up with Henry, asking him if he wanted or had thought about hurting himself. He said, "No, I would never do anything like that. I just said that 'cause I was feeling bad."

Henry's response reassured me. I wasn't really worried that he was suicidal, though I, of course, needed to check it out. What worried me more was this kid was almost too good. I wanted to help Henry not be so perfect about everything, and I wanted to get his parents to help him be a little less good. Henry wanted to be liked by everyone and loved being considered a great athlete. But I noticed both at this session and at earlier sessions that every move he made, every result mattered too much. His parents took every feeling he had too seriously, and Henry absorbed this weight. Now, his feelings took on huge proportions, overwhelming for a little kid.

I also sensed Henry's anger beneath the hurt that he expressed. I thought that getting in touch with his anger might be helpful for this too-good child.

I said, "Yup, kids can be super annoying. I know that both your parents had a lot of experience with annoying kids when they were nine." Janet and Larry seemed to welcome this turn in conversation, which had a playful, freewheeling quality. Larry remembered a guy on his block when he was growing up who really drove him crazy, and Janet weighed in on an incident where she felt betrayed by her best friend in sixth grade. Pretty soon they began talking about all the "pain-in-the-neck" people they could think of, and I joined the conversation, entertaining Henry with stories about people who really irritated me. I was taking the temperature of the room, and I felt that the family heaviness was lifting. I stepped on the gas.

I said, "You know, Henry, when someone pushes me around, or steps on me and I don't like it, I love to curse to myself. That's one of my pleasures!" Henry's eyes lit up. I spit "Bastard!" as one of my favorites. Henry loved it.

This led to a curse word jam session where I invited Dad to talk about his favorite curse words when he feels upset at someone. Dad, a well-trained "good boy," at first reluctantly began sharing some of his moments of irritation with other grownups. I think he was worried that if he showed a less-than-perfect side of himself to his son, he would be a bad influence. Au contraire. Soon Dad got warmed up and revealed that the word "scumbag" was on his top-ten list. Henry went nuts! He had never heard that word and he thought it was one of the best words ever.

Soon Mom joined in on the act and pretty soon we were cursing up a storm. Little Henry looked about twenty years younger. He went from being a worried old man to being a kid. We spent the last twenty minutes of the session like this. Naturally, the grownups in the room felt duty-bound to remind Henry that most of these curse words should take place in our mind. We have to be very selective when we choose to curse out loud.

Everyone left in an upbeat mood. Janet gave me a huge thanks. I think it's because they got a chance to play. There was a sense of freedom in it. We messed around with words that were harmless. Henry—and Mom and Dad—got a chance to step outside the safety zone and they enjoyed themselves. I think Henry got permission to get angry at his friends, instead of only being hurt. Everyone got something out of it, including me. I had a ball.

I got a call from Janet the next week saying that Henry was "much better." He went to school without a problem and was having fun savoring the word "scumbag" which he proudly learned from his father.

Henry was a terrific kid who worried about his folks, and worried about their worry. They were like a circular worry machine. In the cases in this chapter, each family uncovered the story beneath the story, which included their child's anxiety about the family and their attempt to help. The cat is now officially out of the bag. Our children's behavior, even troubling behavior, is almost always an attempt to repair or address family pain.

Most of the time, however, children are sent to therapists on their own, treated as individuals, unconnected to the dynamics of the family. This is the most common way of treating that most popular of all diagnoses—ADHD. In the next chapter we see what happens when the family joins the proceedings.

Questions for Reflection

In "The Case of the Nine-Year-Old Doctor," impossible Eric turned out to be a sweet kid, anxious and helpless about his parents' distress, his mother's loneliness, and his father's absence. When he was "reframed" as the family doctor, it eased the family tensions. Can you think of other stories of "bad" kids that could benefit by reframing?

The family in "A Crazy Teenager Saves the Day" showed how a long-buried tension between the parents played itself out as a proxy battle between the mother and daughter. The mother realized she had displaced her anger toward her husband onto her daughter. This is a common pattern. Can you think of families where you have seen this happen? What leads to this displacement?

In the last story, the therapist thought that little Henry was too worried about being good, about pleasing his parents. He was responding to his parents' anxieties, handed down in part from their own upbringing. The cursefest applied symbolic medicine to this family. How can we know when a child is "too good"? Do you know any such families with a child that is too good?

Chapter 7

ADHD

Replacing Medications with Family Members

LET'S ACT CRAZY

The Keene family was referred to me by their pediatrician. Their son, nine-year-old Evan, had been diagnosed with attention deficit hyperactivity disorder (ADHD). He had been treated for five years by a highly regarded child psychiatrist with expertise in pharmacological treatments of childhood mental disorders. The parents told their pediatrician they were concerned that, despite trying several medication regimens, their son was still a problem at home and at school. The physician who referred them to me explained that this boy was severely disruptive despite treatment. The pediatrician told the family that their son was the most intractable case he had ever seen.

When the family arrived for the first session, I ushered them into my office, then went to talk to my secretary for two minutes while they found places to sit, which is standard practice for me. I typically let families settle in the office without me while I check my mail, etc. When I entered the office, Evan was jumping around pawing at my bookshelf. His dad was scolding, pleading, "Evan, don't do that to the doctor's books. You have to ask him." He was being a too-careful parent and the kid seemed activated by the father's effort to change his behavior. Evan stopped what he was doing when I showed up. I then slipped into being something of an improv actor, that is, a man "acting" like a psychiatrist.

"Ohhh! You must be Evan," I said astutely picking up the father's cue. "I heard you are *very* hyperactive. But you better keep it up, otherwise I might think your parents are fibbing."

He looked at me quizzically, then went into a crazy act, jumping and prancing on his toes, babbling too fast, pawing the books in my bookcase. He was "acting" like a hyperactive kid. His act lost momentum; he slowed down.

I sounded rather let down as I told Evan, "Don't stop yet. I am still not impressed."

He stopped, looked at me, then cuddled up next to his mother on the sofa. Evan remained subdued throughout the session.

Evan's father, Robert, was an anesthesiologist, a quiet but engaged, intelligent, and thoughtful man. Lila, the mother, was a shy, emotionally repressed nurse, who grew up in a Muslim family and was educated in Egypt. Robert was the most active parent. Lila was attentive but spoke little. She was somewhat hesitant, careful about what she said. I did my standard (low) stress first interview. I call it a "stress" interview because I take the focus away from the identified patient and attend to the family's operating systems—how they work. What is anger like in the family? If mother and father are arguing, what do the kids do?

The interview is stressful in the sense that it forces them to talk about relationships that do not include Evan. In this way the interview mildly disrupts their customary way of describing experiences. It stimulates reflection. "How can I be helpful?" "What do you think you need?" "How does the family operate?" I always begin with the father, not because he is most important, but because he usually knows the least about the emotional components of the family. Then I questioned the eight-year-old sister, Annie: "What is your family like?" She tried being silly. I took that to mean she was anxious, so I changed my question: "When you worry about your family what do you think about?" Then I asked Evan similar questions. Then the mother. I always save the mother for last, because usually she knows the most about the family relationships.

The mother answered questions but didn't elaborate. It was almost as if she was involved in a clandestine operation and was hesitant to give anything away. My impression was that her behavior came from growing up in a patriarchal culture—while the family was important, nothing was to be disclosed about it. Robert gave no evidence of being domineering. He was a shepherding father/husband, interested in his family, his wife, and his children. But there was not much evidence of playfulness or intimacy between them.

The mild and modulated "stress" in the first stress interview comes from paying attention to and questioning family living patterns, emphasizing what they ignore and ignoring what they take to be important. This is a *therapeutic* interviewing pattern. I am collecting information, but I am also attempting to lay the groundwork for change. The questions I ask do not have simple answers. Families with symptomatic kids have an easy time talking about the kid and his troubles. When I focus on the family as a system of relationships, they inevitably drift back to talking about the kid and his problems.

The second interview was fairly active. Evan tested me, tried to figure me out by pushing limits. He savagely attempted to hit me in the head with a large wooden toy, attacking me from my blind side. He had selected a toy that would be an excellent weapon. I physically restrained him with ease. I did not just fend him off. I grabbed him and physically held him, tying up his arms and legs so he could not move. In doing this, I am overpowering him, letting him know how much power he doesn't have. I inflict no pain. I did not take him seriously. While restraining him, I talked to the parents about him. In the conversation I nonchalantly referred to him as a "twerp." I treated him with what might be called "pseudo-indifference." He was not the center of attention. He experienced a *deficit* of attention. The problem for many hyperactive children is that they develop the fantasy that they are as big and powerful as the adults in their world. I physically overpowered him without inflicting pain. This way he came to understand how small he was. It is important kids learn that early in life.

The third interview was quiet, not much had happened since the second session. The kids, now familiar with the office, played quietly with my toys while I talked with the parents about how they grew up, how they found each other. I wanted to know how they learned to be parents. Robert, the youngest of three, was the son of a Congregational pastor. He had intended to follow in his father's footsteps, but in college discovered he was most interested in science and switched from pretheology to premed. He hadn't told his parents about the change until he neared graduation, fearing his father would be disappointed. His parents were pleased with the change. After medical school he decided on anesthesiology. Lila was working as a nurse in the surgical recovery room where he was assigned as a resident. That was how they met.

Lila's father was a bureaucrat and, though Muslim, drank too much alcohol, was angry and demanding behind closed doors. That partly explained her hesitancy to speak much about her family. She was the third of four, the only girl. She went to nursing school in Cairo. Her older brother, an engineer, had come to the United States. She wanted to get away from her father, so with her brother's help she joined him in the United States. It was as if she were a refugee. Robert liked her quiet manner and he felt as though he was helping her be more at home in this country.

When they came for the fourth session, all sat silently for five minutes or so. I waited for them to begin. The kids, Annie and Evan, played quietly with some of my now familiar toys.

"Is this helpful?" I asked. "Do you feel you are getting anywhere?"

The parents responded with energy: "Oh yes! We are surprised. Evan has not been a problem during the past two weeks."

I was surprised by the change in attitude. "What do you think happened? How do you explain the change?"

The father answered, "Well, we have seen Dr. Michaels for five years. But he never saw us with Evan. He always talked to us separately. We don't think Evan really understood why we were upset with him. But he is a different boy in the last three weeks. At first, I was uncomfortable talking about him with him in the room, but I believe it made a big difference."

I responded, "That's common. It is impolite, but therapy has rules different from Emily Post. And I have learned that people hear more when they 'overhear' conversations about themselves. They take in more than when we speak directly to them."

Then Lila said, "That day you wrestled him seemed important. I think we have always been too careful with Evan. I think I have been overprotective, thinking he has this sickness, and he is fragile. Then when you picked him up and confined him, I at first wanted to object, but then when you teased him and controlled him, I could feel myself starting to laugh. I enjoyed what you were doing. I was surprised at myself."

This was a good session. Both parents particularly started to feel this was fun.

They wanted to make another appointment. At the fifth interview something very curious happened. Ever-polite, well-behaved seven-year-old Annie went on a rampage in the second half of the session. She was very silly, dancing on my very sturdy coffee table in the middle of the office. Then she danced around, singing and being deliciously sassy, an extended, more exotic version of her brother's behavior in the first interview. She was crazy, way out of character, throughout most of the session. She might have been doing a burlesqued imitation of her brother. It was incredible that it lasted so long. The parents were astounded. Evan wanted his sister to stop, he was parent-like, embarrassed by her behavior. Eventually, he went off to the toy corner and ignored her.

She quieted down by the end of the session, that behavior not seen again. It was her brief flight into madness or ADHD. This phenomenon is not unusual. When change occurs, and the problem child becomes less symptomatic, it is common for someone else to transiently become a problem. But her "act" was impressive because it was so situation specific. We call it "symptom substitution," which is another way of saying that often children in a family (unconsciously) may believe that the parents "need" a child to be a problem, perhaps to deflect conflict between the couple. The brief emergence of symptoms in another child can be a way of testing this.

When the family returned a week later, they began reviewing the past week. There was a pause and Lila, who was always so restrained, stood up. She was wearing her usual outfit—blouse, skirt, and shoes with conservative low heels.

She said, "I feel so strange. This is not me, but I want to do what Annie did last time." She took a few dance steps and then laughing, sat down. "That was fun."

After three more visits the family thought they had what they needed and decided to stop coming. I never saw them again. The doctor who referred them told me six months later that as far as he could tell the situation was stable and Evan's behavior had been altered.

I was pleased about how this case went. As I reflect on it, I believe that one thing that proved helpful was that I did not make Evan's symptoms sacred by overdefining them. Instead of stopping them, I insisted

Evan continue. I do something similar when a kid has a tantrum in my office—I don't try to stop them, I urge them to yell louder. It always disrupts the behavior. What is oppositional and disruptive becomes compliant. The other thing I did was to talk to the parents about the boy while he was present. But I also talk to the brother and sister about the parents, putting the parents in the third person. It is very impolite, but it has therapeutic benefit. I make fun of the patient. I feel free to make fun of everyone—especially fathers. Fathers are inclined to be emotionally distant. Curiously, teasing them helps them to feel included.

It's important to note that all that I do is grounded in caring for the family. I made no effort to be objective, nor did I attempt to be persuasive by referring to science or other outside authority. I kept the experience human. While I believe that all psychopathology is grounded in interpersonal experience, the corollary is that all psychopathologies can be responsive to interpersonal experience.

To repeat, Robert, the father, was the most active parent. Lila was a blend of shy and subservient. As I invited her opinions, Lila became a more active and engaged presence. I think this created some flexibility in their way of operating as a family, which loosened up some patterns that brought pressure on the parents and kids. The family interviewing approach helped them to think more about their family. My style invited them to play. I believe I created a different experience for them in the office, which disrupted their living and thinking patterns and opened the possibility for change. Lila was infected by the invitation to play. As far as I know, she resisted the temptation to become a belly dancer.

This case story highlights one way that overcontrolled, cautious parental behavior becomes an inadvertent reinforcer for upsetting behavior. These parents were somewhat "hypoactive." The kid's hyperactivity might be viewed as an effort to activate the parents. Kids are hungry for emotional response from parents, for connection. If there is a pattern of behavior a parent finds upsetting, and there is a struggle with the kid and the parent gets upset, the child just won the encounter. It's helpful for parents to think about how to do something different. "Ignore" is a too-common response. "Ignore" can work initially because it represents a change in a parental behavioral pattern, but it may be ineffective after a few episodes because ignoring does not provide the emotional component, the connection for which children hunger. It is important for children to be defeated in a loving relational world. It is important for them to learn how much power they don't have.

Evan's parents, educated people in health-care professions, took him to a child psychiatrist where he was diagnosed with ADHD at four years old, and treated for five years with medications. The proliferation of the ADHD diagnosis comes from the model of psychiatry as a medical specialty and its long-cherished belief that psychiatry should be practiced like other medical specialties. But there is a problem. Psychiatry is not like other medical specialties. Good physicians in internal medicine, for example, take a clinical history in the interest of arriving at a diagnosis. While a medical clinical history for mental health may be a review of facts, which are only part of human experience, there are also feelings, and thoughts about how the facts are connected, meaning emerges.

In the standard way of evaluating children with ADHD, a clinical history-taking by a professional mental health practitioner often projects a kind of authority based on objectivity. Our view is that in psychiatry this is pseudo-objectivity. It looks like objectivity, but it is impossible to view another person objectively. We can look at an X-ray of a joint objectively, but not a person. Pseudo-objectivity leads to pseudocertainty. In the perpetual chaos and crisis of modern living, even pseudocertainty is deeply gratifying to people (parents and spouses) distressed by upset and uncertainty in their relationships. But this creates unforeseen problems: the narrowed history-taking method limits what can be known, and prescribing a medication for a child with a "diagnosis" establishes that child in the role of patient and helps to keep them there.

In our work, we carry with us an assumption based on long experience that helps us see through, thus behind, a problem in a family. I have already mentioned this, but I want to describe it more fully. When parents are worried about a child, the child is worried about the parents the same amount plus 10 percent. The children, especially younger children, do not worry with their intellect, they worry with their being, with their whole self. It is as though the child is like a barometer and instinctively knows that they must help their family do well so that the child can do well. The child senses the family must be healthy in order for the child to be healthy. We said, "plus 10 percent." When parents worry about children, they worry about how they are doing in school, what kind of friends they have, will this problem interfere with future happiness? When kids worry about parents, they worry about their parents' happiness, the kind of friends they have. And . . . when will the divorce happen? When will they die? Who will die first? The development of a child's identity in the family is complex, shaped in part by projective identification (i.e., how they are seen by their parents) and by reaction to unconscious patterns of behavior of family members. This next case shows what happens when those unconscious patterns of behavior are exposed.

LIKE FATHER, LIKE SON?

Dr. Stern, a family doctor, prescribed Ritalin and a tranquilizer for nine-year-old Allen at the request of a psychologist specializing in ADHD who had previously evaluated Allen. The family doctor started the meds in an effort to assist in the psychologist's treatment effort. But when the medications did not work, Dr. Stern became uncomfortable and suggested the family get a second opinion. He knew I worked with families and referred them to me.

Ellen, the mother, called for an appointment. As usual, I asked her to bring the family, which included her two sons and their father, from whom she was divorced.

"Would the father come?" I asked. "Yes, he would," she said, "but he is very unreliable."

I suggested she invite him. Ellen and her two sons, Nick, twelve, and Allen, nine, came to the first interview. Ellen said her ex-husband would come, "but he is always late." He never arrived. Ellen, forty, was well dressed, energetic, handsome, articulate, Italian, and Roman Catholic. The boys attended a Catholic school and were neatly dressed like little men in white shirts with neckties and navy pants. Nick was his mother's favorite and her valued partner, the one she "depended on." He got all As. He even talked about how he was trying to help Allen get along better with his mother. Allen was enigmatic. Ellen did not know how to relate to him and his moodiness. And despite his being on Ritalin and Clonazepam, both the family and the school had daily problems with his defiance and passive withdrawal behaviors.

Ellen was obviously a responsible parent and cared deeply for her sons. She was organized, smart, and attentive to details. She was also moralistic and did not like double meanings. Her thinking was clear, but too clear. There was a lack of equivocation and no sense of irony. She suffered from a bad case of irony deficiency. Ellen hid from ambiguity. For example, when I asked her about her family of origin, she acknowledged distress but avoided details about pain.

In my view, the inability to talk about family behavior is a symptom. The inability suggests there is hidden pain, discomfort with reporting subjective experiences. The picture I saw was one of considerable rigidity and emotional restriction. As we neared the end of the interview, I told her to tell the boys' father that it's important that he be included in our next session, adding, "You should warn him to be careful because I'm already mad at him for standing me up this time."

Ellen blushed; tears appeared in her eyes. "I'm sorry, I wasn't telling the truth. I didn't tell him about the meeting. He is a liar. I didn't want him to come."

She confessed she had not told him about the interview because he was so smooth, so persuasive. "I was afraid you would not be able to see my side of the story. That's why he isn't here. I'm sorry."

She was embarrassed. The boys looked at her, puzzled by her upset, not comprehending the cause.

Jim, the father, aged forty, came to the second interview. He was handsome, simultaneously anxious, and cool. An accomplished athlete, he was a local hero from his college days. He got caught up in some eighties schemes for making fast money with stocks and bonds and did two years in a federal penitentiary. My impression was that he had been humbled by his encounter with the law and imprisonment, helped by Alcoholics Anonymous, and was working at being honest with himself and his sons. He was not the con artist I expected from Ellen's description. In fact, with the father there, Ellen, whom I initially liked a great deal, suddenly seemed harsh and overly rigid. She sounded like a "Mother Superior" who did not believe confession really mattered because the priests were too soft-hearted (ironically, she worked as a claims manager for a managed care company). She was good at saying "no," there was not much "yes" in her. She was good at making certain the rules were followed. I felt pressured by her concrete requests for advice and questions about medication and side effects. But in order to shift the focal point, it was important to pressure her by palpating those regions of pain and disappointment she was hesitant to talk about.

The boys' dad was earnest in his concern about Allen. In Allen he saw fragments of himself as a boy and he feared Allen would turn out like him. Allen *was* like his father; he had his father's natural athletic gifts, but he also had his penchant for sudden temper outbursts. Jim worried he never did enough with the boys, but on the other hand, he was concerned his involvement with them was harmful and interfered with their mother's relationship with them.

Some professionals question my interviewing methods, which involve talking about the kids while they are in the room. The fact is everyone gets put into the position of third person at some point during the therapy. Children can gain a great deal from hearing themselves talked about. In the same way, parents benefit by listening when I interview the children about the parents. Allen was always well behaved in my office. But based on his demeanor and the stories they told about him, he seemed like a pet wild cat. The young man looked and sounded as if he had the "it" we call ADHD. He had a nervous energy throughout each interview—an alertness that suggested a nervous system never at rest. Yet he sat like an altar boy on the sofa, legs stretched out, feet not touching the floor. His mother had difficulty talking about anything other than him.

The parents' anxiety about their son shaped my concerns about him. But my assumption, which I shared with them, is that a kid like Allen is in more pain than anyone realizes. In the third interview Ellen was reiterating her great concern that Allen would turn out like his father.

I said, "Well, it could be worse you know."

"What do you mean?" she asked.

"He could turn out like you," I answered, poker-faced, tongue in cheek.

She looked puzzled, started to ask a question, then physically flinched, as if flooded with awareness of what was implied by my comment—how lonely, constricted, and bored she felt.

In the fourth interview I learned the boys had spent the weekend with their father and his new woman partner, who had accepted my invitation to attend the interview. She and Ellen had a cordial relationship. That woman-to-woman relationship is very important in postdivorce parenting.

At one point during the weekend Jim discovered Allen lying in the driveway behind his car. Allen was upset and said he wanted to die. His father was shocked by this. In the interview he asked Allen to say more about what he meant. Allen reiterated that he wanted to die. The parents looked to me for reassurance that he did not mean it. I did not give it to them.

"This is what I am talking about. I believe he hurts a lot. You can only underestimate his pain about all this."

Then to Allen, "What do you think would happen to your family if you died?"

His hands, palms together, were between his knees. He clasped his hands tightly with his knees and shrugged, holding his shoulders up to his ears for a several moments. He didn't say anything.

"When children are suicidal it is because they think someone wants them dead," I said to the parents.

Then to Allen, "Do you think someone would be happy if you were dead?"

He lowered his shoulders and with head down, but eyes on me, nodded yes.

"Who would it be?" I asked.

He held his hand against his chest and surreptitiously pointed at his mother. She gasped. "Allen, no!"

He nodded "yes" again.

"How could you think such a thing?"

The father said he thought Allen was just being manipulative.

"I don't," I said.

I liked it that Jim was uniting with his ex-wife, even though I disagreed with him.

"It is an error to overlook or misunderstand your son's undercover distress."

Over the course of ten weeks and seven interviews, the family doctor who had referred them, weaned him off the medication. I was apprehensive that when the medication was stopped I might see another child. This might be the first case that would force me to see ADHD as something intrinsic, and little affected by family relationships. By the sixth interview Allen was no longer on medication. The quality of the relationship between the family and their family doctor was important. They trusted him. Nothing untoward happened. In fact, all the family members agreed that they had had one of the best weeks in the last year and a half. His father was still concerned that Allen was being manipulative, and I continued to disagree, emphasizing the danger in that position because it underestimated the covert pain of his son.

What happened to Allen's suicidal fantasies? I expanded them with my questions, like, "What will happen to your family when you are dead?" and "Who wants you dead?" He pointed at his mother. That is a powerful experience. "Dead" is a strong word. Hearing it in this context is a bit jarring. Who do you think will be blamed? All these questions expand the suicidal fantasy beyond, "They'll be sorry when I'm dead." These questions disrupt the fantasies. They're questions not asked in the interest of collecting information. Each one of those questions is an experience. They activate the fantasy lives of the whole family, which results in a change in how they think and how they talk about what is happening. I used language to create an experience. That is a therapeutic method.

After the seventh interview in twelve weeks, they decided not to come back. They felt things were going well enough. The ending of therapy may seem abrupt, but sometimes that is the way life goes. If things don't work out well, they can always return. And sometimes that is what happens. They experience a flight into health, which isn't sustained.

I admit I was apprehensive about how they would do. But symptoms of health were emerging in this postdivorce family. I checked in with the family physician from time to time. Allen did well. The doctor reported that the mother, who used to talk about Allen all the time, rarely mentioned him during appointments. It sounded like he remained moody but was not automatically impossible. Both Ellen and Jim developed a parenting pattern that she found very helpful, and her anxiety about her ex-husband was much reduced. That was a few years ago. There hasn't been any long-term follow-up. I seldom get feedback if things go right.

From my clinical experience, this case illustrates the use of family therapy in the treatment of a boy diagnosed with ADHD, a "chemical imbalance," a "brain disorder" in the parlance of child psychiatry and psychology. While medications may be effective in offering "answers," thus reducing ambiguity, they can interfere with growth-producing, integrating encounters with the unknown, the mysteries of being human. The choice to give a medication, to treat the child with their family, are driven by how the practitioner views human experience. This is universally true. There is no "standard" applied to the patient.

The way the problem is viewed is in the eye of the beholder, the doctor/therapist.

Working with this family forced me to consider a few humbling self-reflective questions. I was initially concerned the family doctor was too strong in his skepticism about the medication. I thought he was seeing me as a champion of an antimedication cause. I am not antimedication. I believe in family therapy, and that represents a different way of thinking, thus a different way of talking and behaving. I was surprised things changed as much as they did. But a one-time event can have a strong therapeutic effect.

I noted that Ellen, the mother, had this clarity and certainty about her. Part of this was explained by her character, as well as her Catholic upbringing. But additionally, she had been indoctrinated into the language of ADHD. Alongside the clarity that came from the psychologist's evaluation, I felt a little dumb about my poorly articulated alternative views. I was also nonrationally apprehensive about her connection to managed care.

I felt that the father, from his businessman/athlete's view of experience, was skeptical about me. I am experienced enough to know that anything that causes me to second-guess myself and my methods leads to the temptation to use the ambiguity-reducing medication treatments. This will sound churlish, but one of the advantages of being a biological psychiatrist is that you do not have to question yourself and patients do not have to question themselves. The solutions are in the pharmacy. For family therapists the questions are unending and unavoidable. But the questions are compelling and working on them is implicitly gratifying and humanizing. The way I use language has a destabilizing effect, not only on the family, but on myself. This may be hard to see, but destabilizing can be part of the pathway toward healing.

What was helpful in moving this case forward to its outcome? I questioned the parents and expressed opinions that challenged how they thought. I made a little fun of the saintly mother—I teased her that her son could turn out like her. I challenged the father's way of viewing Allen's suicidal feelings, even as I expanded Allen's suicidal fantasies. I also included some support for the fact that Jim, the father, had changed. He was no longer the man Ellen believed him to be.

Ellen had accused Jim of dishonesty, but then her own dishonesty was exposed. Jim behaved like a thoughtful and responsible parent contrary to Ellen's views, based on her intense earlier experiences with him. I included Jim's new woman partner, so that all the people involved in parenting would be included in the discussion. I mentioned above that the woman-to-woman relationship is important to postdivorce therapy with children. If the two women respect one another, it is helpful to the children of divorce because they will be less plagued by divided loyalties. In fact, I have had more than a few cases where the women become united by their shared upset with the lover-dude's "deficiencies."

I recognize that this kind of interviewing differs considerably from more standard approaches to treating a child with ADHD. I don't do any diagnostic studies. I do not make use of standardized questionnaires. I bring in the whole family for a whole family interview. I use language in a very different way that tends to destabilize how they think about experience. I play with language to stimulate reflection and to activate possibility, alternative ways of thinking and behaving. I don't believe change comes from insight. Insight follows experience. I am attempting to create experiences in my office that induce reflection and lead to change. But, of course, these experiences induce reflections in me as well. In my many years of practice I have never experienced the feeling of being "burned out." I think my skepticism and freedom to be creative and playful have kept my spirit alive. A French philosopher said, "To risk meaning nothing is the beginning of play."[1] In my work, and how I approach families, I am constantly risking meaning nothing. The risk is enlivening.

In today's culture it is virtually routine to give kids medications for ADHD. There is a well-orchestrated industry organized around ADHD with abundant research to create the illusion of scientific certainty. Questionnaires are available to make assessments by pediatricians, family physicians, and nurse practitioners easier. The skeptical side of us is concerned that the diagnosis may be in the interest of serving agendas other than the health of the child. These agendas come from managed care companies, pharmaceutical companies, and professional organizations with psychiatry.

Stories, on the other hand, are clearly made of imagination and metaphor and are understood to be ambiguous. They are embedded in language, like the language of literature, which has much more capacity for describing human experiences. Stories stimulate reflection and lead to the possibility of creative solutions to life's contradictions. They help us to understand ourselves in situations that are tangled in confusion and don't make much sense. Sense comes out of playing with the imagination.

Next, we see how using language to destabilize the family experience leads to a dramatic family altering response. In this case, the child was diagnosed with ADHD shortly after his mother's death. The tensions and grief were still very palpable.

A FAMILY WHO OUTLAWED GRIEF

The father, Frank, called me at the recommendation of his family doctor. His youngest son, eight-year-old Dick, had taken an overdose of aspirin and had been briefly hospitalized. Two months earlier Dick was diagnosed with attention deficit disorder (ADD) based chiefly on his behavior at school. An ADHD clinic treated him with Ritalin. Dick's mother had died from cancer four months earlier, two months before he was diagnosed. Our first session included the father, Dick, and his older brother Paul, age eleven. Frank, an engineer, acknowledged distress about his wife's death, but said they "could not grieve forever" and it was "time to move on." He also minimized the significance of his own hernia surgery, which was scheduled to take place in three weeks. Frank did not grasp the fact that his son, Dick, was naturally concerned that he (the father) might die from the surgery. Dick's mother had had surgery some six months before her death. She did not die as a result of the surgery, but Dick connected it with her death.

Frank had all the expressive range of a robot in a suit. I was concerned Dick's behavior was the result of a fixed communicational impasse in the family and the father's apparent inability to talk about or acknowledge emotional distress. To make matters worse, it seemed the child psychiatrists made their diagnosis without considering the obvious trauma of a wife and mother's death. In my way of thinking, more people were needed so I suggested they bring additional family members to the next session. Frank's father and sister, the most geographically available members of the family, were invited to the next interview. Frank's mother had died two years earlier.

Frank's father, in his late sixties, was a successful engineer who came across as domineering, humorless, and harshly matter-of-fact. He behaved like a military commander with his rigid, autocratic demeanor. I learned his own father died when he was young, and he said that he had "managed just fine." The implication was that grieving was an unnecessary self-indulgence. He encouraged positive thinking in such situations. I pressured him with questions about his growing up.

Then I challenged his rigidity, saying, "It looks like there is a rule against pain or sadness in the family, and Dick is bearing the brunt."

In the manner of many accomplished, domineering positive thinkers, the grandfather sneered, "Psychiatrists don't know anything."

My response, in the manner of an experienced, smart-ass psychiatrist, was, "You don't know much about what I know, or what I have been through in order to be sitting in this chair."

At this point Frank's sister, who seemed suspicious of me initially, joined in.

She turned to her father and brother with tears and anger: "I agree with what this doctor is saying. I wish we had seen him sooner. I cannot believe neither of you shed a tear at either of your wives' funerals."

Frank defended himself: "I needed to set a good example for Dick and Paul."

Suddenly, tears began to flow from all but the grandfather. Then Dick began to describe his worries.

"I'm scared my dad will die from his operation. I thought the aspirin would make me die and then I could go find my mom and help her if Dad dies from his operation."

This is how kids think, and adding clarifying facts does not help them. The kids know too much about the duplicity of adults.

The grandfather smirked and said to no one in particular that I had "planned the whole thing." I thanked the grandfather for having found the humility to acknowledge how smart I am.

Then I complimented him with a bit more irony: "You know you are not only pretty tough, you're also smart. But here's something I don't think you know. Emotions are unbalancing, and I think you are afraid of these emotions you pretend are unnecessary. But even worse, as tough as you seem, I can see your family protects you by not talking about anything emotional. They feel obliged to protect you."

"That's ridiculous, nobody needs to protect me," he said and prepared to walk out, but his son and daughter prevailed upon him to stay until the session ended.

Wow! The fact that the daughter and son stood up to the old man was an important and transforming event.

I saw Frank, his sister, and the boys once more before Frank's surgery and twice afterward. It was curious, but Dick's hyperactivity faded into the background, and not only did Frank's heart begin to beat, but he also gave evidence of being more openly interested in others and less robot-like. This interest showed up in how he talked about people and relationships, how he shared memories of his wife. And now, with his sons and his sister there, he reflected on how much his wife meant to him. Unfortunately, the grandfather would not return.

I immediately felt the impact of my disrupting the family rule system, though I didn't know how it would play out. I broke an implicit family rule that did not allow comment on the patriarch's domineering manner. My remarks sound aggressive, impolite, maybe sarcastic. I was worried they might not come back. But my comments ended up having therapeutic value. I didn't think Frank knew how to get anything out of therapy; he didn't know how to be a patient. He didn't know how to use his relationship with me to question himself. But he learned. He became more human in his behavior. It still troubles me that the child psychiatrist who evaluated Dick did not take his mother's death into consideration.

In each of these three cases, the family had a child diagnosed with ADHD. Though the symptoms varied, each child was being treated with medication but was still symptomatic. This undoubtedly contributed to change with these families. They were all referred to me because treatment wasn't working. This frustration can increase a family's motivation to take the kinds of chances that lead to change.

These sessions reveal a way of working that is way beyond simply talking. We don't like the term "talk therapy," which suggests passivity and somewhat trivializes what we do. Obviously, we "talk," but we are using language, thinking about how language, while usually used to characterize or describe experience, also creates experience. In each case we see how language was used to reframe and create experience. This language was not grounded in science, nor was there any attempt to persuade these families based on "evidence." Instead, the therapeutic approach used language to bring about confusion and disruption in the name of change.

The American Academy of Child and Adolescent Psychiatry publishes treatment guidelines for psychiatric disorders in children. These guidelines mostly say that an evaluation should take no more than two sessions. The child should be on the correct medication by the end of the second interview. We have a different point of view. It takes four to five sessions to determine if the child and family can benefit from psychotherapy. We mention these guidelines because this explains why families who seek help from a child psychiatrist are likely to have their child treated with medication. This pattern is referred to as the "standard of care." If we were cynics, we might refer to this as "monkey see, monkey do." But we aren't cynics.

It is clear by now that, for us, the standard of care, especially with children, means working with the family. There are many ways a family struggles in raising children. One particularly challenging scenario is when the parents' conflicts are concealed, and a child becomes a scapegoat for family tensions. We call this the "mask of family unity."

Questions for Reflection

In the first case, "Let's Act Crazy," the therapist holds and contains the boy Evan when he becomes aggressive. The parents later say this was a helpful experience for them. What do you think about the idea that it's important for children to learn that they don't have much power?

In the second case, "Like Father, Like Son," the therapist addresses the child's (Nick) suicidal gesture by inviting his suicidal fantasies in the presence of the family. The therapist asks Nick if there is someone who wants him dead. Nick points to his mother. This ultimately had a positive therapeutic impact on the family. What do you think about this bold approach?

In the third case, "The Family Who Outlawed Grief," the therapist connected the hyperactivity and suicidal gesture of eight-year-old Dick to the family's repression around the expression of emotion, especially grief. How do you think that emotional constriction in a family can lead to symptoms in children?

Chapter 8

Teens Who Hurt Themselves

Beneath the Mask of Family Unity

THE PROBLEM WITH MR. COOL

Peter called me at the suggestion of his family doctor. He sounded distressed. His only child, fifteen-year-old daughter, Frankie, was cutting herself for the past two years. She had been in cognitive behavioral therapy for a year, with no change. We scheduled an appointment for the family for the following week.

As the family settled themselves on my office couch, Peter, a local Progressive politician, and his partner, Laurie, a writer, wore quietly worried looks. They described how their only child, Frankie, had been cutting herself for the last two years. Frankie had been in individual therapy for the past year, but the cutting continued. Peter presented himself as the cool guy, a long-haired, middle-aged ex-hippie, the understanding, hip dad. Despite his outwardly casual demeanor, he was obviously in pain over his daughter's self-mutilation. The troubling dynamics in the family revealed themselves at this first session. Laurie, the mother, had become the family scapegoat. As the lowest person on the totem pole, apparently, she couldn't get it right, with either her partner or her daughter. Both Peter and Frankie portrayed Laurie as the uptight one, and the Frankie openly showed her disdain for her mother, rolling her eyes whenever her mom spoke, locking eyes with her father as if to say, "See how Mom just doesn't get it?" Despite Frankie's cultivated toughness toward her mom, some of Frankie's comments inadvertently revealed her as a softy at heart. She let it slip that she worried that her mom "seemed tired all the time."

Aside from their daughter's periodic cutting, self-harming both arms and thighs, both parents expressed concern over Frankie's anger at her mother. Most of her cutting took place after a fight with her mother, or when the father was out of town. The dance was almost always the same.

Laurie said, "We would have some kind of argument, and Frankie disappears into her room. She locks her door, and I can't get her to come out. Eventually she does, and, if I beg her, she'll roll up her sleeves. That's when I see the cuts. It breaks my heart."

You could hear the anguish in her voice.

Laurie said quietly, "I'm always anxious after my daughter and I argue. I worry that she'll cut herself. So I try not to say too much. But I'm her mom! I need to guide her!"

Peter described their ongoing battles, saying, "They fight like sisters."

He sounded almost smug. This told me a lot. They weren't supposed to be equals. They weren't peers. I took it as a signal that Laurie didn't have much power with her daughter. I assumed that Peter was involved, probably unintentionally, in keeping Laurie small. And I assumed Frankie's cutting to be a cry for help—not just for herself, but for the family. They were in trouble.

Midway through the session, after I got a sense of this family's drama, I shifted the tone. I wanted to understand these folks in front of me, where they came from, how they began their relationship.

I turned to the parents: "How did you guys meet?"

Laurie said, a slight smile playing on her lips, "He was my knight in shining armor." Fifteen years her senior, Peter appeared, when they first met, to know the ways of the world. He was a big shot political organizer, well known in the community, and Laurie said she felt "thrilled" when he became interested in her.

Laurie said, "When I met Peter, I was struggling."

She was only twenty-four and, though she had gained some recognition for outstanding political writing, she had what she called a "gnawing insecurity" due to her upbringing. Laurie's family had emigrated to the United States from Korea a couple of years after she was born. Her father abandoned the family when Laurie was four years old, and her mother struggled to make a living for Laurie and her older brother.

Her mother was now elderly, financially stable, and, according to the couple, adored Peter.

Laurie said, "I think my mother likes Peter more than me!"

Peter and Laurie had now been together nearly twenty years but never married. They lived mostly together, but Peter retained his own apartment, what he called his "escape pad."

Soon, the patterns that had revealed themselves in the early sessions became abundantly clear. Laurie expressed herself reluctantly, almost apologetically, like she expected to be called out by her husband or daughter. When it came to parenting, she wanted more structure for Frankie, more accountability, in a good way.

She described her concerns: "I worry about Frankie. Not just about her cutting. She resents every suggestion I make, but sometimes I see her confused and I think she needs help. She can't figure out everything herself. She's only fifteen!"

"I can feel the tenderness toward your daughter as you talk about what she needs. You're a wise woman," I said.

I meant this as a move to undermine Peter's disqualification of his partner. Laurie had more of a hands-on, mother-y approach to parenting, which had been repeatedly discredited by Peter. Frankie picked up on, and magnified, her dad's attitude.

From what I observed at the first session, Laurie was right. Frankie was carrying burdens far too heavy for her slight self. This child had a kind of nymph-like quality, with a delicate face and small frame. She had recently been diagnosed with childhood rheumatoid arthritis, which periodically caused her ankles to swell, making walking painful. While Laurie believed her daughter needed guidance, support, and occasional limit-setting, Peter believed in granting Frankie an autonomy that exceeded her psychological and emotional development. He thought Frankie needed to decide almost everything for herself, including how much respect she had to show to her mother. Everything was negotiable.

Every time Peter, Mr. Laid-Back Guy, talked about his wife, it carried some veiled criticism. He expressed himself in such a way as to sound caring, but this was the proverbial knife-inside-the-velvet-glove routine. All of Laurie's ideas regarding their daughter—most of which were sane and helpful—were dismissed by the father as too strict, too this, too that. When Laurie said, "I think Frankie should have a regular time to be in bed," Peter would counter, with a smug reasonable-ness,

"I think she is mature enough to figure out what she needs to do. She's pretty good at knowing what she needs." Laurie would then withdraw, overruled. Frankie, the sensitive young soul that she was, clearly found these tensions unbearable. Her cutting brought these tensions to the surface—and the family into therapy.

Strange as it might sound, the parents were largely ignorant of these patterns. Laurie must have been distressed by her low status in the family, the way Peter always subtly undercut her, but she clearly did not have the ability to address what must have been a very painful experience for her. Though these family tensions were palpable, they were also nearly invisible to the naked eye, buried beneath the well-oiled social veneer of these well-meaning folks. My job was to bring these problematic patterns into the open so they could change.

Therapy lasted around six months with semiregular meetings. As familial patterns began to open, Frankie's self-mutilation unceremoniously stopped. By the third session she no longer cut herself. In nearly every session, I found ways to challenge Peter's self-satisfied dismissal of his wife and support Laurie's positions. I began to therapeutically flip the script. When Laurie spoke, and Peter and Frankie jumped in to correct her, I interrupted this dance with, "Laurie, you clearly know what your daughter needs. You've got this incredible intuitive sense. You see everything. How come Peter doesn't see what you see? Can you help him out?" This was not as easy to do as it sounds since the family had been unconsciously practicing their unwholesome patterns for quite a while. Peter, especially, appeared invested in the family script. In fact, part of his attraction toward his wife was how she admired him for what they both believed were his many wonderful attributes.

Their patterns as a couple clearly needed some updating. There was a fair amount of (polite) kicking and screaming on Peter's part. He would say, "You may not realize it, but I'm the one everyone in my community looks to for guidance. I'm pretty good at knowing how to solve problems." Though Peter clung to his self-importance, he gradually surrendered to my suggestions that, in fact, he had a wonderfully competent wife whose ideas about parenting would be good for their daughter. Slowly, Peter accepted an expanded, more complex—and more human—view of himself, someone who, like his daughter, needed guidance from Laurie. As I openly enjoyed Laurie and her perceptive, stable parenting, Peter began to talk to her differently in our sessions, more respectfully, with more care. It looked like a more alive partnership was beginning to emerge.

Frankie's cutting did not resume except once, very briefly, after several months. Without much explicit talk about her cutting, I reframed her self-harm as part of a troubled relationship pattern. The cutting was a symbolic act of aggression against her mother.

I told both parents, "I think it's very confusing for Frankie. She has two parents who have different ideas about her. She's got a mother who is perceptive and caring, but for some reason doesn't get much credit. And Dad, it looks like you're pretty skeptical about Mom and her approach, which is crazy to me. You married a brilliant woman. Only you, and now your daughter, don't know it."

The fact that Frankie's cutting stopped rather quickly is not unusual: it's part of the power of introducing the subtly dominant family dynamic underlying the child's distress. Previously, Frankie had spent a year with an individual therapist for cognitive behavioral therapy. When the family came to see me, the parents appeared both overwhelmed and helpless in the face of their daughter's seemingly intractable self-harming behavior. The couple had no idea how they contributed to Frankie's pain. That is part of what distinguishes this therapy experience from an individual model, and what can make it so powerful. The family becomes the patient.

Broadening the lens from just Frankie to her family as a whole had an almost instantaneous antidepressant effect on this teenager. I'm pretty sure she felt relieved that someone—an adult professional—was seeing what she was seeing, and understood the bind she was in. These intimate family undercurrents were brutal for her. Though she wasn't fully aware of this bind and couldn't articulate it, Frankie felt it. The unacknowledged imbalance of power in her parents' relationship resonated with her.

Early in therapy, I observed how Frankie was not free to love her mother openly: she absorbed her dad's powerful message of Mother as "not good enough" and acted as his spokeswoman. Frankie would risk betraying her powerful dad—and the family script—if she were closer, and nicer, to her mom. Not an easy road for a teenager to walk. Of course, the therapy was not always smooth sailing. For quite a few sessions Peter seemed to resent my promotion of his wife, and my demotion of him. And it took a while for Frankie to absorb this new model of a mother, one who was competent and caring. She fought it, though not quite as hard as her dad.

In my therapy with this family, I did what I could to bring these powerful family tensions to the surface, where they could be exposed, explored, and reworked. This delicate part of the healing process meant that the family, especially the parents, needed to know I was on their side. That I accepted them, even as I rather rudely challenged Peter and his subtly superior ways. As the therapist, I needed to regularly check in with myself to make sure my caring was intact. It was.

It should be said that this therapy process, arduous as it was at times, was not grim. We had some fun along the way. Though I proved to be a real therapeutic pain in the neck for Peter, we also enjoyed many moments of humor: Peter and I grew up in the same midwestern city, and we enjoyed bantering about the ups and downs of the city's sports teams, as well as sharing our perspective on a variety of life's absurdities. I liked this guy and respected him, even though I didn't like how he was with his wife. I believe these people felt cared for: I conveyed to them a shared humanity as I lightheartedly revealed my own parental blunders, even as I exposed, and questioned, some of their less attractive qualities as a family.

Several months after our last therapy meeting, I got a call from Peter. Frankie was enjoying a better relationship with her mom, and the cutting had not resumed.

As I offer the abbreviated version of a rather common therapy experience, it's important to emphasize that young people like Frankie typically feel relieved to find an adult professional who understands their worry about their family: their symptoms become a part of the family dynamic, of the broader suffering in the family, and the child no longer feels so alone, or so uniquely responsible. The pressure on them is reduced.

I enjoyed working with this family and sensed from early on that I could be helpful. Of course, any therapist's pleasure grows when the couple or family responds well to the therapy. The initial test came when I realized that Peter allowed me to therapeutically push him around a little bit. At first, I wasn't sure. I observed that despite his casual presentation, he was the powerhouse of the family, the covert CEO. I saw that Laurie's second-class status created a wound for the couple and family, a painful state that the daughter was well aware of.

I sensed that the original unconscious marital contract between Peter and Laurie meant that he was "top dog." But now the marriage was straining at the edges and drastically needed an update. I watched, and experienced, Peter's reactions as I challenged his cool, rather unyielding authority and gradual opening to my provocations. The fact that Frankie's cutting stopped early in the therapy operated like a GPS for me, acknowledging that I was on course in my observations. For the remaining therapy I just hoped they, and I, could keep it up.

When push came to shove, Laurie and Peter showed the strength of their family integrity: they opted for honest, difficult, self-exploration, which gradually reduced their suffering and opened the door to new freedoms in their family, hopefully paying dividends for years to come.

When families come to therapy, worried about their self-destructive children, what we typically see is how the family's attempt to solve the problem ends up reinforcing the problem they are trying to solve. Most often, latent conflict between the parents has been unacknowledged, or swept under the rug, often with a pretense of family togetherness. This mask of family unity, though largely unconscious, emerges in the way a family tells its story. This enforced unity restricts, rather than expands, the family spirit. The need to protect a family image or story may be motivated by a history of trauma, too much despair, anxiety, or perhaps pride or ego.

Sometimes a family member, usually a child, may be sacrificed to maintain this appearance of group unity. Sometimes families *need* a child to be a problem: it gives the family something to be mad about. There is security in having something to be mad about. But when security is rooted in anger, it limits the resilience and creativity that contribute to health.

In families where a child becomes the designated problem, often the parents, either one or both, avoid the inevitable and necessary self-questioning that is the hallmark of healthy living.

Enter the adolescent. Geniuses at detecting and unmasking parental coverup, the difficult adolescent shows up as a discordant note in the story the family wishes to tell. It seems to be part of Nature's design that our teenagers are perfectly—though painfully for parents—created to reverberate with family stress, especially stress that remains unacknowledged and unresolved. When families are stuck in unhealthy living patterns, our young people show exceptional creativity and commitment when it comes to challenging the deadness that can develop in marriage and family life, exposing the cracks and putting pressure on the parents. Teenagers are hypocrisy busters. It's a good idea to pay attention to these young people: they are usually trying to tell the parents something important—something the folks need, but may be loath, to learn.

These dynamics play out in dramatic fashion in the following case of a self-harming seventeen-year-old teenage girl with an eating disorder. The family, two parents with their two teenage daughters, were referred to me by their family doctor. The parents were worried about their eldest daughter's anorexic behavior. Here's what happened when I held up the therapeutic mirror for this family.

THE FAMILY WITH A SMILE ON ITS FACE

I first saw seventeen-year-old Melinda and her family at the urging of their family doctor. Melinda had been practicing the dubious art of anorexia for several years, and at the time of our first meeting she was consuming a carefully controlled four hundred calories a day. She had stopped menstruating, a classic symptom of anorexia. If she kept going in this direction, Melinda would end up in the hospital. She had just begun working with a nutritionist, and their family doctor recommended seeing a family therapist. The parents reluctantly agreed to call me for a consultation.

My first couple of meetings with this well-groomed, picture-perfect family was both intriguing and infuriating. The mom, Cassandra, was a Swiss-born beauty with porcelain skin and blond hair swept up in a knot. She radiated an anxious need for approval and harmony. Each time she spoke she looked at the family for signs of confirmation. She clearly didn't want anything to disturb this image of lovely family harmony. And her husband, John, cooperated by appearing to agree with everything his wife said. "Agreement" was his middle name.

John, German-born and in his late forties, worked in advertising for an international finance magazine. He looked like an aging punk rocker. This was his second marriage. He described his previous wife as "unstable." He had a twenty-five-year-old son, Frederick, from this marriage who continued to be what John described mournfully as "a hand-full." Frederick had been hospitalized for drug addiction and was struggling to stay clean. John appeared to carry a lot of guilt toward his son, whose behavior created a fair amount of disruption in the early part of John's marriage to Cassandra.

During the first few meetings with this family, I felt at times like Alice in Wonderland, trapped in an absurd world where normal responses are regarded as suspect. The dictates of the family culture, unconsciously promoted by the parents, looked to me something like this:

1. No one will disagree.
2. No one will raise their voice.
3. We will be happy.
4. We will have fun.
5. We will think alike.
6. We will love each other all the time.

This pattern first appeared when I noticed that every time Melinda spoke, her parents and fifteen-year-old sister, Lucia, disqualified her. Melinda, an academic superachiever, was enrolled in an advanced high school for bright, hardworking kids. She was hugely perceptive, but her point of view didn't gain any traction in the family. Melinda had zero credibility. She was a poster child for what a scapegoat looks like. Scapegoating, of course, is a relatively common phenomenon. Anyone who has worked in an organization has seen it—how everyone focuses on one person as the problem to avoid looking at larger institutional dysfunction. It's the same in families. The subliminal function of scapegoating is to avoid responsibility: as long as THAT PERSON is the problem, we don't have to address the underlying problems of our group.

In her family, Melinda would try to lobby for some relatively mild change related to her own privacy. This was an "open door" family; they lived in a loft—one big, open space—and the parents, especially the father, would often keep the bathroom door open when he showered. Privacy in this family was seen as an affront, an act of aggression toward other family members. In one session, Melinda talked about wanting to have time in front of the bathroom mirror without her younger sister honing in.

"I'd love to be able to put on my makeup without Lucia telling me to move over or hurry up. She's always hovering around when I'm trying to get ready."

In response, Lucia muttered under her breath, "Selfish."

Melinda weighed in, politely of course, on wanting her parents (i.e., mother) to treat her differently, to let her spend time in her room alone instead of magically appearing in the living room to watch a popular television show with the rest of the family.

"Sometimes, Mom, I just want to be left alone, to do my own thing. I may not be interested in that show."

Melinda always, from what I saw, expressed these preferences respectfully, in an almost hypermature manner. No adolescent pouting for her. But she was clearly out of step with how this family did things. She apparently hadn't gotten the memo. Any comment about a personal preference was treated like an assault on the family. The slightest challenge to her mother was responded to as a betrayal. Melinda doubled as family scapegoat *and* troublemaker. I was pretty sure that her eating disorder related to her inability to have an autonomous voice in this family of supertogetherness.

As I gathered information about the parents' individual backgrounds, one feature stood out. Cassandra had been raised in a home where her own mother acted as the peacemaker, constantly softening her husband's rules to accommodate the children. Apparently, Cassandra's mother spent much of the time containing her husband, worried that he'd be too hard on Cassandra and her brother, and always ran interference between the children and their father. Cassandra's mother wanted to avoid conflict at all costs. I never found out how she learned this, but it must have come from some trauma or pain in her own past. It sounded like Cassandra's mother didn't want any anger, or even heat, coming from her husband. When Cassandra turned sixteen, she started giving her father a hard time by staying out late and disobeying his rules. Of course, Cassandra knew her mother would back her up.

I spent the first few sessions of the therapy hoping to disrupt the stifling togetherness of this family, sharing my observations in a way that challenged the family norms. I used my whole being to try to create a sense of differentiation in this family. I encouraged, actually begged, for different opinions, different voices. I chided John for his "Mr. Agreement" persona and said, "Dad, I'm having trouble telling what you're really thinking. It looks like you're worried about having a different brain than Cassandra's."

Naturally, he disagreed with me. I wanted, needed, to challenge Cassandra's hyperpeacemaking.

I told her, "You have a Band-Aid for everything. It looks to me like no one should ever be upset over anything. No one should ever feel hurt, or angry."

Every comment I made that had a bit of tension in it was blocked by Melinda's mother. If I challenged the family togetherness Cassandra would look around innocently, like I was an invader coming to hurt her tribe. She didn't want to believe that there was a problem in how the family was operating. Melinda was the problem. Couldn't I see that? This pattern was (inwardly) infuriating for me. I began to feel like Melinda. Nothing could get through in this family. It was one voice or no voice at all. Then we had what, I thought, might be our final session.

The parents showed up with just Melinda. They decided to leave their younger daughter at home, stating that something had happened over the weekend with Melinda that they wanted to discuss "privately." (I inwardly took this as a personal challenge, since I made it clear that everyone needed to be at our sessions. I decided not to take the bait.) Cassandra recounted her version of what happened.

"We had an uproar at our home a couple of days ago," she said. She went on to describe an argument with Melinda that ended with Melinda smashing a plate on the ground and throwing some silverware for good measure. The family was calm (of course) when recounting this story.

Cassandra, Band-Aid in hand, said, "We had a good discussion afterward."

I thought that this might be some health breaking through. Melinda's anger turned outward, openly directed at her parents. It sounded more dramatic than dangerous. I asked about what transpired that led to the escalation. Melinda volunteered her version.

"I came down after dinner and felt quiet. I just didn't feel much like talking. My mom wouldn't leave me alone. She kept asking what's wrong, what's wrong, what's wrong. I didn't know what was wrong. I just didn't feel like having a big smile on my face."

Bingo! I wanted Cassandra to explore her daughter's perspective, but her mother shut it down. She didn't want to go there. Instead, Cassandra tried to redirect her daughter to a "happier" thought so I stopped the conversation.

"Melinda is trying to help you to understand what she needs as a seventeen-year-old. It sounds like she needed some space."

Cassandra, of course, took this as a minor insult, and kept anxiously talking, mostly ignoring my comment. I stopped her again and said, "Nothing gets digested in this family" (semi-intentional metaphor). "Melinda is incredibly perceptive and caring. Your daughter says many important, valuable things that would help you to know what she needs from you. She is her own person, with her own ideas, her own desires, her own needs. But nothing gets digested. You just keep going without stopping to learn anything from her. You're missing a crucial opportunity."

I insisted on a few minutes of silence. I felt that if I could amplify Melinda's voice, she might gain some real, healthy control in her relationship with her mother instead of the pseudocontrol of starving herself.

I could almost see the steam coming out of Cassandra's ears. I knew she was furious at me, and I wanted to tease her a bit, to show that I saw her upset.

"You know, I feel like such a Scrooge with your family. I feel like the bubble-buster, the one who came to rain on your parade. The groove-blower. I feel like 'Angry Guy.'"

I called myself out with a smile and the tension lessened.

Then Melinda launched into a gorgeous soliloquy that contained so much wisdom, and so much health. I felt like I had a front row seat at a powerful Broadway show. She looked at her mom.

"It's not that I don't want to be part of this family. I love you. I WANT to be in the family. But if I say I want to do something myself, like wake myself up in the morning, you say, 'Well, then you can just do your own laundry.' You act like if I want to do something my way that I'm hurting you. And then I feel guilty."

This soft-spoken young woman continued in this vein for a few minutes, telling her folks everything they needed to know for healing to begin. If I could have applauded, I would have. But I did the next best thing and held my hand up for silence. I nodded, signaling my respect for Melinda and her courage. I didn't want Cassandra to move in and smooth over her daughter's comments. I wanted to let Melinda's description of her experience in this family ring out in the room without distortion.

Since we neared the end of the session, I thought it was a good time to end. I could see that Cassandra was mad. She refused to look at me. I was interfering with the script that she had so meticulously honed. I knew she saw herself as the family doctor and my support of her daughter's troublemaking probably offended her pride, at the very least. But I greatly admired Melinda and wanted to help her stop hurting herself. I had to risk her mother's animosity if we were going to get anywhere.

We ended the session without scheduling another one. I didn't know if I would see them again. I heard from their family doctor that they were "shopping around" for another therapist. But then the mother called two days later.

She said, "You know, I was very angry at you the other day. We interviewed some individual therapists for Melinda, and they all told us to stick with the family therapy." She added, "This is difficult for me. It's not at all what I expected. But I'm starting to think it's very helpful. So, we'll stick with you through this painful journey."

I could hear the smile in her voice. I was glad to have the opportunity to affirm her. Despite her exasperating ways, I liked Cassandra.

"I'm impressed by how you're responding. I know our meetings feel difficult, but you're an intelligent and thoughtful person. I'm impressed."

She needed that from me, and I was glad to give it to her.

"I know our other daughter doesn't want to come, but I'm going to make her attend. I don't care if she's mad at me. That's what we're supposed to do as parents, right?" Now it was my turn to smile.

At the end of the fourth session, Melinda and her family reported that she was now eating 1,200 calories a day. She looked much better.

I continued to see them for several visits, about seven sessions in all. One improvement went unnoticed, except by me. When I first met them the two sisters were fighting so intensely that they could barely leave the house as a family. According to John, the family couldn't go to a movie or restaurant together without the daughters battling so intensely that the parents nearly collapsed in shame. This led to them avoiding family outings.

That problem resolved quickly, by the third session. I knew that the source of the conflict between the sisters had to do with the fact that

Lucia was playing on her parents' team, correcting and criticizing her older sister, which, of course, Melinda resented. I needed to rebalance this relationship and get the sisters back on the same team. Lucia needed to stop protecting her parents, which was both bad for her and continued to isolate Melinda.

I lightly chided the younger daughter for her goody-goody ways with her parents.

"Lucia, you're only fourteen but you sound like you're forty. You know, you have a very cool older sister. You can learn a lot from her if you'd just open yourself to it. She's much cooler than the old folks over there," motioning to her parents sitting on the couch.

Lucia had unfortunately picked up on the instruction manual that called for disapproval of Melinda. Lucia was embarrassed, in a good way, which eased tensions between the sisters.

Despite these apparent improvements, especially Melinda's looser grip on food control, I don't fully consider this case a success. At around the sixth session Melinda returned from travel abroad where she relapsed slightly in terms of her anorexia. I was looking forward to continuing to work with this family, to go deeper and solidify the early gains by continuing to address underlying family patterns, but Cassandra had recently obtained an individual therapist for Melinda whom she had begun seeing.

Our sessions ended with a whimper, not a bang. School was over, summer had begun, and the family planned to leave town for a couple of months. Cassandra said she would call when they returned. I never heard from them again.

What a difficult case! I felt like I had been through a war, but one with the intention of healing, not destruction. I'm not sure if I adequately conveyed here what it felt like to sit with this family. The invisible rules mandating conformity in all things felt intense and oppressive. My approach to diagnosis includes both observation of family interactional patterns and my experience of being with a family, testing both for points of rigidity and of flexibility. By flexibility I mean self-questioning, imagination, curiosity. The more flexibility, in general, the more health. By contrast, the repetitive, static quality of this family, with Cassandra in the leadership position, felt the opposite of life-giving.

Unlike with Peter and Laurie, the previous family discussed, I wasn't at all sure I would be able to help them. Cassandra proved tougher than Peter. Her reaction to my disruption of their script was more intense, and I never felt whether she respected or trusted me. I tried to balance my unsettling approach by continuing to affirm, nonverbally, my respect for the integrity of the family. My challenges were never directed at Cassandra or John's personhood, just what they did, how they operated. I knew I needed to hold firm in my efforts to remove this family's mask of unity, and it is probably only the confidence that comes with many years of experience that allowed me to withstand Cassandra's anger toward me. I carried the conviction that I couldn't give in to the family pressure to change my tune. I had to tolerate the loneliness of being the wrong one in the room. I'm quite sure that's how Melinda felt. And her life was potentially at stake.

The two previous cases show what can happen in therapy with a family where the adolescent is actively engaged in self-harming behavior. But what about the more subtle cases, those situations where a young person might be hurting themselves indirectly? Reckless behavior, excessive drinking, or dangerous neglect of health issues can be just as damaging to them.

In this next story we meet Brianna, a recent college graduate, who was referred by her family doctor. The doctor was worried that she was not taking care of her type 1 diabetes, and her carelessness toward her health posed some potentially disastrous health consequences for her.

WHY IS IT SO HARD TO LOVE MYSELF?

Brianna, a lanky twenty-three-year-old, had been referred to me by her family physician because of her depression and inconsistent management of her diabetes. Diagnosed with type 1 diabetes at eight years old, Brianna knew everything about the disease, but she still struggled to get her sugar under control. When I first met her, Brianna had just graduated from college, the kind of place that rewards being outspoken and "different," and now, like many young people postcollege, she was floundering a bit as to her next move. She was considering applying to graduate school and studying architecture. She loved design and had fantasies about making her mark as a female avant-garde architect.

Working with Brianna was interesting but challenging. I admired her intelligence and self-awareness, though I found her a bit intimidating. If I chose a word she didn't like or offered an opinion that she found "lame," she would let me know. She wasn't afraid to bite. In fact, I think she rather enjoyed it. I sensed early on that she was testing me, wanting to see if I was strong enough for her. She wouldn't have respected me if I were a pushover, since as she put it, talking about her former roommate, "I find weak women a turnoff." I kept this in mind and made sure I stayed true to myself. Occasionally, sparks flew when I didn't agree with her. I didn't worry about it. I knew it was important for Brianna to have a therapist who had their own voice and used it unapologetically.

We spent a good deal of time talking about Brianna's family. The middle child of three, her older brother lived in the city and worked in finance. I'm never quite sure what that means, except that they focus on making a lot of money. Her sister had recently moved out of the parents' house to begin her freshman year at college. Brianna's parents lived several hours away in a neighboring state where her dad was a philosophy professor and her mom worked as a specialist in early childhood education.

Throughout my sessions with Brianna, her struggles with her parents figured prominently. She was confused as to how to establish her autonomy with them, including around her diabetic care. Sometimes she felt like a kid, and at other times like she should have all the answers. While the process of growing into adulthood is a normally clumsy matter, Brianna's struggles seemed to have something specifically to do with her family's dynamics. She described chronic tensions between her parents, and her mother's periodic bouts of drinking. Brianna worried about her folks and felt stressed by her relationship with them. I believed this had contributed to her depression. I suggested a family meeting. They agreed to come into town for a session so we set up a meeting for the following week.

Both parents and Brianna's brother came for the session. There was tension in the air as the family seated themselves in my office. Articulate and well-meaning people, there was a stiff quality in how they related to one another. The first eruption came when Anna, the mom, talked to Brianna about her worries about her daughter's inconsistent attention to her diabetes. Brianna and her brother immediately attacked their mother for being "too abrasive" and "too intense."

A mental flag went up. Anna's concern was realistic, and she expressed her concern with feeling and emotion, not at all over-the-top. In fact, her distress was well founded since Brianna's self-care was episodic and somewhat freewheeling. Brad, the father, then chimed in, echoing the kids' refrain.

"Mom doesn't calibrate her reactions, but she means well," he said.

His patronizing comment, hidden behind the veneer of a calm voice of reason, looked to me like a well-honed pattern of which this intelligent family was unaware. These kids sat on their dad's shoulders, taller than their mom, who was disqualified as an alarmist. As we talked further, I saw that Anna was small in this family.

I commented wryly, "If your mom cried 'fire,' you all would have to see the evidence before you evacuated."

Anna was guilty until proven innocent.

I began to talk openly, but with care, about these patterns as they emerged in the session.

"In the short time we've been meeting I've been struck by Anna's intelligence and thoughtfulness. She's right to be worried about Brianna but instead she gets painted as a crazy person."

Anna and Brad, believers in the benefit of psychotherapy, with their own individual therapists, reacted as if this were new to them. Brad appeared a little taken aback by my comment.

"My wife gets too emotional. That's what I find challenging." He added, "It's overwhelming for me how intense she gets sometimes."

I said, "She seems like she's pretty healthy, not emotional in a bad way. Why are you so worried about her intensity?"

Brad, with his almost exaggerated calm, looked to me like he might be afraid of his own irrationality, of his strong feelings.

I asked him, "Where did you learn to be worried about emotional intensity?"

Brad paused, then said, "My home was a bundle of chaos when I was growing up. My parents fought a lot. And my parents were heavy drinkers. It wasn't a picnic."

His brief description sounded like his childhood memories were still a source of pain for him.

I said, "It sounds to me like you feel like you need to keep your wife's emotions in check, otherwise disaster might ensue."

Brad didn't respond, but I could tell he was thinking about what I said.

Anna looked at me. "That's an interesting comment. I never thought about it like that."

Even though Anna wouldn't have framed it like that, I was pretty sure she felt the pain of being emotionally stepped on, first by her husband, then by her kids. And it looked like Brianna's mom had given up fighting with her husband, Brad. With her husband's supreme self-assurance, I think she felt outclassed. Brad had unconsciously enlisted his children in this unresolved impasse.

I continued to emphasize Anna's good judgment and praise her emotional freedom. In response to my affirmation of her, Anna began to speak hesitantly about her frustration at feeling "unheard." A poignant picture emerged.

"I have a hard time getting anybody to take me seriously. First my husband, then my kids. This has been going on a long time."

I said, "That sounds lonely."

She nodded. The room was quiet. I turned to both parents.

"I can imagine that this made it hard for Brianna growing up, trying to learn about how to take care of her diabetes. It sounds like a lot of mixed messaging going on. Kind of a muddle."

The opening of these tensions, while empowering for Anna, had an almost immediate therapeutic effect. These were thoughtful, intelligent people, trapped in patterns that were unrewarding and unproductive. It was almost as if the family had been holding its collective breath. Now they started to breathe. Brad gave his version of a "thumbs-up" to the session.

"Boy, I wish we would have had some family therapy when Brianna was young. It could have saved us years of grief," he said.

Brianna's confusion over how seriously to take her diabetes was borne out of this parental dysfunction.

She weighed in on how this affected her as a child with diabetes: "Yeah, it was a real crap shoot when I was a kid. I wasn't sure WHAT I was supposed to do. I remember my mom trying to get me to avoid sweets, but Dad was, like, 'What's the big deal? Let the kid have a cookie.'" The parents' mutual and unresolved dance equated to

Mom = Too Intense, Anxious

Dad = Calm and Rational

which played itself out again and again around Brianna's diabetes. This young girl couldn't escape the conflicting message about how to care for herself.

To the family's credit, they responded to this session by starting to do things differently. Shortly after our meeting, Brad apparently became an activist around Brianna's diabetes, contacting her physician and others involved in her care. He said he wanted to make sure he was "updated" on the latest numbers so he could help with problems if they arose. Brianna's family physician called me to complain about the father's "intrusiveness." I briefly described the family's dynamics and explained that this was progress for the family, and for Brianna. In fact, the father's interest was key to Brianna's developing a healthier desire to care for herself. The doctor got it.

I continued to meet with Brianna alone for several months, until she decided to enroll in a graduate program in design that took her out of state. During this time, her diabetic care became more consistent as she addressed her disease more openly and deliberately. While not yet perfect, the numbers indicating control of her diabetes were better than they'd been. She had finally begun taking care of herself.

On the family front, Brianna described how her phone conversations with her mother changed.

"My mom never used to be able to stand up for herself. If I argued with her, she would just get quiet, she wouldn't say anything. She never argued back or put me in my place." Brianna smiled. "Now if I'm a pain she pushes back."

I said, "That sounds better for both of you."

"Absolutely!" she replied.

Brianna was aware of these patterns. She reported this new development with pleasure in her voice. She now had a mom who seemed more capable of standing up for her own point of view. And Brianna now had a dad who was a bit of a pain in the neck regarding her diabetic care. But Brianna didn't fight it—she was finally getting the kind of care she needed.

This case is an example of how a single consultation can help get a family's circulation going, allowing them to begin to move off a subtle, nearly invisible impasse that can trouble people for many years. The fact that the parents, Brad and Anna, responded so quickly to our meeting told me a lot about their underlying good health. They were both self-questioners, involved in therapy, curious about themselves. But the individual therapy setting cannot capture what I saw. Brad couldn't report on his patronizing behavior toward his wife. He didn't know about it. And Anna could not describe how trapped she felt, how her drinking provided her with an escape. This was an unconscious, interpersonal pattern, so subtle it needed to be observed to be detected.

Brianna certainly didn't know that she risked betraying her father if she were to take her diabetes seriously. She felt, but couldn't have articulated, how her parents' ongoing, but undeclared, battle in their relationship spilled on to her, creating a low-grade depression. It also helped that the parents, therapy-wise as they were, came in predisposed to listen and learn. Brad and Anna also demonstrated the kind of intelligence that left room for questions. They didn't need everything to be neat right away; they could tolerate the confusion that came from looking at their situation from a new perspective.

I had no further contact with this family after our session, nor have I seen Brianna since she left for graduate school. I can only hope that they continued to show the imagination and resilience that characterized their response to our one and only therapy session.

As we reflect on these cases, one thing stands out: these parents, Laurie and Peter, Cassandra and her husband John, Anna and Brad, loved their children. These were good, caring people who would not intentionally hurt them. But the grownups in these families were blind to the damage that they were causing. And their children ended up hurt or hurting themselves.

By telling these stories we do not intend to suggest that healing is easy. However, once we broaden the lens on the problem to include the family, change is possible. In all three of these families the symptoms presented by the young person resolved rather rapidly. This is not uncommon. In each case it meant the family needed to allow for the excavation of buried tensions. Most important, each parent had to be willing to look at themselves, to question themselves from a different, unfamiliar angle. They had to take responsibility for their living patterns in the family. None of us can really afford to think of ourselves as innocent, at least after age thirty. That's really not so bad, when you think of it.

In each of these families, themes of control emerge as strong elements of the story. Control issues are often generated, at least in part, by residual trauma, which may be passed down through several generations. In the next chapter, we see how this trauma/control dynamic shows up in three different families. How they respond makes all the difference.

Questions for Reflection

In the first case, "The Problem with Mr. Cool," the therapist viewed Frankie's cutting as an act of aggression toward her mother. How did this interpersonal framework help resolve Frankie's self-destructiveness? What is the difference between this perspective and the framework of an individual therapy?

In the second case, "The Family with a Smile on Its Face," Melinda's eating disorder was seen as an effort to have an autonomous voice where "togetherness" was the motto. How did the therapist recognize that this family had a policy of enforced family unity? How can you recognize those traits in a family? When does this become a problem?

In the story of Brianna's family, "Why Is It so Hard to Love Myself?," the parents responded quickly to the therapist's challenges. What were the ingredients in this family that allowed them to use this therapy so well? What did their health look like? What are some of the ingredients in a healthy family?

Chapter 9

Control Freak

Transmission of Intergenerational Trauma

A MOTHER LEARNS TO LOVE HERSELF

The first call came from Trish's father, Arthur. He said Trish, an eighteen-year-old high school senior, had "bipolar disorder" and was "completely out of control." The family had gotten my name from a pediatric neurologist who had referred other families to me. Part of this neurologist's practice included writing prescriptions for kids with psychiatric diagnoses, after the diagnosis had been made elsewhere. She was a thoughtful doctor and when she sensed a hard-to-define problem in the family, referred them to me for family therapy. Trish's father elaborated: "She's not obeying her curfew. Last Friday she didn't come home until dawn. I don't know if she's drinking or on drugs or what. She quit taking her bipolar medications four months ago. Maybe that's what's causing this."

Based on my phone conversation with the father, I expected a very disturbed, probably manic, young woman. A very different Trish arrived. Instead of being "out of control," this young woman was composed and thoughtful in an appealing, graceful way. She was tall with fine skin and long, straight reddish-blond hair pulled back into a ponytail. I sensed right away Trish was a self-owning young woman. She did not blame others for her recent behavior.

She said, "I know I haven't always been easy lately. I came home too late the other night. But my parents overreact to every little thing!" Her mom and dad appeared tense and agitated in contrast to Trish. It was easy for Trish's folks to talk about her, but not about themselves. In this first interview I noticed that Trish seemed far more capable of self-observation than either of her parents. When I asked, "How can I help?" both Arthur and his wife, Carol Marie, began talking about their frustration with Trish.

Trish responded with that universal eye roll of adolescents. "I just wish they'd chill out a bit," she said.

Arthur said Trish had quit taking her medications the preceding October, a month after he, an executive in a large corporation, had been "downsized." He acted as if it was not a big deal.

"They gave me a severance package. It was only a business decision."

Dressed in suit and tie, Arthur came across as conservative and repressed, not good at paying attention to what was happening inside him. I sensed he relieved any uncertainty about himself by being angry with Trish or his spouse.

Carol Marie, on the other hand, was upset by his nonchalance. Her anxiety about her husband's job loss was palpable, like she felt their ship had been torpedoed and was slowly sinking. Carol Marie was hesitant to reveal anything about herself but was very articulate about her daughter's behavior. There were times when she appeared almost cruel, smirking as she described how Trish dressed, her messy bedroom, her coming in late last Friday night. Her smirk suggested to me that she got some covert gratification from Trish's behavior. I suspected it may have provided her with a distraction for what looked to me, as an initial impression, like an emotionally barren marriage.

These parents, despite being in their fifties, appeared to be somewhat naïve about relationships. They were polite suburbanites with little imagination, little capacity or language for self-observation. They did not know how to question themselves. But they were clear about Trish and what was wrong with her and her behavior.

The parents asked me to see Trish alone for a couple of visits, which I did, though this isn't something I usually do. Trish's parents seemed like cautious, fearful people and I thought this might help them to trust me and my way of working. During these visits Trish, again, impressed me with her mental health. She was thoughtful about herself and was clearly enjoying her expanding group of friends.

She told me, "I like these people. I am having fun. I never knew how to have fun before. I don't think my parents have ever been happy. I don't want to turn out like them."

In the sessions with Trish, she talked about being worried about her parents. I assume this to be true of all children. When parents are worried about a child, the child is worried about the parents the same amount plus 10 percent. The extra 10 percent comes from worrying about who will have the nervous breakdown, when will the divorce happen, and who will die first. It seemed to me that Trish was trying to help her mother grow up a little, to become more of a person, to find satisfaction in her own life. She was concerned her mother was trapped, didn't have any friends, and didn't know how to go about finding them. Trish was trying to get her mother connected to the mother of one of her girlfriends who lived on a farm.

She said, "My friend's mom has a great sense of humor and really seems to enjoy her life. I think she'd be a good influence on my mom."

Trish was also concerned about father.

"I don't have much of a relationship with him. He is always working. He is bossy, ordering us around, trying to control me and my mother. He was making a lot of money until he got 'downsized.' I'm nervous about what might happen next."

My sessions with Trish suggested that while inexperienced, she was, emotionally, more mature than her parents. She had far more tolerance for ambiguity than they did. Trish's implicit maturity pointed to the presence of some underlying health in this family. I guessed Arthur's recent firing, or "downsizing" seriously disrupted the family balance and contributed to the current crisis. He seemed to have no capacity to acknowledge this, though Carol Marie was clearly devastated, apprehensive about what would come next.

Arthur and Carol Marie came in for the next session and I continued to see the family for about twelve sessions over the next five months. I wondered what had happened in this family that Trish, a mature, sensitive young woman had acquired the label of bipolar disorder and had been on medications most of her young life. I sensed a caution, a deep fear from the parents, that I didn't yet understand.

Arthur came from a family where his father, who had grown up on a farm, was successful in a small-town auto parts business. He portrayed his mother as domineering, harsh, and emotionally unpredictable, the Queen of Hearts incarnate ("Off with their heads!"). As a byproduct, Arthur hated emotion, and acted to quell it in himself, his spouse, and his children. His demeanor and behavior were both repressed and repressive, but this concealed an unarticulated fear. Emotion, especially expressed by a woman, made him feel like an overwhelmed little boy. Arthur did not take the severance from his job personally. He acted like he took nothing personally. This was learned in his upbringing. He was emotionally distant, humorless. His personal style is what I think of as "culturally invisible pathology." It's valued in the workplace but fails miserably in the land of intimacy where families live.

Carol Marie came from a timid, frightened family. She grew up with a lot of insecurity. She had a passive father, who was nearly invisible in her memory. She talked about how her mother protected her father but was herself fearful and depended on religion and her daughter for emotional sustenance. Carol Marie had been a security blanket for her mother. At first, Carol Marie was a careful patient in our sessions, but soon she seemed to come alive. She began to enjoy becoming a patient. I think of a "patient" as someone who learns to use a relationship to question themselves. Much of her life had been characterized by apprehension, fueled by a fear of an undefined catastrophe. I learned more about the source of her fear, which for her meant going through life waiting for the other shoe to drop.

According to Carol Marie there had been a major business failure, an economic trauma, in her father's family long before she was born, which apparently had a devastating impact on her parents. This failure created a fear that something like that could happen again. I think of those experiences as "catastrophe fantasies." They are like a shadow that is cast over the family, not always visible but creating an ominous backdrop. These fears often stem from encounters with death, serious illness, psychosis, financial collapse, warfare, other kinds of trauma.

When Trish was three years old her brother, Chad, was born. Both children were unexpected. Arthur and Carol Marie had tried to conceive for the first ten years of their marriage. Then suddenly, unexpectedly, Carol Marie became pregnant with Trish, a miracle baby. Carol described wistfully the soothing intimacy she felt with her new baby.

When the second child was born the family naturally became more emotionally chaotic. We think God likes it that way. God finds perfection interferes with being human. When a baby arrives in a family, intimacy increases. That should be good. But there are those who have trouble tolerating the warmth that comes with intimacy, and they move back. During couples therapy is usually when we learn that a fault line appeared in the marriage just after the birth of the first baby.

In the case of Trish's family, Arthur responded to the birth of his children by working progressively longer hours. Arthur's reaction was to become more distant, more repressive, and more demanding. Carol Marie interpreted Arthur's response to the birth of Chad like this: "You keep quiet. You know I hate it when you get so emotional. And keep those kids quiet. Dammit! Can't you see that Chad needs changing? You didn't iron my shirt. I told you I needed that shirt this morning."

Carol Marie, remembering this painful time, said softly, "I felt overwhelmed and isolated. And lonely, incredibly lonely."

Like most children, Trish undoubtedly felt her parents' emotional upset. Her behavior assuredly resonated with the anxiety and turmoil in her parents' marriage. In addition, Trish had been the center of the universe for three years, until this little thief Chad showed up.

Carol Marie said, "I thought if only my four-year-old was not so difficult, things would be better."

They were referred to a well-known, highly regarded child psychiatrist who said that Trish "might" have bipolar disorder and "deserved" a trial of Lithium. The "trial," however, was a one-way street and never ended, until a month before they came to see me—fourteen years later. I had a chance to look at the notes from this initial evaluation: there were no specific findings. The diagnosis was based on a psychiatrist's *impression*, but the impression became a fixed, unquestionable conclusion.

As an institution, conventional modern child psychiatry has little capacity or language for thinking about, let alone working with, families, except in cursory ways. They saw the best child psychiatrist in the area, but he never inquired about the family. A four-year-old was upsetting her mother. In effect the psychiatrist was treating the mother's anxiety by medicating the child. The child psychiatrist who saw her then did not have any language for considering the silent distress in the marriage that had its origins in both family's backgrounds, and was covered by polite, orderly suburban success.

When the diagnosis was attached to Trish, it explained why Carol Marie felt so overwhelmed: her daughter had a mental illness. The child's diagnosis helps them avoid feeling responsible or confused about themselves. "Trish is 'sick,' it's not me (or us)." The parents' anxiety, passed down over a couple of generations, now had an explanation that they were hesitant to disrupt. I learned when I saw them that the diagnosis helped to stabilize the parents' marriage. But reflecting on multigenerational history, as I induced them to do in our sessions, opens a new kind of awareness.

We continued to meet for several months, until Trish left for college. Arthur attended all the sessions. During the time I worked with them, he surprised Carol Marie by doing the laundry several times. Trish helped him acquire this new, unfamiliar skill: a daughter teaching her father. Of course, Arthur was clumsy at his first forays into domesticity, but he figured it out. It may seem like a small matter, but it was an important shift in the marriage. Arthur also cooked a few meals; again, a small matter, but a huge transition for him. His participation was part of a new pattern. I had teased him, "You should learn to think like a woman. You have two excellent teachers, your wife and your daughter." I wasn't suggesting that domesticity is the essential purview of women, but rather, this expanded sense of his role was an improvement for everyone.

The Reverend William Sloane Coffin used to say, "The woman most in need of liberation is the woman inside every man." This applied perfectly to Arthur. I was also pretty sure that his new, slightly looser way of being, helped Carol Marie feel like she had more of a partner. These were remarkable changes for him. He found a new way to enjoy his family and Carol Marie was deeply gratified by these small changes.

By the time Trish left for college there was a marked change in the family. Everything, and everyone, appeared lighter, less fraught. The way I treated Trish, my curiosity and appreciation of her, the way I treated her as if she were healthy, helped the parents respond differently to her. Carol Marie seemed to feel cared for by me—safe—and she responded by becoming more self-aware and learning to question herself. It looked like she got some much-needed soothing from our meetings. Carol Marie seemed invigorated and amused by our interactions and her husband looked like he enjoyed this new, freer wife. I could tell Trish was gratified by her mother's behavior. And Carol Marie, who at first had seemed envious of her daughter early on (remember Snow White?), showed evidence of genuine appreciation for her daughter. We ended the therapy as Trish left for college. Then, one month later, Carol Marie called me. I was surprised. She wanted to come to therapy for herself. I suggested that she bring Arthur, but she said he was busy hunting for another permanent job and was now working as a car salesman. It sounded to me like something had come alive for Carol Marie in our earlier sessions and she liked it. She wanted to see if there was more where that came from.

Carol Marie said she was "intrigued" by a suggestion I made during their initial sessions as a family.

"When we first met you said maybe I could find a way to love myself. I'm not sure what that means, but I'd like to find out."

I said, only semijokingly, "You know, to some Christians, loving oneself is an almost sinful proposal. But I have other ideas."

I described my experience of bottle-feeding my children as infants. They would suck from the bottle; their eyes were fixed on mine. It was a very moving experience for me. I felt I was feeding their bodies with the bottle, but with my eyes I was feeding their souls. And I was learning something new about love.

I said to Carol Marie, "Why don't you use your imagination and a mirror to look into your own eyes that way?"

She was silent, with a slight smile on her face. I could tell she was taking it in.

Much to my surprise, Carol Marie took to the therapy experience like she was born to it. She would arrive for an interview feeling surprised about something she had done. One important symptom of emotional health is the ability to be surprised by yourself. Occasionally, the subject of Trish arose. She was away at college and sometimes her poor judgment made her a source of distress. She did have the college freshman's way of doing dumb things. Carol Marie tended to see these things as symptoms of bipolar disorder. But bad judgment in a college freshman is not yet a diagnostic category. In her case, the troubles she got into were more symptomatic of naïveté and an unusually soft heart.

At the end of six months Carol Marie decided to end therapy. She felt better about herself and thought she had learned enough for the time being. During the time we met, she had shed the "Marie" part of her name, thinking that it was too prissy. One day she came into the session describing the delight she felt at her latest adventure: over the weekend she went on a walk, got lost, enjoyed getting lost, and ended up returning home quite late. As Carol became a patient on her own, her struggles mirrored her daughter's. Her getting lost and being gone for a time was a milder model of Trish's staying out all night long.

This case shows what can happen when fear and its cousin, anxiety, take hold of a family and bury themselves within. This family's cautious living pattern, driven partly by residual trauma from Carol's family and the fear-based upbringing that characterized Arthur's childhood, ended up embedding itself in this family, which created a powerful, though nearly invisible, distress for the family. While I never learned what made Arthur's mother so tyrannical and harsh, I'm guessing that there was some residual trauma in his mother's family of which he was unaware.

I've always thought, "If you can't stand guilt, don't have kids." Love and guilt go hand in hand in the struggle to be human and to raise humans. I never regard a parent's difficulty as a moral failing, but as an (unconsciously) learned way of being, handed down through genera-tions. I think my caring for Trish's family, in effect, showing them how to be patients, how to wonder and be less reactive, took some of the fear away from them. Originally, while polite, Arthur came across as kind of a rigid guy with little imagination. That gradually changed as we got around to talking about his family and how he grew up. They learned to question themselves, which gave them a degree of newfound freedom. The pressure from the fear that had governed their lives, going back generations, finally lifted.

Sometimes, when residual, unconscious fear or anxiety grips a fam-ily, it can show up as physical symptoms, not just psychological dis-tress. It used to be called psychosomatic medicine, though that phrase has fallen out of popularity. The next case shows how tricky addressing intergenerational trauma can be.

THE BOY WHO IS SCARED TO BE SICK

This family was referred to me by their friends who had previously seen me in therapy. Annie and James were worried about their only child, eleven-year-old Logan, who had been showing a variety of OCD-type symptoms the last couple of years. They were also concerned about his rather fresh mouth and tendency to be a wise guy, especially with his dad. On the phone Annie said that she worried that the couple's fraught relationship was creating anxiety for their son.

Annie and James, an artistic couple in their midforties, had been together for over fifteen years. Annie worked as a set designer for theater productions on Broadway, and James was a moderately well-known actor. They had never married, mostly because, as Annie said, "James has commitment issues." But commitment, or lack thereof, is usually a bilateral affair, so I suspected that perhaps Annie, too, had her own fears about intimacy, which she may not be aware of. Sometimes choosing a partner who "can't commit" can be an act of self-protection.

At the first session with the family, the couple talked about how Logan made every decision difficult. He argued with his parents, mostly his dad, challenging his authority on a regular basis.

"Nothing is easy with Logan," Annie claimed.

Logan was a handsome, well-behaved, articulate kid, adult in his language and demeanor in the way single children often are. Observing the family in this first session, I saw that Logan inhabited the pressure-cooker position between his parents. He looked at both of them each time he responded to a question I'd asked, like he wanted to be sure he wasn't upsetting anybody. Logan seemed especially protective of his mom and wary of his dad.

It looked like his dad was the heavyweight in this couple, judging by several dismissive comments James made toward Annie. These mostly took the form of, "Annie needs to learn to control her emotions" or "Annie doesn't do well under stress." I was pretty sure that Logan was tuned in to what looked like a rather dramatic power imbalance in the couple, and I suspected that his frequent jousting with his father was a way for Logan to bring his old man down a peg. I suggested meeting alone with the parents for the second visit to get a better handle on the nature of their relationship.

The first visit revealed a couple filled to the brim with tension, though everything looked placid on the outside. No overt fighting was taking place, but a well-honed conflict avoidance system was evident. They had never married because, basically, they could never decide if they were a couple or not. They kind of drifted together and remained in a kind of amorphous state. Early on, Annie, a lovely, warm, emotionally astute type of woman, had pushed for more of a commitment. James resisted. He had a lot of reasons, mostly due to Annie's inadequacy.

She said wryly, "He always found something wrong with me, and finally I gave up," meaning asking for marriage.

James appeared to occupy the "expert" position on all things, with Annie as the emotional/intellectual lightweight. Despite James's pseudo superiority complex, I liked both of them immediately. They were smart, thoughtful, and seemed engaged in the therapy from the beginning. Early on, Annie proved to be much more attuned to the dynamics of the duet. James tended toward more self-protection, though he was generally receptive to my observations. Though James projected a cool, "above-it-all" demeanor, he began to open up about his own history of anxiety that had been nearly crippling at various points in his life.

James's backstory included an ongoing, quiet fight to prove his father wrong. This fight persisted silently to this day. James described his father as "an incredibly uptight guy" who dominated his mother, adding bitterly, "And she caters to his every wish." James told how his paternal grandfather died suddenly of a heart attack when James's dad was only nine. This set up a pattern where James's dad became a "control freak," who as James said, "made everyone's life miserable." He described his dad as an "anxious wreck," albeit a closet wreck since he was highly functional and built a hugely successful business. James said his father, whose life has been hampered by severe chronic psoriasis, attempted to cope with his anxiety by becoming a compulsive jogger.

James was much more like his father than he knew. His anxiety was palpable, especially in the way he wanted to keep all tensions at bay. He wanted everything, every conversation, to be smooth and unruffled. I thought that James clearly inherited his father's residual trauma, and he didn't even know it. The man whom James saw as his nemesis showed up as a newer, slightly improved version in his son. Although James was so distressed over his parents' marriage, he had unwittingly created a similar model in his own life. He was the boss man, the carrier of superior knowledge and wisdom, and Annie muted her own desires in her attempt to please him.

We talked about these themes for several weeks. I would have liked to have said to James, "You're like your dad, including how you throw your weight around with Annie." Instead, I amplified Annie's voice, implicitly challenging James's patronizing attitude toward her.

"James, you feel like you have to carry all the responsibility. You have an incredibly competent, intelligent partner and you don't appreciate her." Another time, when Annie was placating James's ego, I turned to him and said, "Annie is so nice to you, James. She lets you believe you're smarter than her. Do you need her to comfort you that much?" Of course, James interpreted these comments as a challenge, but he didn't leave the therapy, so I still had a chance to try to rebalance this out-of-whack duet. I knew I needed to challenge James's "expertise," and I did this partly by enjoying and underlining Annie's considerable expertise in all matters relational. This wasn't phony on my part. Annie, indeed, revealed herself to be an incredibly thoughtful, intuitive woman. She just didn't know it. Or believe it.

Things seemed to be moving slowly, almost imperceptibly, in the right direction. There was slightly less caution between them and a bit more openness in conversation. Then, a couple of months into the therapy, they again began expressing concern about Logan. While the couple described their home life as slightly more harmonious, their son seemed to be dealing with lots of anxiety. Logan called Annie several times from school, worrying about his anxiety, and accompanying stomachaches. He believed that something was wrong with him and sounded seriously stressed. I was puzzled. I wasn't sure if Logan had some worry about changes in his parents' relationship that might have triggered this or whether something was going on that I wasn't aware of.

During one session, Annie said, "Something happened over the weekend. We're worried about Logan."

"I'm all ears," I said.

Logan had stayed at his cousin's house and another kid had gotten sick and threw up. Logan called his parents and was freaking out over the phone that he might throw up, and he was terrified at this prospect. As I listened to Annie and James describe this event, I was struck that they sounded as worried as Logan. James in particular seemed triggered by his son's health anxieties and reacted with alarm.

"Why didn't you reassure Logan that he was okay?" I asked.

This set in motion a conversation that reflected a dynamic that dominated their relationship from the beginning.

"I would love to do that. But I can never be calm when Logan is sick. I never could be. James would always accuse me of neglect," Annie said. She looked at James, "You would never trust me. I always felt that every little health-related thing became a huge crisis."

James didn't deny it. This was the legacy of his own childhood, where James's father had the rug pulled out from under him with the traumatic sudden death of his own dad. This created a fear that has reverberated through three generations. James was mostly unaware of the powerful nature of this residual trauma.

I said, "Let's have Logan come for the next session."

The three arrived at the next session with Logan looking somewhat listless. He had a fever and looked like he was struggling to be a part of the session. (Annie called and told me that he had a slight fever and wondered if they should cancel. I left it up to her.) Early on, Annie said she had to leave a bit early because of work, so I knew this would be a somewhat abbreviated session. After some initial conversation about the recent sleepover event, I asked Logan a bit about his parents' response when he gets sick.

He said, "My dad is crazy overprotective. It's almost scary. My mom only worries once in a while."

I nodded. "Yeah, I've noticed your dad's worry is typically B-I-G."

Despite being a bit under the weather, I could detect a lot of anxiety coming from Logan. This was a good kid—too good. He operated in a way that signaled emotional caution, often looking at his dad, and as we began to explore his stomachaches and his worry, he seemed to always want to give the "correct" answer, the pleasing answer. This was a worrying kind of kid. Worrying about his health. Worrying about his dad's approval. Worrying about his mom's ability to take care of herself. Worrying about his worry.

Annie turned to Logan, hoping to minimize his anxiety, "I'm not worried about your health. There's nothing dangerous going on."

I asked James if Logan knew about his own history of worrying. I knew Logan, like other people, saw James as a cool guy, a no-problem, everything's-under-control-type of person. On the surface, Logan's dad acted like nothing in the world bothered him. He had a snarky sense of humor that made it seem like he was looking down at the world from his high perch. At my invitation, James began to talk about his anxiety that he probably picked up from HIS father. Suddenly, James began to cry. We were all still. I'm pretty sure Logan was taken aback. He didn't react though and sat stiffly on the couch. I wasn't sure he had ever seen his dad cry.

James, stealthily wiping away tears, looked at me.

"You know, I missed out on having a close relationship with my own dad. I didn't want that with Logan. I wanted him to have a different relationship with me than I have with my dad."

He paused for several minutes. We were all silent. James looked at Logan.

"I'm sorry that I created so much worry for you about your health." James smiled. "My bad," he said.

Logan looked uncomfortable. I turned to Annie.

"I'm touched by James's openness, by his tears. What are you thinking?"

I wanted to reassure Logan that his dad wasn't falling apart. He was getting better.

Annie sounded like she meant it when she said, "Oh, yes! This is good! This is much better for all of us!"

Annie had to bolt from the session for a work thing, but James stayed on for a few minutes with his son. James's tears seemed to release a kind of uptightness from his body. He looked at Logan and said, "I want you to be able to say what you feel."

I knew what he meant. Logan looked wooden, frozen. I'm not sure if it's because he was sick or scared. They decided to leave since Logan politely said, "I'm not feeling well." As they left, I felt some anxiety. While I knew that James's show of vulnerability was a healing step in the right direction, I was troubled by Logan's response. He seemed so uncomfortable, and I didn't know what that meant. And the fact that the session ended so abruptly left me with an unsettled feeling. I wondered if James's emotional candor with his son felt heavy for the kid. Logan seemed so stiff. Maybe he was just sick. We agreed to meet again soon.

I wish I could say that this session signaled the beginning of something new for the family, but that's not what happened. That was the last I saw of the entire family. I didn't hear from them for a while, and then Annie reached out by phone. She said James was really worried about his son's anxiety, so they took Logan to a psychiatrist who started him on antidepressants as well as medications for anxiety. Both Annie and James had a predisposition toward the use of these drugs, and Annie seemed especially fond of her antidepressant medications, which she had taken for nearly twenty years.

I felt sorry, and inwardly upset, that they bailed on the therapy. I wondered what, if anything, I could have done differently. As I reviewed my work with them, I think I should not have moved to working with the couple alone so quickly. I should have kept Logan as part of the therapy for a longer period. This family was very much a threesome: two parents in a rather ambiguous, undeclared relationship plus their child. I would have had the opportunity to get to know Logan better, understand the way he participated in the family dance, and been in a better position to address his struggles. This young man needed help, not just his parents, and I missed the opportunity to do that early in our work by just seeing the couple.

As I pondered our last session, I recalled how the family had shown what looked like the beginning of a breakthrough. I thought, and hoped, this opening could have begun to shift the three-generation transmission of anxiety from James's father to James to Logan. I really felt for this kid and the burdens of bearing his father's mostly unacknowledged anxiety.

I also wondered about my own unsettled feelings that I experienced at the end of our last session. I believe I may have been picking up on apprehension from the father. I think James's tears may have left him feeling unmasked, his "cool guy" cover blown. For many years he had been unconsciously carrying the undigested grief and trauma of his own father. This created a great deal of internal pressure for him, which had never been adequately addressed, on any level. James's momentary tearful breakdown may have created some anxiety for both father and son. Above all, James didn't want his son to be scared, and I think he may have been concerned that his tears would upset his son.

Logan, perhaps, worried that his father would be upset at being so exposed. His dad never, ever let himself fall apart. I think the move to see a psychiatrist was designed to "protect" Logan from being exposed to his father's vulnerability, removing the family and the father's pain from the equation, focusing solely on Logan. This would reestablish the family homeostasis, the pseudo stability that had characterized the family's way of operating. James and Annie could carry on, not addressing James's anxiety, as he and they had done for many years. I believe that

James worried that his son would be hurt if he saw his father's pain. Of course, the opposite is true.

I still see Annie from time to time about various personal/professional issues, but I never saw James or Logan again. Annie reported that they weren't happy with the first psychiatrist, so they began psychiatrist-shopping, including with a preeminent expert on OCD. All of these psychiatrists prescribed medication, including antipsychotic medication, for Logan. His anxiety and OCD symptoms apparently remained as they continued to shop for the right medication fix for their son. I learned from Annie that James had been suffering from a variety of psychosomatic troubles, including severe stress-related skin rashes, like his father, as well as digestive disturbances. According to Annie, he was not interested in therapy at this time.

Anxiety is a tricky, nearly invisible pattern that resides in the nervous system of families. This pattern is usually passed down through at least one generation, often more. Nothing overtly may appear to be wrong in the family, though a child, especially a "good" child, may show up with anxiety. Most often they are responding to—picking up on—an anxiety, often resulting from trauma, that has been handed down to the parents, undigested from their parents or grandparents. Children are great emotion-detectors, sensing parental anxiety even when the parents themselves may be unaware. This can feel heavy for kids, which often gets expressed in their behavior, rather than words.

The experience of trauma is widespread. Many people the world over have been the unfortunate recipients of traumatic experiences through war, famine, poverty, injuries inflicted by culture, as well as more intimate, interpersonal wounds like unexpected loss. The next story shows how trauma can trickle down through two generations undetected, but as a powerful force.

THE CASE OF THE MEAN DAD

I first heard Dana's soothing voice when she called me requesting family therapy. "We're not communicating very well," she said. She wanted to come for the first visit with her husband alone to talk about how, as she put it, "incredibly stressful" family life had been lately. We arranged an appointment for the following week.

When I went out to the waiting room to greet Dana and her husband, Jacob, I could smell an odor of resentment coming from the husband. He looked like he expected me to find him guilty of something. Uh oh. This may be a rough first visit. The couple looked lovely on the outside—well-heeled and in their midforties. Dana was casually, but elegantly, dressed. Jacob sported a gorgeous, well-tailored, and obviously expensive suit. The husband's quiet surliness gave me (inward) pause.

Dana initiated the therapy because she was worried about her husband's difficult relationship with their kids. She described it like this: "He walks around like he's angry at the kids, especially at our oldest daughter. He's got an incredibly harsh way about him."

Dana and Jacob had four kids, seven-year-old Mia, an eleven-year-old daughter Jenna, and two teenagers, a fourteen-year-old boy named Lance and seventeen-year-old Lila. Dana described how Jacob was especially hard on Lila, the oldest. She said, "He's obsessed with her weight and hounds her about it constantly." Surprisingly, Jacob nodded. He apparently agreed with his wife's characterization. To me, he had the air of a strong guy going down to defeat.

I noticed something early on in my conversation with these folks. Jacob was really funny. He had an off-beat, self-deprecating sense of humor even though he found himself in a painful predicament, in part by his own making. His well-developed sense of irony was especially appealing. He referred to himself as a "bastard" more than a few times. Though he repeated several times "I know why I'm here," meaning as the guilty party, he clearly was looking to remedy the suffering for him and his family. He recounted how one of their best friends recently called him and spelled it out: "She told me all the things I was doing wrong with my family. I appreciated her honesty."

Wow. This guy was not the jerk that he had apparently become in his family. Bona fide jerks, male or female, reveal themselves in the office. People cannot hide their true colors, no matter how hard they try. I conjectured that Jacob's behavior with his kids had something to do with context, with family dynamics. The guy that Dana described—aggressive, angry—didn't show up in my office, so I assumed that whatever went on at home, the family's underlying relationship patterns contributed to making the dad such a "mean guy" in his family life. Dana also didn't tiptoe around her husband. She didn't seem worried about offending him. It looked to me like she came as the spokesperson for the team, which included the kids. I guessed that she was the captain of the team. Her message was clear: Jacob was wrong with the kids. Wrong, wrong, wrong. I observed that Jacob listened to her without showing the slightest defensiveness.

At this first meeting I showed my appreciation for both of them. Dana came across as a thoughtfully expressive and appealing woman. I said to her, "My guess is that Jacob's troubling issues have more to do with the family operating system; this guy sitting in my office is pretty appealing." I added, "It looks to me like he might be isolated from the team, a painful place to be."

Jacob nodded. I often frame a first session in this way, to set the stage for the work to come—expanding the family's view of its reality. I think this took some pressure off Jacob, and Dana didn't challenge me.

Thus began my work with this family, which included about fourteen visits over approximately ten months. The battleground where Jacob fought, mostly ineffectually, with his oldest daughter, revealed itself at the start. Early in our family sessions I noticed that Lila was the obvious CEO of the sibling operation. Demonstrating the calm competence of a surgeon leading an operating room, she often kept the youngest child, Mia, occupied in our sessions while simultaneously checking on her younger siblings Jenna and Lance. In one session, Lila began talking about how her dad is "always on my case," about exercise, diet, "you name it," she said. Jacob muttered something about wanting Lila to "take better care of herself." He cited her refusal to go to an early morning spin class as a symbol of her personal neglect. An avid triathlete, Jacob had voiced fears about his own potential for "falling apart," and he seemed to be projecting these fears onto his oldest child. Lila, by the way, was a pretty, round-faced, five-foot-ten, big-boned, healthy-looking young woman. She was slightly overweight, but in no way would one think of her as fat.

Lila looked at her mother as she said, "My dad always has something to say. He's got this crazy control thing going on."

As she spoke, I began to wonder if Dana was a ventriloquist. She appeared to be throwing her voice to Lila. In fact, every time Lila spoke, or occasionally when the other kids offered their thoughts, they looked at their mom as they spoke, silently getting her approval. Or maybe reassuring her that they were on her side. Dana was an absolute powerhouse in this family, and I believed she was completely unaware of this. Jacob knew it, though.

Dana (unconsciously, of course) controlled the kids through her eye movement and body language; she was tracking and monitoring every word they said, though she was sitting silently across the room. Jacob tried responding a few times, but Dana had a subtle way of "shushing" him, putting her hand on his arm indicating that she wanted the kids to speak. I was pretty sure that Dana, the peacemaker, wanting everything calm at all times, worried that conflict might erupt and wanted to keep a lid on it. I knew Dana meant no harm, but this tight circle Dana drew around her and her children was a toxic pattern for the family: mother saint and father sinner. This kind of rigid polarization fueled Jacob's feeling of impotence, which I knew increased his fury and need for control.

I teased Dana about her close monitoring of her children. I said, "I'm exhausted just watching you. You are on duty every second. Where did you learn that?"

This looked like a well-honed pattern that probably predated her marriage. At my invitation, Dana began describing the stresses in her upbringing, particularly in her parents' marriage, her father's unpredictability, and some turbulence with her younger sister. As the eldest, Dana had been enlisted early on as the "family doctor," the fixer of all things.

She said, "I was the 'go-to' person for all problems in our family."

She obviously got some status and ego-boosting from this job, but it became a prison for her in other respects.

I chose to focus on the latter.

I commented quietly, "You never had the luxury to get it wrong." I added, "It sounds like you've been carrying your family on your shoulders for many years, that you never had the freedom to show weakness or confusion. Your hand needed to be on the wheel at all times."

She seemed to be taking it in. She nodded. Jacob chimed in: "Even now, if she misses the exit to Newark Airport and ends up in Connecticut, she can't admit she made the wrong turn."

His voice was full of humor and tenderness. Dana didn't laugh.

I knew that in order for this family to heal, Dana needed to stop acting as a fixed buffer between her husband and their kids. She didn't realize that she was unwittingly *increasing* Jacob's control issues. I motioned for her to rest, and let Jacob talk to his kids in his own way.

I wanted to reassure her that it wasn't dangerous. Slowly, Lance began to address his dad, telling him about how "pissed" he was at some of his father's behavior at home. Lance really laid into the old man; he didn't hold back, letting him have it for what he described as his dad's strong-arm tactics, especially with him and Lila.

Thus began a beautiful piece of music in this session—Jacob and Lance, head-to-head, going back-and-forth, hashing it out. Lance didn't pull any punches.

"Dad, you can be a real douche sometimes."

Jacob didn't even flinch. He looked so happy just to be having this conversation with his son, without his wife in between, that he didn't even mind being called a douche. Jacob gave Lance a plaintive look and said, "I worry so much that you won't be able to take care of yourself. Sometimes it seems like your head is in the clouds. I worry about all you guys, and I don't know what to do to protect you. I feel so helpless."

They looked like two guys at a bar, with that kind of hushed intimacy. Jacob acknowledged his heavy-handed approach at times.

"Sometimes I just don't know what else to do!" Jacob turned to me and, nodding to his son, said rather wistfully, "We never get to talk like this."

By now the theme of Jacob's control issues with his kids was clearly pronounced. And Dana's attempts to intervene, to "protect" her kids clearly exacerbated the problem. After about six months of intermittent visits, we had a powerful session that cast Jacob's parental anxiety in a new light. The couple came to the session alone. Shortly after Dana and Jacob settled in on the office couch, Dana described a turbulent episode in the family before the kids left for camp.

She recounted how Jacob "lost it" with Lance. After ferreting out the details, it seemed that Jacob became upset after Lance failed to download some pictures onto Jacob's computer, as he'd asked him–several times–to do.

Jacob said, "I can't believe he didn't do it. What do I have to do to get this kid to get his head out of the clouds?"

Dana, as usual, provided both context and a defense of their son, who apparently did complete the download but in a different format than Jacob requested. It sounded to me like Lance made a real effort to do as his dad asked, and that his teenage computer wizardry mistakenly didn't allow Jacob to see the pictures. I was puzzled.

I turned to Jacob, "It sounds like Lance tried to do the job, he did his best. It looks like you way, way, overreacted to a slight mishap. What do you think?"

Without missing a beat Jacob responded, "Absolutely!"

He knew his reaction—loudly berating his son for too many minutes—did not fit the crime.

"Do you feel bad about what happened?"

"Absolutely!" he said. He added, "I worry that this kid won't be able to function in life. He just doesn't get it sometimes. He seems clueless."

Of course, their son was a fourteen-year-old boy—"clueless" goes with the territory. Jacob's response sounded like some kind of primal anxiety about one's children not being able to care for themselves. Or about being blindsided. I felt something in the air. Something I had not picked up on before. This anxiety sounded, and felt, different from the normal, albeit painful, anxiety we, as parents, have about our kids. I shared my puzzlement. What was behind Jacob's extreme worry? Did he have any idea?

The next words out of his mouth sounded like he was joking. "The Holocaust."

"Really?" I said.

He then danced around it for a while, describing how his younger sister didn't know how to take care of herself and her life was "shitty." He referred to several other close family members—parents and a sister—who had died, which I knew, and how their lives had been difficult.

I circled back, "Were you joking about the Holocaust?"

Silence.

Dana said, "Our whole life is because of the Holocaust."

Jacob still had a semijokey expression on his face.

"Please explain," I said.

The rest of the session became a very painful one for me and, I'm quite sure, for Jacob. For the first time I heard the story of Jacob's Polish father, who, when nineteen, was drafted into the Polish army, just as Hitler's forces were entering Poland. As soon as army officials discovered Jacob's father was Jewish, they sent him home. Upon his return, he found that both parents and seven siblings had disappeared. He later learned that they had been sent to a concentration camp where they all perished. The entire family wiped out. Jacob recounted this story in an unsentimental, breezy, almost lighthearted manner.

I felt a stone in the pit of my stomach. While I had heard similar stories before, it never got any easier, at least for me. I wanted Jacob to know how I was feeling. I didn't want to hide my grief at such a profound and barbaric loss. In fact, I thought that Jacob's jocularity perhaps prevented him from digesting the grief and fear from this trauma, passed down from his father. Jacob, unknowingly, projected these unconscious fears onto his kids. I realized, as I listened, that Jacob's anxiety sounded like he worried that his son's "not being aware" could have disastrous consequences. Jacob responded to normal adolescent idiocy like it could become a matter of life and death. I shared how, when I visited Europe's oldest synagogue in Prague, I heard the old Jewish guides talking about how the Czech Jews tried to accommodate the Nazis; they couldn't believe human nature could be so evil. They had experienced brutally the dangers of being naive, or unaware.

I said to Jacob, "I will never hear your anxiety about your kids with the same ears again."

Jacob, who had been with me up until now, started to get antsy. He clearly wanted to move away from grief to problem-solving. He started to talk about something that felt mundane by comparison. He was a bit of an escape artist, and now I had a better understanding of its meaning.

At the risk of having Jacob hate me, I said, "I need to stay quiet for a minute."

We had a few minutes left in the session, and I felt the need to maintain the spell. It felt like we were honoring the dead in Jacob's family. Jacob almost burst out of his skin. He started fiddling with his phone. Dana clearly enjoyed the imposed rest. She sat still, a slight smile on her face, basking in the silence, not needing to solve any problems.

Jacob muttered, "I hate this! It's like a retreat!"

I had to smile.

The session was over. The room was still. As they left, Dana mouthed the words, "Thank you."

While it's impossible to say if this was a turning point, which in therapy, like in life, is often subtle, this session seemed to change the tone and tempo of the therapy. We met a few more times, both with the family and with the couple alone. Then Jacob and Dana came for what turned out to be our final session. The atmosphere in the room felt light. No crisis. No drama. Not much palpable tension.

Dana was fresh off a minibike marathon in which she performed really well. She talked about her riding in almost transformative terms: the beauty of the scenery, the unexpected power in her speed and of her lungs, her surprising endurance.

She said with a smile toward Jacob, "And I love being the last man standing."

I enjoyed hearing Dana crow about her personal achievements, having nothing to do with her family. She wasn't busy trying to monitor Jacob's moods or worrying about the kids. She was basking in the glow of her unexpected strength and the enjoyment of establishing her own pace. I nodded appreciatively.

I said to her, "Watch out! Next time you come in here you'll be talking about starting your own company!"

"I know!" she said.

This was new—Dana openly selfish, enjoying her autonomy and purely personal pursuits.

Jacob referred to the current state of relative peace in the home.

"I learned I'm not an asshole. If I really was the kind of asshole they painted me as, I would have killed myself!" Jacob's colorful commentary alluded to what had been healing for him in our discussions. "I realized I can be myself. That's all I can be anyway, but it's a relief to be able to do it."

As I reflect on our work over that year, I think a couple of things may have helped move this family to a different place. A lot had to do with my being a friend to Jacob. He had no friends when they first arrived. He was, indeed, "the asshole." A team of one. But my appreciation of his humor, his self-reflection, his commitment to his family, and his emotional intelligence helped shift his wife's perception of him. And, in the "trickle-down theory" of family life, this helped with the kids as well.

I think Dana may have gotten more freedom to not be so protective of her kids. She realized that she wasn't responsible for every single thing that went on in the house. She seemed to be less fearful of tensions and arguments. Having a somewhat lighter sense of her responsibilities, I think, allowed her to listen to Jacob more as a buddy, without having to "fix" whatever he was upset about. In one session, Dana remarked that their daughter Lila complains about her parents "being a team" all the time, but, although she claims to be irked, everyone seems to be having more fun. Lila was no longer the object of her father's obsessive worry, and Jacob talked about how he and his daughter were planning on competing in a bike marathon together.

The household was calm, in a good way. Not a forced calm, but the kind that comes from understanding and connection. We decided to meet again as needed. Jacob, especially, seemed to want the reassurance that it was okay to call whenever he wanted to, to check in at any time. I think our sessions helped affirm the value of his voice, something that was missing when I first met them.

It's been a few years now since I've heard from them. Except for one phone call. Dana phoned to tell me Lila had been accepted at the college of her choice, a small midwestern liberal arts university, located not too far from Dana's parents. Both Jacob and Dana were excited about this new adventure for their daughter.

Questions for Reflection

In the first case, "A Mother Learns to Love Herself," how did the diagnosis of this child give the parents a name for their stress? How did this affect the growth of the family and its members?

The second case, "The Boy Who Is Scared to Be Sick," ended in disappointment for the therapist. Why do you think the family stropped the therapy? Is there something the therapist could have done differently? How might the picture have been different if the family remained in therapy?

In the last case of "The Mean Dad," the mother didn't realize how powerful she was. How did she inadvertently increase the dad's control issues? What happened to create a change?

Chapter 10

Looking for What's Right

BEWITCHED

The Jackson family came to see me with their therapist, a social work intern, for a single consultation. The family included the mother, father, and their seventeen-year-old son, Bob. There were two older sisters who no longer lived at home and didn't come for the session. Bob was upsetting everyone because he was interested in witchcraft. He dressed in a dark, goth manner, painted his fingernails black, and hung around with kids who dressed and behaved like him. Elizabeth and Robert Sr., his parents, were right out of central casting as middle-class, stiff, uptight suburban folks. Embarrassed by their son, they assumed everyone thought of him as an idiot. With the help of the school and their pastor, they came to view Bob's role-playing as a mental disorder.

Halfway into a very tense first interview with me as consultant, I turned to the parents.

"It seems like it's easy for you to talk about Bob, about what you don't like and what you think is wrong with him. But you don't seem very good at talking about yourselves and what your family is like."

It occurred to me that Bob did not have a thought disorder—he was trying to learn something about how to be in this world and this "inspired" behavior turned him into a disturbing and annoying adolescent. After taking the initial history, in which I connected with each family member, I said "You know, I sense Bob is a creative kid, but what worries me is that he has turned into such an isolate."

I turned to Bob, "Had you thought of trying to cultivate some of your pals into a coven, so that you have some disciples? You know you can't be a successful witch without a coven."

The mother, a very humorless sixth grade teacher, lips pursed in permanent disgust, went after me like I was one of her students.

"That's ridiculous. We didn't come here for more silliness." She paused. Then challenging me, as though it were her classroom and she was in charge, said, "Why are we here anyway?"

Smiling, and without pause, I answered, "I'll tell you something. I have been ridiculous for a long time, and I'm good at it. I suppose you're here to learn a different way to be ridiculous."

The content of this clumsy message had abrasive and rude elements, but simultaneously and nonverbally it was nondefensive, ambiguous, playful, and inviting. But most important, it was an oddly self-deprecating comment, which set the tone for a new kind of conversation.

I turned to the mother, "So, Elizabeth, how did you manage to upset your parents when you were in high school?"

She hesitated. Then, as she began talking, this previously no-nonsense mother appeared to relish recapturing a version of her teenage self. For the next ten minutes Elizabeth went on to describe some of her own exploits as a high school senior, laughing as she recalled some of her antics. She loosened up and smiled as she talked about pretending to forget about her curfew, sneaking alcohol into a school dance, a few episodes of playing hooky—all fairly typical escapades in the adolescent rebellion repertoire. Her husband and son looked on, amazed. I don't think they had ever seen this woman before. As she reminisced, it looked to me like, in her heart of hearts, she liked her son's way of being idiosyncratic and found herself a little jealous. Elizabeth feared he would grow up to be scared like his father. As the dominant mother/teacher role stepped aside, in her amused, nonanxious remembering, the family, and I had access to her personhood in an entirely new way. Our conversation felt like play with a freedom in it that, I think, surprised the family. As they turned to leave at the end of the hour, Elizabeth looked at me and said, "I almost forgot why we came. I had a good time. I didn't expect that. Thank you."

I smiled, a silent acknowledgment that I also enjoyed our time together. Several weeks later I checked in with the social work intern who was the therapist for the family. She said they decided not to continue the therapy. The mother reported that they were doing better.

This brief vignette, a single consultation, reveals what can happen when we don't try to make progress toward specific goals in therapy trying to fix a problem. It should feel more like parallel play. We work with families in ways that help them change their living processes by creating a context where they experiment with the unwritten rule system they live by—a system that dominates their relationships. Conscious purpose and preset goals interfere with being therapeutic.

In this case, I entered the family as a kind of temporary family member, as I always do, hoping to subtly disrupt their unconscious rule system that was causing distress. It appeared that when Elizabeth, the mother, was angry, everyone went silent. But I didn't stay silent, I teased her. I think this gave her permission to enjoy a bit more freedom than she usually allowed herself. As she began to explore her own rebellious behavior as an adolescent, this helped to shift and soften the parents' attitude toward their son.

Crucially, I didn't ally myself with the idea that Bob, a teenager, was exhibiting a mental disorder. Instead, I did a bit of what we call "reframing," where I wondered if the problem was that Bob didn't have enough followers, not that he was indulging in witchcraft. I implied that he was actually falling down on the job. This type of depathologizing tends to change the game, creating new possibilities in relationships. Pathology can have a stabilizing, but costly, effect on a family. One of my mentors once told me, "Where there is caring, all pathology is sharing or repairing." What we do is similar to play therapy in which a special space exists for having a special experience. That special space is my office.

It can be helpful, as with the Jackson family, to try stepping outside of our own efforts to be consistent in our roles as enforcer and monitor, frustrated parent, disappointed or angry spouse. Instead, being self-deprecating, telling stories about our own experiences, can bring about the kind of changes that alter disturbing behavior in our relationship sphere. It also reduces the tension we might be inadvertently inducing, which contributes to the problem. Family problems can inhibit and obstruct growing. Families identify problems and then set out to solve them. What we are describing as problems often begin as solutions. That is, a family's attempt at solutions can create additional problems.

We are giving alternative ways to look at experience. It's tempting to use these ways to figure out your spouse or your kids. But the harder and more critical part is paying attention to what your contribution to any situation that frustrates you might possibly be. Consider it. Think about what the pain behind the problem might be. It's useful to think about our children's behavior as a struggle for maturity, not a moral failing. Experiment with changing what you do.

How does this translate into our experience of living? It applies most particularly to adolescents who are causing trouble with their behavior. They are subject to endless criticism that induces distance; they are pushed out of the family, which contributes to the problem. A key to making life better is to catch them doing something right! And to remember that as a parent you are the only source of a unique kind of needed loving in their world. There are plenty of people around who can and will dismiss, criticize, or punish them, but no one but you can give the loving you do. No one can make up for a lost parent. By the way, in case you hadn't noticed, it is always easier with other people's children.

In our therapy we look for undercurrents of health not as a denial of the problems that are present, but as a way to increase possibility, as a counterbalance to what is disturbing, as a way to disrupt single-mindedness. If I characterize you as doing something and I enjoy or appreciate it, it will likely take pressure off of you. And you are likely to do more of it. If health is nurtured, it can expand.

We often see people in our office who suffer from wounds in their childhood—wounds that have not healed. In fact, everyone has some kind of childhood wound, since we are all raised by human parents, with human frailties and suffering, inherited from their ancestors. This is the human condition. Our next story shows what can happen in a family when these wounds are explored and embraced.

IT'S NEVER TOO LATE TO HAVE
A HAPPY CHILDHOOD

Thirty-five-year-old Daisy was referred to me for depression by her family doctor. When I first met her, she was steeped in anguish following the separation from her alcoholic boyfriend shortly after the birth of her daughter. Her mother, Janet, flew in from Florida to live with her, which Daisy both appreciated and feared, given her mother's history of being critical of her.

Daisy's childhood was characterized by a lot of turmoil and hurt. Her parents separated when she was twelve, and Daisy's mother moved away to try to establish a stable home for Daisy and her younger brother. Daisy lived with her alcoholic father for over two years, then began shuttling back and forth between her parents. She described these painful years, feeling neglected by her father and harshly judged by her mother. Daisy remembers how she always felt fat and ugly, not able to live up to her mother's southern standards of beauty. The turbulence of these years and her mother's flight from Daisy's childhood home created an ever-present wound of abandonment for Daisy. Even as an adult, Daisy often felt like she was "in the way" with her mother.

During the course of the family therapy, I began seeing Daisy with her newly sober boyfriend, John. They eventually reunited, and were slowly working things out. Daisy, John, and their baby now lived together with Daisy's mom; Daisy still felt emotionally fragile with her mom, however. Janet proved to be a formidable, and sometimes troubling, presence for her daughter. Janet became a part of the therapy process, and we'd had several sessions where I observed how she still threw a few wild, emotional punches without fully realizing it. This sent Daisy reeling, silently.

Janet was, indeed, a real pistol. With her bright, spiky red hair, even brighter blue eyes, and rapid-fire, peppery southern speech, Daisy's mom can make you feel like you've run into a hurricane. Janet, though intelligent and kindhearted, didn't have much experience with introspection. Daisy had historically tiptoed around her mom emotionally, saving her "hurts" and storing them. Our therapy sessions brought some of these tensions to the surface, and their relationship improved. But I knew many of Daisy's old wounds remained.

One day Daisy surprised me by appearing for our session with her mom. Janet had moved out, and I hadn't seen them together for a while. I gave Janet a warm greeting. She explained why she came.

"I thought I should come today because I want Daisy to know we are on the same team. Sometimes I feel like she doesn't know we're on the same team. And I want her to know it."

Nice opening. I encouraged her to continue.

Daisy opened by saying she'd been "taken aback" that her mother decided to volunteer at a shelter on Christmas Day instead of spending the day with the family. The room grew silent.

Janet said, "I could tell you were upset."

Daisy continued with some casual-sounding response about wanting the family to be together on Christmas. Daisy snuck in the phrase "that cut deep" and then continued talking as if nothing had happened.

Her mom didn't let it go.

When you said, "That cut deep," were you referring to your old hurts about me? About when I left? About those years when I wasn't around for you?"

Silence. I got a feeling in my gut that we had just entered dangerous emotional territory. I had seen Janet become explosive in previous sessions. I made sure my seat belt was buckled; I was ready. The tension in the room was palpable. I wanted to let it develop.

Janet turned toward her daughter and, slowly, began a nearly twenty-minute soliloquy as she attempted to recapture the drama of the difficult period of separating from Daisy's dad, moving out, and leaving the entire family. Janet recounted the pain of that crazy time. She described her own blindness, anguish, and inability to ask for help.

She said, "I never knew you could get help for problems like mine. I never knew you could go someplace and learn how to talk to people. I never knew there was a way to address pain other than to escape it."

Janet smiled, describing her joy at now knowing that you could work through problems with people you loved without having to run away. Then she grew quiet, she looked at Daisy and said, "I never, ever, wanted to hurt you. I was so stupid. I didn't know how to tell you how much I loved you, that you and your brother were the most important things in the world to me. I was in so much pain, the only thing I knew how to do was to grab you by the arm [she imitates the motion] and drag you with me, instead of holding you and comforting you."

Daisy was looking at her mom. She said, "I don't know what I'm supposed to say."

I shook my head, meaning, "nothing."

Then, with a smile on her face, Daisy said in almost a whisper, "I want my mommy."

Janet pulled her daughter close, cradling her in her arms. Daisy repeated this phrase a couple of more times. Janet held her daughter closer. It was long overdue.

They stayed like that for quite a while.

Janet said, "Those are the best words you can say to me."

Then referring to one of our past sessions, Janet reminded her daughter that she didn't need to protect her.

"I won't break," she said.

I noted to myself, then out loud to Daisy, that she now had "a whole Mommy."

A strange sensation came over me as I watched this exquisite duet. I could almost see Daisy's wounds healing. It was as if I had an X-ray that showed where the empty and broken places were, and I watched as they healed. I shared this crazy image with Daisy, and she nodded, smiling.

I mostly stayed out of the way, only adding a small admiring or encouraging comment here or there. I was thinking of the great Austrian conductor Herbert von Karajan who wrote that he understood a lot about conducting after he learned to fly a plane. He said he learned how not to get in the way when the plane was flying by itself. In this session, the plane was doing just that.

As the session ended, I inwardly applauded these brave women. I think they felt it. Daisy looked stunned. I was emotionally exhausted, in a good way. I knew that I had been a part of some exquisite relationship music that was full of imagination, some risk-taking, caring, and commitment. And, again, I was reminded of the healing power that resides within families. You just have to look for it.

This story, and the others included in this book, all carry assumptions about ourselves and our fellow humans, about what contributes to distress and how to create change. People come to our offices because they are frustrated or distressed about how their lives are going. The stories they tell are about problems made up of painful and disruptive fragments. What's wrong? Where's the pain? are what practitioners typically focus on. But we pay attention to what's right as well.

All therapists have assumptions that influence their work. It is not unusual for therapists and physicians to inadvertently become part of a problem. A fairly obvious one is the use of antipsychotics for treating angry or aggressive behavior in children and teens. New antipsychotics have metabolic effects, one of the most common being rapid and substantial weight gain. I once heard a child psychiatrist say to a mother who was upset with her daughter's weight gain, "Well, I guess you have to make a choice. Either you have an obese child or an angry one." That comment is based on the child psychiatrist's assumptions. There are many more alternatives than what her assumptions allow her to see and to consider. An obvious one is that she knows nothing about the importance of including the whole family. Her solution has become a problem.

Everyone, not only therapists, has assumptions that guide them in their living in the world and influence their understanding of it. Our assumptions are often experienced as beliefs and steer our thinking. But what are thoughts made of? They are, in part, memories of experiences that were connected with emotion. But they are also made up of assumptions of which we are not aware. Assumptions tend to be buried. We do not state them, but they guide what we do. They come from past experience and from our families. They may even be based on family experience that occurred before we were born. Here is a sampling of assumptions that guide us in our work with families:

> Health is rooted in the group morale of the family. It is like a team. Good morale leads to more victories. Poor morale, because of dissension, results in the likelihood of more defeats.

> Kids worry about their families—always. Sometimes their anger is connected to the fact that they don't have the power needed to bring about change.

> The healthy family has a four- to five-generation intrapsychic family that acts as a reference library for family decision-making and the construction of the family image.

> You can only underestimate the pain of the family scapegoat (problem child).

> Symptoms belong to the family, not just the symptomatic individual.

These are only a few assumptions behind our attention to areas of health in a family. This is not to say there is no problem. We do not want to minimize difficulty. Instead, we pay attention to the dynamic impact of the problem—the kaleidoscopic complexity. We sense there is a problem, but from where and what does it arise? What keeps it going? What counterbalances are there in the relationship system? Health is a counterbalance to problems. Finding aspects of health does not suggest that a problem, along with pain or frustration, does not exist. It is a way to complicate how the problem is seen and how the problem is viewed. We do this in the name of health.

Connecting with a person's health gives us a way to appreciate a patient even more. Being appreciated is good for anyone if it is administered in the proper dose. It is important to nurture these fragments.

The next case tells the story of a young woman who grew up believing there was something fundamentally wrong with her. She first developed this belief when she was an adolescent suffering from depression and an eating disorder. Her brief experience in therapy challenged the story she had learned to tell herself.

ALREADY PERFECT

I knew something was different as soon as Katie walked into my office. A tall blond beauty with creamy skin and lively blue eyes, Katie typically moved slowly, cautiously, as if she might break something. Today, her movements appeared freer, lighter. The difference in her energy was palpable. Had she fallen in love? Landed her dream job as a fashion designer?

Katie was referred to me for recurring depression by her family physician. She said, "I guess I've been depressed off and on since I was a teenager." Soft-spoken and hesitant, Katie radiated a mix of intelligence and wisdom that made her seem older than her twenty-three years. I hadn't seen her in several weeks when she came to the office. This was our fifth session,. As soon as she sat down, I noticed a different quality to her demeanor. She seemed more animated and livelier, less remote. I soon learned why.

A bit of background may be helpful. Katie came from a close-knit Canadian family where she was the youngest of three and the only girl. She described how she always felt different from her brothers, more cautious and sensitive.

"My brothers were perfect. They did everything they were told," she remembered.

Katie thought her mother was bewildered as to how to deal with her and became very protective. Katie went through a fairly painful—for everyone—adolescence. She became anorexic at age fourteen, though not severe enough to require hospitalization.

She recalled, "I was angry a lot, though I kept it mostly inside. I felt like I was supposed to go along to get along. My parents never understood if I was upset. So I gave up and stayed in my room a lot of the time."

It sounded like a stormy and challenging time both for Katie and her folks.

I guessed that Katie, just by being the emotional being she was, had upset the rather constricted dynamic in the family by pressing her folks to deal with more emotion than had been required in the raising of her (nontroublesome) brothers. During this period Katie's parents sent her to a therapist, who started her on antidepressants, which she continued to take for the next eight and a half years. She emerged from this turbulent teenage passage and came to the United States to attend the Chicago Art Institute to study fashion design. Katie continued therapy on an intermittent basis and regularly renewed her antidepressant medication.

In our first several sessions, Katie and I explored her family background, constructing a map as best we could without the family present. Katie's parents had been married thirty-plus years, and like all long marriages, had undergone several incarnations. Her father, a successful industrialist, occupied the place on the family pedestal. Katie described him as "a combination of free spirit and ambitious and hard-driving." Her mother was seen as the flawed one in the marriage, as she was given to angry outbursts that left Katie rattled and shaken. Both of Katie's older brothers were models of propriety. They did well in school and kept whatever troubles they had to themselves. In fact, this seemed to be the family theme. They may as well have had a plaque on the door to the house that read, "NO FEELINGS ALLOWED."

As we talked over a period of a few weeks, I began to understand where the family's unofficial motto came from. Katie described her mother's background as one marked by tremendous deprivation, both physical and emotional. Her mother came from a poor family in rural England. Their poverty became so acute that Katie's mother's parents were forced to place their daughter and her siblings in an orphanage at a young age. They remained in the orphanage until they were young adults. Katie did not know many of the details of this family tragedy, but clearly her mother learned early on not to complain or cry about her own fate. This set the stage for a "no feelings" policy that permeated Katie's household.

Katie recounted these stories in a way that made it seem as if her family members were in the room. She described these painful episodes in her family life in a curious, open-ended way that suggested she was looking for connections to her own life. Her keen observing eye and willingness to reflect on her own responses related to the family dance, of someone willing to embrace the messy process of growing into adulthood. Katie impressed me with her courage and creativity, and I told her so. I shared my observations of her as a healthy, multidimensional young woman, someone with ample emotional resources. Katie seemed taken aback by my comments.

She said, "It's strange to hear you say those things. I've gotten so used to thinking of myself and my emotions as sick. Or maybe just wrong. Like I'm damaged."

I was struck by Katie's vivid language to describe her experiences. I told her, "You should write." She said, "As a matter of fact, I've begun journaling again." She agreed to share her reflections with me.

Katie's fight with herself is reflected in her journals:

I have been trying, my entire life, to be something I am not. I have tried and tried to push myself into a box of organization, a semblance of normalcy and hesitation. I cannot do this anymore. I do not live in a square, I live in a circle, part of me thrives on chaos. I need to be let out of the box, I need to give myself the permission to fall, to let go and fall into life.

When Katie walked into my office that day looking lighter and freer, the puzzle created by her new demeanor soon cleared up. I quickly realized I had guessed wrong. Nothing new like a boyfriend or a job offering had happened. She sat down on the pink couch in my office.

"By the way, I stopped taking my antidepressants."

Gulp. I immediately felt guilty. Though we'd never spoken directly about her medications, I wondered if I had unconsciously conveyed my skepticism about these drugs and worried that Katie might be trying to please me, her therapist. I thought to myself, "I've only seen her a few times. Who am I to (unconsciously) instigate this drug rebellion?"

"I hope I didn't have anything to do with that decision," I asked. Katie set me straight.

"I decided I wanted to feel my feelings. I'm not scared of my feelings anymore. I feel like I've been on 'mute' for eight years now."

I relaxed. It looked like, through indirect conversations that took place in the therapy office, Katie was daring to expand her own self, her personhood beyond the original family rules. It seemed that Katie now felt that the straight and narrow, nonmessy, obedient path was hurting her. Continued use of these drugs signaled, on some level, an accommodation to a pattern of living that didn't support Katie's fully dimensional self. Without talking explicitly about her use of medications, I had openly connected to, and admired, Katie's healthy/messy self, who often felt like she was "too emotional," too this or too that. I liked her "too-ness," which I believed gave Katie permission to risk being more herself.

Her journal reflects the emotional release she experienced after she discontinued her antidepressant medication:

This has given me the freedom to trust myself, the freedom to let go and really and truly let go—trust me to trust myself. Trust myself in that I will make the right decisions for me. To own it, and love it. The freedom to be honest with myself, to love and hate and get angry and make a terrible mess and love it and do it again until it is perfect.

Sitting there in my office, her lips in a slightly upturned smile, Katie looked beautiful. Fearless, yet vulnerable. After bowing to my professional duty to advise her to check with her physician, I allowed myself to enjoy watching this butterfly emerge from her cocoon. She talked about the relief she felt from this chemically induced detachment where she often felt like a spectator in her own life.

Katie writes sorrowfully in her journal about her straitjacketed emotional responses to her beloved grandmother's death:

Every emotion I have felt these past years have felt fake, aside from flat indifference. It was incredibly confusing and distressing. To have my grandmother die and only be able to cry once. That even was a little forced. To read a letter from her at my brother's wedding and not cry while every last guest was in tears, it broke my heart. I was cold—I felt no pain, no joy no desire.

I didn't expect this case to go the way it did. I frankly wasn't even thinking about Katie's use of antidepressants—we never really talked about it, except when she mentioned it initially as part of her history. Instead, I believe that my full engagement with Katie and her emotions, her life, and my appreciation for her high-quality personhood, operated as an unexpectedly powerful medication for her. I treated Katie as if she were a healthy, evolving young woman whose confusion, questions, and yes, even depression, formed a whole dynamic self, worthy of respect and care. I believe she absorbed my rather casual approach to her in the therapy office. I wasn't worried about her depression, but taken by her competence, her curiosity, her resilience.

Katie's emerging connection with her estranged self could be dismissed as unique to just her. One could argue that the persistence of her depression meant she was wrongly medicated, or that she had a "chemical imbalance." But it is more than that. We live in a culture that suggests that human experience can be quantified and measured. The exclusive focus on measuring symptoms ignores the human truth that suffering is normal, inevitable, and meaningful. We can't be truly alive without it. The "brain chemistry" model of depression reduces and distorts the way we think about our human experience—that scary, exhilarating, confusing, imperfect experiment—with living and loving.

We see Katie's increased sense of aliveness, which I observed in our sessions, reflected in her journals.

We'll let her have the last word:

When I die, which eventually I will, I do not want my gravestone to say: she was afraid. She never took chances. We barely knew her. Because I have something to say. I was not put here to hide. I was put here to show beauty. I was put here to help people feel. To feel things they didn't know were there. . . . If nobody likes it, if everybody hates it, I will take my pain and turn it into something beautiful. I am powered by something much larger than myself. I was born to be different. This I know for certain. I may be drowning but I can swim.

Notes

CHAPTER 4

1. *The Enchiridion* by Epictetus. Written 135 A.C.E. Translated by Elizabeth Carter (1).
2. John R. Neil and David P. Kniskern, *From Psyche to System: The Evolving Therapy of Carl Whitaker* (New York: Guilford Press, 1982), 187.

CHAPTER 5

1. Jenifer McKim, "Savage Toll of Abuse for Children in DCF Care: More than 95 Have Died since 01, Reports Say," *Boston Globe*, February 2, 2014, https://www.bostonglobe.com/metro/2014/02/02/massachusetts-children -under-state-protection-die-from-abuse-with-alarming-frequency/2TcwcpIb-WnrANkKKQs1CVP/story.html.
2. Katie Couric, *What Killed Rebecca Riley?* (New York: Columbia Broadcasting System, 2007).
3. Tolstoy, Leo. *Anna Karenina*. Translated by Aylmer Maude and Louise Maude. (New York: Wordsworth Classics, 1995).

CHAPTER 7

1. *Deconstruction in a Nutshell: a Conversation with Jacque Derrida.* Caputo, J. ed. (New York Fordham: University Press. 1997).

Bibliography

Astor, Maggie. *The 2020 Democrats Were Told to Give a Gift or Ask Forgiveness. Guess What the Women Chose* (New York: New York Times, December 20th, 2019), https://www.nytimes.com/2019/12/20/us/politics/klobuchar-warren-democratic-debate.html.

Caputo, J. ed. *Deconstruction in a Nutshell: a Conversation with Jacque Derrida* (New York Fordham: University Press, 1997).

Couric, Katie. *What Killed Rebecca Riley?* (New York: Columbia Broadcasting System, 2007).

Epictetus. *The Enchiridion.* Written 135 A.C.E. Translated by Elizabeth Carter.

McKim, Jenifer. *Savage Toll of Abuse for Children in DCF Care: More than 95 Have Died since 01, Reports Say* (Boston: Boston Globe, February 2nd, 2014), https://www.bostonglobe.com/metro/2014/02/02/massachusetts-children-under-state-protection-die-from-abuse-with-alarming-frequency/2TcwcpIbWnrANkKKQs1CVP/story.html.

Neil, John R. and Kniskern, David P. *From Psyche to System: The Evolving Therapy of Carl Whitaker* (New York City: The Guilford Press, 1982).

Tolstoy, Leo. *Anna Karenina.* Translated by Aylmer Maude and Louise Maude (New York: Wordsworth Classics, 1995).

Wehrwein, Peter. *Astounding Increase in Antidepressant Use by Americans* (Cambridge: Harvard Health Blog, October 20 2011), https://www.health.harvard.edu/blog/astounding-increase-in-antidepressant-use-by-americans-201110203624.

Whitaker, Robert. *Anatomy of an Epidemic.* (New York: Broadway Books, 2010, 2015), 268, 272, 275.

Index

ADD. *See* attention deficit
  disorder (ADD)
ADHD. *See* attention deficit
  hyperactivity disorder (ADHD)
affair, 56–57
affair repair, 51–68; affair in, 56–57;
  apology in, 56; guilty of betrayal,
  51–57; polite betrayal, 57–60;
  postaffair, 61–68
aggression, 155. *See also* self-
  mutilation case
anger, 9, 18–21, 36, 47, 49, 52, 55,
  66, 93–94, 96, 102, 124, 128,
  130–32, 134, 144, 148, 152,
  157, 160–61, 165, 184, 191,
  193, 202, 204
anguish, 38, 109
Anna Karenina (Tolstoy), 103
anorexia, 158
antidepressant medications, 3, 7, 10,
  14–16, 23, 155, 185–86, 206–9
antipsychotics, 94, 97
anxiety, 24, 27, 74, 93–95, 100–101,
  109–10, 117–18, 120, 126–27,
  132, 142, 144, 157, 174, 177–78,
  180–87, 191–93

apology, 56
attention deficit disorder (ADD), 147
attention deficit hyperactivity
  disorder (ADHD), 133–50; family
  therapy in treatment of, 136,
  142, 144–47; with family who
  outlawed grief, 147–50; irony
  deficiency case, 140–47; kid with,
  133–50; standard of care, 150;
  treatment guidelines for, 150
autonomy, 153, 166, 194

behavior problems in kids, 3–4
betrayal, 61–62, 78;
  acknowledgment/apology for, 63;
  guilty of, 51–57; polite, 57–60
Biederman, Joseph, 96–97
bipolar disorder kids/seniors (cases),
  89–110; eighteen-year-old high
  school senior, 173–80; five-year-
  old boss, 98–104; little prince
  and waif, 104–10; littlest victim,
  94–98; nine-year-old doctor, 113–
  18; three-year-old, 89–93
The Boston Globe, 94

215

Carter, Betty, 123
chemical imbalance, 3
childhood rheumatoid arthritis, 153
childhood wound, depression
    and, 200–205
child's mood/behavior, 113–18
Clonazepam, 140
Clonidine (blood pressure
    medication), 95
conflicts, 14–15, 17, 22, 28, 31, 59,
    63, 81, 96, 102–3, 123–26, 150,
    157, 163–64, 169, 190; avoidance,
    11, 41, 55, 68, 87, 116, 124, 181;
    breastfeeding, 48; fear of, 22
control freak, 180–95
Couric, Katie, 95–96
crazy teenager (case), 120–27

Depakote (antiseizure drug), 94
depression, 1–5, 7; affair repair
    and, 51–68; cases, 1–3, 7–25.
    See also specific cases; chemical
    imbalance, 3; childhood wound
    and, 200–205; family therapy,
    4–5, 10–25; good, 23; predivorce
    couples in, 27–48; recurring, 205–
    10; in relationships, 7–25; sexual
    disconnection and, 69–78; suicide
    attempt and, 23; symptoms, 1, 3,
    7; teenager case, 165–71
distress: emotional, 147; of falling
    short, 78–87; individual, 4; in
    intimate patterns of relationship,
    69–87; kids and their families.
    See under kids; marital, 51–87;
    mental, 3, 51–87

eating disorder, 158–65
emotional distress, 147
emotional rigidity, 90
emotional stoicism, 51–52
emotional sustenance, 176

emotions, 148, 176
escape pad, 153
extramarital affairs, 51–68

family operating system, 113–14,
    123, 126, 134, 188–89
family scapegoating, 16, 18, 48, 111,
    148, 150–51, 159–60, 204
family therapy, 4–5, 10–25, 29–32,
    36–43, 109, 119–20, 144–45,
    163, 168, 173, 187, 201. *See also
    specific cases*
family unity, 158–65
fears, 74, 77, 118, 128, 136, 142,
    176, 184, 189, 193; about
    intimacy, 181; of conflict,
    22; of emotions, 90; from the
    parents, 175–80
forgiveness, 57
freedom, 20, 67, 71, 75, 77–78, 85,
    92–93, 109, 127–28, 131, 146,
    157, 168, 180, 190, 194, 198–99

gnawing insecurity, 152
good depression, 23
grownup, act like, 89–93
guilty of betrayal, 51–57

Haley, Jay, 119
happy families, 103
hieroglyphics, 109

ignore/ignorance, 138
impossible behavior. *See* out-of-
    control behavior
infidelity, 78–79
inspired behavior, 197–200
intergenerational trauma,
    transmission of, 173–95;
    OCD-type, eleven-year-old
    with, 180–87

interview: Biederman, Joseph, 96; with Couric, Katie, 95; with individual therapists, 163; with patients, 113–14, 134–38, 140–47, 150, 174, 179, 197; stress, 134–35 irony deficiency case, 140–47

juvenile bipolar disorder, 103

kids: with ADHD, 133–50; behavior problems in, 3–4; bipolar, 89–110; OCD-type, eleven-year-old with, 180–87; out-of-control behavior, 113–20; stress, 95–96; "too-good," 127–32
Kifuji, Kayoko, 95

Leaving Home (Haley), 119
libido, 78
lupus, 120

marital distress, 3–4, 27–48, 51–87
marriage preaffair, 56–57
mental distress, 3, 51–87
Milquetoast, Casper, 116
mood disorder, 7
mood of relationship, 10–12
mother-daughter battles, 120–27

OCD-type, eleven-year-old with, 180–87
openness in relationship, 57–60
out-of-control behavior, 113–20
overprotectiveness, 127–32

parental dysfunction, 168
parental hypocrisy, 122
patriarchal culture, 135
Paxil, 95
polite betrayal, 57–60
postaffair repair, 61–68
preaffair relationship, 61–63

predivorce couple in depression, 27–48
preseparation therapy, 86
pseudocertainty, 139
pseudo-indifference, 135
pseudo-objectivity, 139
psychiatric diagnoses, 95–97
psychiatric disorders in children, treatment guidelines for, 150
psychiatry, 139
psychopathology, 138

recurring depression, 205–10
relationships, depression in, 7–25; affair repair, 51–68; distress of falling short, 78–87; man with stone-faced mask, 18–25; nice boyfriend, problem of, 7–12; predivorce couples, 27–48; sexual intimacy and, 69–87; woman who misplaced her voice, 12–18. See *also specific cases*
Ritalin, 140, 147
romantic overtures, 69–70

scapegoating, family, 16, 18, 48, 111, 148, 150–51, 159–60, 204
self-acknowledged control issues, 71
self-assurance, 80–81, 85
self-care, 23, 165–71
self-conscious, 36
self-contained child, 90
self-deprecatory quality, 83
self-esteem, 22, 37–38
self-harming behavior, 127; depression case, 165–71; eating disorder case, 158–65; self-mutilation case, 151–58
self-mutilation case, 151–58; family integrity, 157; family role, 152–56; symptoms, 151–52; therapy for, 155–58

self-observation, 174
self-protection, 181–82
self-reflection, 16
Seroquel (antipsychotic), 94, 97
sexual deadness/dysfunction, 70–71
sexual disconnection, 69–78
sexual intimacy, 69–87; distress of
    falling short, 78–87; wife and
    husband, lack of, 69–78
stress, 27–34, 95–96; interview,
    134–35. *See also* lupus
suicide, 23, 143
symptom substitution, 137

talk therapy, 149
teenagers, 151–71; depression case,
    165–71; with diabetes, 165–71;

eating disorder case, 158–65; self-
    mutilation case, 151–58
togetherness, 158–65
Tolstoy, Leo, 103
"too-good" child, 127–32
tranquilizer, 140
twerp, 135

unconscious hubris, 33
unhappy families, 103
unhappy sexual duet, 69–78

violence, 94–96
von Karajan, Herbert, 203

Whitaker, Carl, 76
wild sex, 73–74
women, 57

About the Authors

Amy Begel is a family therapist who received her family therapy training over thirty years ago with one of the creators of family therapy, Dr. Salvador Minuchin. Since then, she has maintained a busy private practice in New York and New Jersey. Until 2011, Amy was Senior Faculty at The Minuchin Center for the Family where she conducted family therapy training nationally and internationally. In addition to her clinical practice in family therapy, Amy is on the teaching faculty of the Department of Family Practice, The Institute for Family Health at Mount Sinai Hospital, and the Departments of Internal Medicine and Cardiology at Maimonides Medical Center where she teaches resident physicians how to look at relationship dynamics in the context of medical care. Amy has authored numerous professional articles and posts, including for *Psychotherapy Networker* magazine, the popular medical blog *KevinMD*, and HuffPost. She writes the blog *Most Human*. She lives in Teaneck, New Jersey.

David Keith is Professor Emeritus of psychiatry at SUNY Upstate Medical University, Syracuse, New York. He has been in practice for forty-five years. He was on the psychiatry faculty at Wisconsin for eight years, then entered private practice for five years with the Family Therapy Institute in St. Paul, Minnesota. It was at the University Wisconsin that Dave met Carl Whitaker, MD, considered to be one of the important forefathers of the family therapy movement. He became cotherapist, coauthor, and therapeutic collaborator with Dr. Whitaker, working with him for over twenty years. Dave is board certified in child and adolescent psychiatry. Dave has published twenty-two book chapters and thirty-one papers. He coauthored *Defiance in the Family:*

Finding Hope in Therapy (2001) and *Family Therapy as an Alternative to Medication: An Appraisal of Pharmland* (2003). He is the author of *Continuing the Experiential Approach of Carl Whitaker: Process, Practice & Magic* (2015). He lives in Manlius, New York.

9 781538 182727